AF522285

Global Competitiveness in Supply Chain Management

Global Competitiveness in Supply Chain Management

Baldev Singh Chhikara

RANDOM PUBLICATIONS
NEW DELHI (INDIA)

Global Competitiveness in Supply Chain Management

ISBN 978-93-5111-660-8

Published in 2015 in India by

RANDOM PUBLICATIONS

4376-A/4B, Gali Murari Lal, Ansari Road
New Delhi-110 002
Phone : +9111-43580356, 011-23289044, 011-43142548
e-mail: sales@randompublications.com,
info@randompublications.com, randomexports@gmail.com

Reprinted 2019

Type Setting by : Friends Media, Delhi-110089
Digitally Printed at : Replika Press Pvt. Ltd.

Preface

A Supply Chain encompasses all activities in fulfilling customer demands and requests. These activities are associated with the flow and transformation of goods from the raw materials stage, through to the end user, as well as the associated information and funds flows. There are four stages in a supply chain: the supply network, the internal supply chain, distribution systems, and the end users. Moving up and down the stages are the four flows: material flow, service flow, information flow and funds flow. E-procurement links the supply network and manufacturing plant, e-distribution links the manufacturing plant and the distribution network, and e-commerce links the distribution network and the end users. The supply chain begins with a need for a computer. In this example, a customer places an order for a Dell computer through the Internet.

With the globalization of the business, the dimensions of business are changing rapidly. With the emergence of competition at global level, the customer is the one who is benefited the most. He has now options, as he can choose, what he would like to buy from various alternatives, and also he can dictate terms. In order to attract customers, companies are introducing products with innovative features. This leads to the products with lower life cycle. The ability of a company to introduce new models at short notice depends heavily on the ability of its suppliers to provide support by way of supply of components at the right time.

As an operations management major, it is my concern to know how supply chain works for making an organization globally competitive. First of all, globalization is a challenge and an opportunity. The options for companies that are experiencing sustainable global competition are to develop workable strategies in supply chain and processes to survive and thrive or die. Moreover, supply chain management is considered as a competitive weapon due to the significant effects that supply chain activities have on all elements of an organizations financial performance, including operating costs, revenue growth, and asset management. By this, we can see that supply chain can really affect any corner of an organization.

This book focuses on concepts, principles and real life experiences which improve understanding of the Supply Chain Management (SCM).

I would like to thank my team for standing beside me throughout my career and writing this book. My special thanks go to "Random Publications" who have published the book.

– Baldev Singh Chhikara

Contents

1

Supply Chain Management

OVERVIEW OF SUPPLY CHAIN MANAGEMENT

A Supply Chain encompasses all activities in fulfilling customer demands and requests. These activities are associated with the flow and transformation of goods from the raw materials stage, through to the end user, as well as the associated information and funds flows.

There are four stages in a supply chain: the supply network, the internal supply chain, distribution systems, and the end users. Moving up and down the stages are the four flows: material flow, service flow, information flow and funds flow.

E-procurement links the supply network and manufacturing plant, e-distribution links the manufacturing plant and the distribution network, and e-commerce links the distribution network and the end users. The supply chain begins with a need for a computer. In this example, a customer places an order for a Dell computer through the Internet.

Since Dell does not have distribution centres or distributors, this order triggers the production at Dell's manufacturing centre, which is the next stage in the supply chain. Microprocessors used in the computer may come from AMD and a complementary product like a monitor may come from Sony. Dell receives such parts and components from these suppliers, who belong to the up-stream stage in the supply chain. After completing the order just as to the customer's specification, Dell then sends the computer directly to the users through UPS, a third party logistics provider.

In this supply chain, Dell Computer is the captain of the chain; the company selects suppliers, forges partnerships with other members of the supply chain, fulfills orders from customers and follows up the business transaction with services.

Now, consider a case of purchasing a pack of Perdue chicken breast at Sam's Club. When customers buy trays of chicken breast at Sam's Club, the demand is satisfied from inventory that is stocked in a Sam's Club distribution centre.

Production at a Perdue Farms manufacturing facility is based on forecasted demand using historical sales data. Perdue Farms runs a vertical supply chain starting from the eggs, to the grains that feed chicks proceeding to manufacturing, packaging, and delivery.

Packaging materials come from suppliers. These two different types of supply chain, responsive supply chain and efficient supply chain.

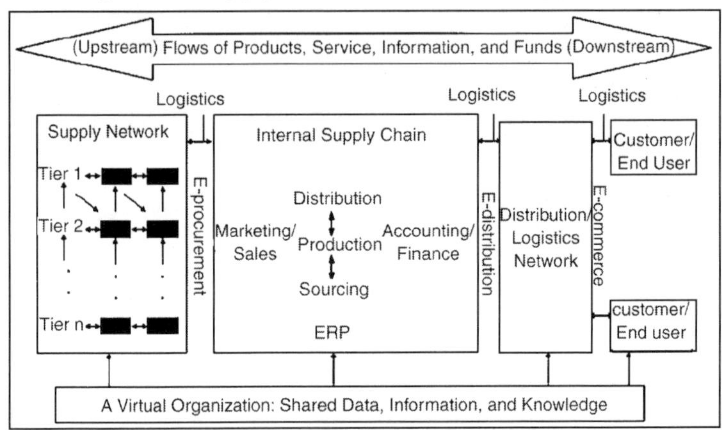

Fig. Supply Chain in e-business Environment

Supply Chain Management is a set of synchronized decisions and activities utilized to efficiently integrate suppliers, manufacturers, warehouses, transporters, retailers, and customers so that the right product or service is distributed at the right quantities, to the right locations, and at the right time, in order to minimize system-wide costs while satisfying customer service level requirements. The objective of Supply Chain Management is to achieve sustainable competitive advantage. A company's supply chain in an e-Biz environment can be very complicated. Logistic function facilitates the physical flow of material from the raw material producer to the manufacturer, to the distributor, and finally, to the end user. Sourcing or purchasing of the company is responsible for selecting suppliers, negotiating contracts, formulating purchasing process, and processing order.

Production is responsible for transforming raw materials, parts or components to a product. Distribution is responsible for managing the flow of material and finished goods inventory from the manufacturer to customer. Enterprise Resource Planning systems integrate the entire company's information system, process and store data, cut across functional areas, business units, and product lines to assist managers make business decisions. As an IT infrastructure, ERP influences the way companies manage their daily operations and facilitates the flow of information among all supply chain processes of a firm. For example, a computer manufacturer's supplier network includes all the firms that provide items ranging from such raw materials as plastics, computer chips, to subassemblies like hard drives and motherboards. A supplier of motherboard, for example, may have its own set of suppliers that provide inputs that are also part of the supply chain. Distribution management involves the management of packaging, storing, and handling of materials at receiving docks, warehouses, and retail outlets. A major part of distribution management is transportation management, which includes the selection, and management of external carriers or internal private fleets of carriers.

E-commerce uses advanced technology to assist business transactions in a web-based environment and facilitates the transaction of information flow and fund flow. E-commerce involves business-tobusiness transaction such as Covisint, business-to-customer transaction, customer-to-business transaction, and customer-to-customer transaction such as e-Bay auction.

E-commerce is conducted via a variety of electronic media. These electronic media include electronic data interchange, electronic funds transfer, bar codes, fax, automated voice mail, CD-ROM catalogs and a variety of others. E-distribution instructs where to locate the sources of supply and advises how to access them, as well as how to move the materials to the retailers via the Internet or a web-based environment. E-procurement is a part of E-commerce. E-procurement completely revolutionizes a manufacturing or distribution firm's supply chain, making a seamless flow of order fulfillment information from manufacturer to supplier.

Now we have characterized the nature of supply chain management, we are ready to make a few relevant points:

- The role of supply chain management is to produce products that conform to customer requirements.
- The objective of supply chain management is to be efficient and cost-effective through collaborative efforts across the entire system.
- The scope of supply chain management encompasses the firm's activities from the strategic level through the tactical and operational levels since it takes into account the efficient integration of suppliers, manufacturers, wholesalers, retailers, and end users.

THE CONSUMER GOODS INDUSTRY

Traditionally, manufacturers were the dominant forces in the supply chain in the consumer goods industry. With the trend towards retail consolidation and the emergence of large retailers, power in the supply chain has been shifting towards the retail level. Whereas manufacturers previously designed, produced, promoted and distributed their products or brands and retailers depended on their leadership, with this power shift, retailers have been able to exert pressure back into the supply chain. They have forced manufacturers to change their supply chain strategies and, for example, include tailored pallet packs, scheduled deliveries, continuous replenishment systems, etc.

The supply chain in the consumer goods industry includes all parties directly or indirectly involved in receiving and fulfilling customer requests, *e.g.* manufacturers, suppliers, wholesalers, retailers, third party service providers (transporters, warehouses) and customers. Supply chains are dynamic and involve the constant flow of products, in formation and finance between the different stages). The first flow (products and related services) is one of the main elements in supply chain management.

Traditionally, it is the major topic in logistics, because customers expect their orders to be delivered on time, reliably and damage free. Information flows comprise, for example, orders, inventory, demand or sales data. These flows are important for replenishment and (demand) forecasting at all stages of the supply chain. Financial flows include the transfer of funds or cash between the supply chain partners.

DEFINE THE SUPPLY CHAIN MANAGEMENT

Supply chain management is defined as the planning and management of all business activities involved in fulfilling customer requests, such as sourcing, procurement, operations, marketing and logistics management. It not only focuses on processes or functions within one particular company, but also includes coordination and collaboration with other parties in the supply chain.

The main goal of supply chain management is to facilitate the integration of supply and demand management for the purposes of improving the performance of individual companies and the supply chain as a whole. The objective of supply chain management is thus to maximise overall value generated and it focuses strongly on supply chain profitability.

Supply chain management (SCM) is the process of planning, implementing and controlling the operations of the supply chain as efficiently as possible. Supply Chain Management spans all movement and storage of raw materials, work in process inventory, and finished goods from point-of-origin to point-of-consumption. The definition one American professional association put forward is that Supply Chain Management encompasses the planning and management of all activities involved in sourcing, procurement, conversion, and logistics management activities.

Importantly, it also includes coordination and collaboration with channel partners, which can be suppliers, intermediaries, third-party service providers, and customers. In essence, Supply Chain Management integrates supply and demand management within and across companies. More recently, the loosely coupled, self-organizing network of businesses that cooperates to provide product and service offerings has been called the Extended Enterprise. Some experts distinguish Supply Chain Management and logistics, while others consider the terms to be interchangeable. Supply Chain Management can also refer to Supply chain management software which are tools or modules used in executing supply chain transactions, managing supplier relationships and controlling associated business processes. Supply chain event management (abbreviated as SCEM) is a consideration of all possible occurring events and factors that can cause a disruption in a supply chain. With SCEM possible scenarios can be created and solutions can be planned.

PROBLEMS OF SUPPLY CHAIN MANAGEMENT

Supply chain management must address the following problems: Distribution Network Configuration: Number, location and network missions of suppliers, production facilities, distribution centers, warehouses, cross-docks and customers. Distribution Strategy: Including questions of operating control (centralized, decentralized or shared); delivery scheme (*e.g.*, direct shipment, pool point shipping, Cross docking, DSD (direct store delivery), closed loop shipping); mode of transportation (*e.g.*, motor carrier, including truckload, LTL, parcel; railroad; intermodal, including TOFC and COFC; ocean freight; airfreight); replenishment strategy (*e.g.*, pull, push or hybrid); and transportation control (*e.g.*, owner operated, private carrier, common carrier, contract carrier, or 3PL).

Information: Integration of and other processes through the supply chain to share valuable information, including demand signals, forecasts, inventory, transportation, and potential collaboration etc.

INVENTORY MANAGEMENT

Quantity and location of inventory including raw materials, work-in-process and finished goods. Cash-Flow: Arranging the payment terms and the methodologies for exchanging funds across entities within the supply chain. Supply chain execution is managing and coordinating the movement of materials, information and funds across the supply chain. The flow is bi-directional. Activities/functions Supply chain management is a cross-functional approach to managing the movement of raw materials into an organization, certain aspects of the internal processing of materials into finished goods, and then the movement of finished goods out of the organization towards the end-consumer.

As organizations strive to focus on core competencies and becoming more flexible, they have reduced their ownership of raw materials sources and distribution channels. These functions are increasingly being outsourced to other entities that can perform the activities better or more cost effectively. The effect is to increase the number of organizations involved in satisfying customer demand, while reducing management control of daily logistics operations. Less control and more supply chain partners led to the creation of supply chain management concepts. The purpose of supply chain management is to improve trust and collaboration among supply chain partners, thus improving inventory visibility and improving inventory velocity.

Several models have been proposed for understanding the activities required to manage material movements across organizational and functional boundaries. SCOR is a supply chain management model promoted by the Supply Chain Management Council. Another model is the SCM Model proposed by the Global Supply Chain Forum (GSCF). Supply chain activities can be grouped into strategic, tactical, and operational levels of activities.

Strategic

Strategic network optimization, including the number, location, and size of warehouses, distribution centers and facilities. Strategic partnership with suppliers, distributors, and customers, creating communication channels for critical information and operational improvements such as cross docking, direct shipping, and third party logistics. Product designs coordination, so that new and existing products can be optimally integrated into the supply chain, load management Information Technology infrastructure, to support supply chain operations.

Where-to-make and what-to-make-or-buy decisions Aligning overall organizational strategy with supply strategy. Tactical Sourcing contracts and other purchasing decisions. Production decisions, including contracting, locations, scheduling, and planning process definition. Inventory decisions, including quantity, location, and quality of inventory. Transportation strategy, including frequency, routes, and contracting. Benchmarking of all operations against competitors and implementation of best practices throughout the enterprise.

Milestone payments focus on customer demand. Operational Daily production and distribution planning, including all nodes in the supply chain. Production scheduling for each manufacturing facility in the supply chain (minute by minute). Demand planning and forecasting, coordinating the demand forecast of all customers and sharing the forecast with all suppliers. Sourcing planning, including current inventory and forecast demand, in collaboration with all suppliers. Inbound operations, including transportation from suppliers and receiving inventory. Production operations, including the consumption of materials and flow of finished goods. Outbound operations, including all fulfillment activities and transportation to customers.

Order promising, accounting for all constraints in the supply chain, including all suppliers, manufacturing facilities, distribution centers, and other customers. Supply chain management Organizations increasingly find that they must rely on effective supply chains, or networks, to successfully compete in the global market and networked economy. In Peter Drucker's management's new paradigms, this concept of business relationships extends beyond traditional enterprise boundaries and seeks to organize entire business processes throughout a value chain of multiple companies.

During the past decades, globalization, outsourcing and information technology have enabled many organizations, such as Dell and Hewlett Packard, to successfully operate solid collaborative supply networks in which each specialized business partner focuses on only a few key strategic activities. This inter-organizational supply network can be acknowled-ged as a new form of organization. However, with the complicated interactions among the players, the network structure fits neither "Market" nor "Hierarchy" categories. It is not clear what kind of performance impacts that different supply network structures could have on firms, and little is known about the coordination conditions and trade offs that may exist among the players.

From a system's point of view, a complex network structure can be decomposed into individual component firms. Traditionally, companies in a supply network concentrate on the inputs and outputs of the processes, with little concern for the internal management working of other individual players. Therefore, the choice of an internal management control structure is known to impact local firm performance. In the 21st century, there have been a few changes in business environment that have contributed to the development of supply chain networks.

First, as an outcome of globalization and the proliferation of multi-national companies, joint ventures, strategic alliances and business partnerships, there were found to be significant success factors, following the earlier "Just-In-Time", "Lean Management" and "Agile Manufacturing" practices. Second, technological changes, particularly the dramatic fall in information communication costs, which are a paramount component of transaction costs, have led to changes in coordination among the members of the supply chain network.

Many researchers have recognized these kinds of supply network structures as a new organization form, using terms such as "Keiretsu", "Extended Enterprise", "Virtual Corporation", Global Production Network" and "Next Generation Manufacturing System".

In general, such a structure can be defined as "a group of semi independent organizations, each with their capabilities, which collaborate in ever changing constellations to serve one or more markets in order to achieve some business goal specific to that collaboration".

DEVELOPMENTS IN SUPPLY CHAIN MANAGEMENT

Six major movements can be observed in the evolution of supply chain management studies:

- Creation, Integration, and Globalization, Specializa-tion Phases One and Two, and SCM 2.0.
- *Creation Era:* The term supply chain management was first coined by an American industry consultant in the early 1980s. However the

concept of supply chain in management, was of great importance long before in the early 20th century, especially by the creation of the assembly line. The characteristics of this era of supply chain management include the need for large scale changes, reengineering, downsizing driven by cost reduction programmes, and widespread attention to the Japanese practice of management.

- *Integration Era:* This era of supply chain management studies was highlighted with the development of Electronic Data Interchange (EDI) systems in the 1960s and developed through the 1990s by the introduction of Enterprise Resource Planning (ERP) systems. This era has continued to develop into the 21st century with the expansion of internet based collaborative systems. This era of SC evolution is characterized by both increasing value added and cost reduction through integration.
- *Globalization Era:* The third movement of supply chain management development, globalization era, can be characterized by the attention towards global systems of supplier relations and the expansion of supply chain over national boundaries and into other continents. Although the use of global sources in the supply chain of organizations can be traced back to several decades ago (*e.g.* the oil industry), it was not until the late 1980s that a considerable number of organizations started to integrate global sources into their core business. This era is characterized by the globalization of supply chain management in organizations with the goal of increasing competitive advantage, creating more value added, and reducing costs through global sourcing.
- *Specialization Era-Phase One-Outsourced Manufacturing and Distribution:* In the 1990s industries began to focus on "core competencies" and adopted a specialization model. Companies abandoned vertical integration, sold off non-core operations, and outsourced those functions to other companies. This changed management requirements by extending the supply chain well beyond the four walls and distributing management across specialized supply chain partnerships. This transition also refocused the fundamental perspectives of each respective organization. OEMs became brand owners that needed deep visibility into their supply base. They had to control the entire supply chain from above instead of from within. Contract manufacturers had to manage bills of material with different part numbering schemes from multiple OEMs and support customer requests for work-in-process visibility and vendor managed inventory (VMI). The specialization model creates manufacturing and distribution networks composed of multiple, individual supply chains

specific to products, suppliers, and customers who work together to design, manufacture, distribute, market, sell, and service a product. The set of partners may change according to a given market, region, or channel, resulting in a proliferation of trading partner environments, each with its own unique characteristics and demands.

- *Specialization Era-Phase Two-Supply Chain Management as a Service:* Specialization within the supply chain began in the 1980s with the inception of transportation brokerages, warehouse management, and non asset based carriers and has matured beyond transportation and logistics into aspects of supply planning, collaboration, execution and performance management. At any given moment, market forces could demand changes within suppliers, logistics providers, locations, customers and any number of these specialized participants within supply chain networks. This variability has significant effect on the supply chain infrastructure, from the foundation layers of establishing and managing the electronic communication between the trading partners to the more complex requirements, including the configuration of the processes and work flows that are essential to the management of the network itself. Supply chain specialization enables companies to improve their overall competencies in the same way that outsourced manufacturing and distribution has done; it allows them to focus on their core competencies and assemble networks of best in class domain specific partners to contribute to the overall value chain itself–thus increasing overall performance and efficiency. The ability to quickly obtain and deploy this domain specific supply chain expertise without developing and maintaining an entirely unique and complex competency in house is the leading reason why supply chain specialization is gaining popularity. Outsourced technology hosting for supply chain solutions debuted in the late 1990s and has taken root in transportation and collaboration categories most dominantly. This has progressed from the Application Service Provider (ASP) model from approximately 1998 through 2003 to the On Demand model from approximately 2003-2006 to the Software as a Service (SaaS) model we are currently focused on today.
- *Supply Chain Management 2.0 (SCM 2.0):* Building off of globalization and specialization, SCM 2.0 has been coined to describe both the changes within the supply chain itself as well as the evolution of the processes, methods and tools that manage it in this new “era”. Web 2.0 is defined as a trend in the use of the World Wide Web that is meant to increase creativity, information sharing, and collaboration among users. At its core, the common attribute that Web 2.0 brings is it helps us navigate the vast amount of information available on

the web to find what we are looking for. It is the notion of a usable pathway. SCM 2.0 follows this notion into supply chain operations. It is the pathway to SCM results – the combination of the processes, methodologies, tools and delivery options to guide companies to their results quickly as the complexity and speed of the supply chain increase due to the effects of global competition, rapid price commoditization, surging oil prices, short product life cycles, expanded specialization, near/far and off shoring, and talent scarcity.

- SCM 2.0 leverages proven solutions designed to rapidly deliver results with the agility to quickly manage future change for continuous flexibility, value and success. This is delivered through competency networks composed of best of breed supply chain domain expertise to understand which elements, both operationally and organizationally, are the critical few that deliver the results as well as the intimate understanding of how to manage these elements to achieve desired results, finally the solutions are delivered in a variety of options as no touch via business process outsourcing, mid touch via managed services and software as a service (SaaS), or high touch in the traditional software deployment model.

Supply chain business process integration Successful SCM requires a change from managing individual functions to integrating activities into key supply chain processes. An example scenario: the purchasing department places orders as requirements become appropriate. Marketing, responding to customer demand, communicates with several distributors and retailers, and attempts to satisfy this demand. Shared information between supply chain partners can only be fully leveraged through process integration. Supply chain business process integration involves collaborative work between buyers and suppliers, joint product development, common systems and shared information. According to Lambert and Cooper (2000) operating an integrated supply chain requires continuous information flows, which in turn assist to achieve the best product flows. However, in many companies, management has reached the conclusion that optimizing the product flows cannot be accomplished without implementing a process approach to the business. The key supply chain processes stated by Lambert (2004) are: Customer relationship management Customer service management Demand management Order fulfillment Manufacturing flow management Supplier relationship management Product development and commercialization Returns management.

One could suggest other key critical supply business processes combining these processes stated by Lam-bert such as: Customer service management Procure-ment Product development and commercialization Manufacturing flow management/support Physical distribution Outsourcing/partnerships Performance measurement

- Customer service management process: Customer Relationship Management concerns the relationship between the organization and its customers. Customer service provides the source of customer information. It also provides the customer with real time information on promising dates and product availability through interfaces with the company's production and distribution operations. Successful organizations use following steps to build customer relationships: determine mutually satisfying goals between organization and customers establish and maintain customer rapport produce positive feelings in the organization and the customers
- *Procurement process:* Strategic plans are developed with suppliers to support the manufacturing flow management process and development of new products. In firms where operations extend globally, sourcing should be managed on a global basis. The desired outcome is a win-win relationship, where both parties benefit, and reduction times in the design cycle and product development are achieved. Also, the purchasing function develops rapid communication systems, such as electronic data interchange (EDI) and Internet linkages to transfer possible requirements more rapidly. Activities related to obtaining products and materials from outside suppliers requires performing resource planning, supply sourcing, negotiation, order placement, inbound transportation, storage, handling and quality assurance, many of which include the responsibility to coordinate with suppliers in scheduling, supply continuity, hedging, and research into new sources or programmes.
- *Product development and commercialization:* Here, customers and suppliers must be united into the product development process, thus to reduce time to market. As product life cycles shorten, the appropriate products must be developed and successfully launched in ever shorter time schedules to remain competitive. According to Lambert and Cooper (2000), managers of the product development and commercialization process must: coordinate with customer relationship management to identify customer articulated needs; select materials and suppliers in conjunction with procurement, and develop production technology in manufacturing flow to manufacture and integrate into the best supply chain flow for the product/market combination.
- *Manufacturing flow management process:* The manufacturing process is produced and supplies products to the distribution channels based on past forecasts. Manufacturing processes must be flexible to respond

to market changes, and must accommodate mass customization. Orders are processes operating on a just-in-time (JIT) basis in minimum lot sizes. Also, changes in the manufacturing flow process lead to shorter cycle times, meaning improved responsiveness and efficiency of demand to customers. Activities related to planning, scheduling and supporting manufacturing operations, such as work-in-process storage, handling, transportation, and time phasing of components, inventory at manufacturing sites and maximum flexibility in the coordination of geographic and final assemblies postponement of physical distribution operations.

- *Physical distribution:* This concerns movement of a finished product/service to customers. In physical distribution, the customer is the final destination of a marketing channel, and the availability of the product/service is a vital part of each channel participant's marketing effort. It is also through the physical distribution process that the time and space of customer service become an integral part of marketing, thus it links a marketing channel with its customers (*e.g.* links manufacturers, wholesalers, retailers).
- *Outsourcing/partnerships:* This is not just outsourcing the procurement of materials and components, but also outsourcing of services that traditionally have been provided in house. The logic of this trend is that the company will increasingly focus on those activities in the value chain where it has a distinctive advantage and everything else it will outsource. This movement has been particularly evident in logistics where the provision of transport, warehousing and inventory control is increasingly subcontracted to specialists or logistics partners. Also, to manage and control this network of partners and suppliers requires a blend of both central and local involvement. Hence, strategic decisions need to be taken centrally with the monitoring and control of supplier performance and day-to-day liaison with logistics partners being best managed at a local level.
- *Performance measurement:* Experts found a strong relationship from the largest arcs of supplier and customer integration to market share and profitability. By taking advantage of supplier capabilities and emphasizing a long-term supply chain perspective in customer relationships can be both correlated with firm performance.

As logistics competency becomes a more critical factor in creating and maintaining competitive advantage, logistics measurement becomes increasingly important because the difference between profitable and unprofitable operations becomes more narrow. A.T. Kearney Consultants (1985) noted that firms engaging in comprehensive performance measurement realized improvements in overall productivity. According to experts internal measures are generally collected and analyzed by the firm including Cost Customer Service Productivity measures Asset measurement, and Quality. External performance measurement is examined through customer perception measures and "best practice" benchmarking, and includes

- Customer perception measurement, and
- Best practice benchmarking.

Components of Supply Chain Management are

- Standardization
- Postponement
- Customization

Theories of Supply Chain Management Currently there exists a gap in the literature available in the area of supply chain management studies, on providing theoretical support for explaining the existence and the boundaries of supply chain management. Few authors such as Halldorsson, et al. (2003), Ketchen and Hult (2006) and Lavassani, et al. (2008) had tried to providc theoretical foundations for different areas related to supply chain with employing organizational theories. These theories include: Resource based view (RBV) Transaction Cost Analysis (TCA) Knowledge based view (KBV) Strategic Choice Theory (SCT) Agency theory (AT) Institutional theory (InT) Systems Theory (ST) Network Perspective (NP) Components of Supply Chain Management Integration

THE MANAGEMENT COMPONENTS OF SUPPLY CHAIN MANAGEMENT

The SCM components are the third element of the four square circulation framework. The level of integration and management of a business process link is a function of the number and level, ranging from low to high, of components added to the link. Consequently, adding more management components or increasing the level of each component can increase the level of integration of the business process link.

The literature on business process reengineering, buyer-supplier relationships, and SCM suggests various possible components that must receive managerial attention when managing supply relationships. Lambert and Cooper (2000) identified the following components which are: Planning and control Work structure Organization structure Product flow facility structure Information flow facility structure Management methods Power and leadership structure Risk and reward structure Culture and attitude However, a more careful examination of the existing literature will lead us to a more comprehensive structure of what should be the key critical supply chain components, the "branches" of the previous identified supply chain business processes, that is, what kind of relationship the components may have that are related with suppliers and customers accordingly.

Bowersox and Closs states that the emphasis on cooperation represents the synergism leading to the highest level of joint achievement. A primary level channel participant is a business that is willing to participate in the inventory ownership responsibility or assume other aspects of financial risk, thus including primary level components. A secondary level participant (specialized), is a business that participates in channel relationships by performing essential services for primary participants, thus including secondary level components, which are in support of primary participants.

Third level channel participants and components that will support the primary level channel participants, and which are the fundamental branches of the secondary level components, may also be included. Consequently, Lambert and Cooper's framework of supply chain components does not lead us to the conclusion about what are the primary or secondary (specialized) level supply chain components.

That is, what supply chain components should be viewed as primary or secondary, how these components should be structured in order to have a more comprehensive supply chain structure, and to examine the supply chain as an integrative one. Baziotopoulos reviewed the literature to identify supply chain components. Based on this study, Baziotopoulos (2004) suggests the following supply chain components:

For customer service management: Includes the primary level component of customer relationship management, and secondary level components such as benchmarking and order fulfillment. For product development and commercialization: Includes the primary level component of Product Data Management (PDM) and secondary level components such as market share, customer satisfaction, profit margins, and returns to stakeholders. For physical distribution, manufac-turing support and procurement: Includes the primary level component of enterprise resource planning (ERP), with secondary level components such as warehouse management, material management, manufacturing planning, personnel manage-ment, and postponement (order management).

For performance measurement: Includes the primary level component of logistics performance measurement, which is correlated with the information flow facility structure within the organization. Secondary level components may include four types of measurement such as: variation, direction, decision and policy measurements. More specifically, in accordance with these secondary level components, total cost analysis (TCA), customer profitability analysis (CPA) and asset management could be concerned as well. For outsourcing: Includes the primary level component of management methods, and the strategic objectives for particular initiatives in key areas of information technology, operations, manufacturing capabilities, and logistics (secondary level components).

REVERSE SUPPLY CHAIN

Reverse Logistics is the process of planning, implementing and controlling the efficient, effective inbound flow and storage of secondary goods and related information opposite to the traditional supply chain direction for the purpose of recovering value or proper disposal. Reverse logistics is also referred to as "Aftermarket Customer Services". In other words, anytime money is taken from a company's Warranty Reserve or Service Logistics budget that is a Reverse Logistics operation.

The Bullwhip Effect

The fundamental idea of supply chain management is that all parties in volved should coordinate their activities and collaborates, thus improving the profitability of all supply chain partners. If each value added partner is considered in isolation, inefficiencies in the supply chain can occur. They result mainly from the isolated planning of materials or order quantities along the value chain and are described as the bullwhip effect. This occurs when sales or order quantity fluctuations swing upwards through the various value added stages, with the amplitudes increasing at each stage.

The bull whip effect results from the fact that customer demand is often unstable. Thus, each company in the supply chain must forecast demand. Because of incomplete information and uncertainties, forecasting errors are common and companies therefore usually carry safety stock in their inventory. Moving up the supply chain from the consumer to the suppliers, each participant in the supply chain observes higher fluctuations in demand and therefore has a greater need for inventory buffers.

If demand rises, supply chain participants tend to increase stock and orders. On the other hand, if demand declines, companies tend to reduce inventory stocks. The bullwhip effect is characterised by variations amplifying the further one moves up in the supply chain from the consumer to the suppliers. The effect demonstrates how pervasive inefficiencies can arise mainly from delays caused by uncoordinated planning cycles (*e.g.* because of order batching, price fluctuations or the rationing of quantities by manufacturers), in consistent and possibly out of date customer information or sales data.

This then impacts planning and reduces the transparency of supply and material quantities beyond the specific value added stage. The main approach to solving these difficulties is the implementation of comprehensive inters organisational information and planning systems, developing an information flow in the supply chain which reduces inefficiency. Apart from information sharing, other sales and marketing practices in the supply chain, such as the price schedule offered by the manufacturers, frequency and depth of price promotion, demand forecasting methods, allocation rules in case of shortage, etc., are important.

Efficient Consumer Response

The consequence of the problems encountered with isolated planning is that cooperation and collaboration among the supply chain participants are at the core of industry efforts to attenuate the bullwhip phenomenon. The concept of efficient consumer response (ECR) is significant in this context. ECR comprises a number of collaborative strategies and operating practices between retailers and suppliers that focus on fulfilling consumer needs better, faster and at less cost. The ECR concept implies a shift from the traditional push oriented view of the supply chain that relied on "pushing" merchandise through the supply chain, initiated and performed in anticipation of customer orders, to a pull oriented supply chain.

Pull processes, in this view, are triggered by consumer demand and are executed in response to consumer needs. ECR is thus a demand driven pull system that has an affinity to the concept of just in time. Efficient consumer response is central to the development of concepts for exploiting inter organisational potential through the structuring and control of value chains and offers a range of supply side and demand side oriented concepts based on retailer supplier collaboration.

Supply Side Concepts in ECR

Whereas demand side oriented concepts focus on cooperation in marketing, supply side oriented concepts strongly emphasise logistical issues. Following the pull oriented view, they relate mainly to the satisfaction of demand in terms of delivering the right products to the right destinations at the right time and in the right quantities ("4r") throughout the supply chain at lowest possible costs. The emphasis is on minimising logistics costs, such as transport costs, in particular inventory costs, and costs related to asset commitment.

The main areas of collaboration on the supply side are:

- *Efficient administration (EA):* EA focuses on efficient administrative processes between the supply chain parties. Very important in this context are electronic data interchange (EDI) and other technologies that enable, for example, process automation.
- *Efficient operating standards (EOS):* The objective of these concepts is to enhance efficiency by establishing industry wide standards.
- *Efficient replenishment (ER):* The main goal of ER is to synchronise manufacturer and supplier operations with retail sales in terms of a just in time pull oriented supply chain driven by retail sales.

Order and Delivery

The super ordinate concept in inventory management for ECR is continuous replenishment (CRP) which implies the continuous flow of merchandise based on consumer demand (*i.e.* retail sales). The fundamental idea is to transfer the just in time concept to retail outlets and thus reduce overall inventory at all stages of the supply chain. Continuous replenishment systems require integrated information systems (*e.g.* EDI) that enable close to real time transfer of sales and inventory data between retailer and supplier.

This information transfer enables suppliers and retailers to reduce lead times in production and delivery. Quick response (QR) is a specific type of CRP, and a concept which has been developed to accelerate product flows in the supply chain. The concept was developed in the textile industry to reduce replenishment lead times and is especially well suited to markets with high volatility in demand and a rapidly changing assortment.

The main objective is to decrease the number of over stocks and of out of stocks in the fashion industry, which is characterised by a high number of product variants and short fashion cycles with low demand predictability and a high share of impulse purchases. By allowing for multiple orders to be placed in the selling season, quick response enables a better match between demand and supply. A manufacturers' postponement strategy is closely linked to this concept and refers to the delay of product differentiation until temporarily closer to the sale of the product.

Inventory Management Concepts

Inventory management strategies in efficient replenishment can be classified according to the party responsible for maintaining inventory levels in vendor managed inventory (VMI), buyer managed inventory (BMI) or co managed or jointly managed inventory (CMI). The focus of attention is on vendor managed inventory, which is characterised by the vendor being responsible for maintaining the retailer's inventory in the retailer's distribution centre or in each of the outlets.

The main objective is to reduce out of stocks in the stores, and inventory in the supply chain, by centralising forecasting at the supplier and shortening of supply chain. For the retailers, VMI is sometimes associated with a loss of control in the supply chain. VMI requires a continuous information transfer between both parties in terms of sales and inventory data, and the vendor generates the orders (*i.e.* reverse purchase orders). Under ideal conditions, inventories are replenished in quantities that meet the retailer's immediate demand, reducing out of stocks with minimal inventory.

Buyer managed inventories imply retailers maintaining the suppliers' inventory. They are thus inversely related to VMI. Jointly managed inventories entail cooperation between vendor and retailer in inventory management.

Transport and Distribution

Several transport and distribution strategies are applied in efficient replenishment. They serve mainly to guarantee continuous product flows in the supply chain). For example, cross docking allows for stockless distribution processes and transport optimisation. Direct store delivery (DSD) means that merchandise is shipped directly to the outlets and transport pooling helps to use transport capacities to the full extent.

COLLABORATIVE PLANNING, FORECASTING, AND REPLENISHMENT (CPFR)

Collaborative planning, forecasting, and replenishment is a concept which integrates the idea of supply side and demand side concepts in ECR. The concept focuses mainly on promotion processes and thus relates primarily to HiLo pricing strategies that, in contrast to EDLP pricing strategies, are usually characterised by a high risk of running out of stock, because of high demand uncertainty.

The main goal of CPFR is to increase sales forecast accuracy by joint sales planning by manufacturer and retailer, using all available data from both parties. Based on this forecast, production, delivery, warehousing and advertising are coordinated to achieve higher product availability and reduce inventory costs. Additionally, as information on customer behaviour is available simultaneously to all participants, reaction to sudden, unanticipated, changes in demand is possible.

Enabling Technologies

Supply chain management requires efficient information sharing processes between the parties at each stage of the value chain. Many available technologies enable such information flows. In order to facilitate an inter organisational data exch-ange, electronic data interchange (EDI) and communication networks that enable instantaneous, real time information transfers such as Internet, intranet or extranet are necessary. Standardisation and automation are important to increase efficiency of such information processes.

Other particularly important enablers of inter organisational information exchange are, therefore:

- *Automated identification systems:* Important auto id systems are bar codes, optical character recognition or RFID. They are based on coding systems such as global trade item numbers (GTIN) that identify each SKU (item) in the supply chain, the global location numbers (GLN) for identifying each participant in the supply chain or the serial shipping container code (SSCC) for identifying shipping units.
- *Communication standards:* Standardised message formats that can be processed by the IT systems of all involved parties are important for inter organisational data transfer. Examples are UN/EDIFACT (United Nations Electronic Data Interchange for Administra-tion, Commerce

and Transport), EANCOM (a subset of UN/EDIFACT in the consumer goods industry) or GS1 XML, which is a more flexible message format.

- *Master data:* Master data are the basic data in information processing. They characterise each object in the supply chain, for example, each customer or supplier. Customer and supplier master data are usually company specific whereas article master data are usually exchanged between the parties. Thus, standardisation in this field is very important.

INFORMATION MANAGEMENT

As the bullwhip effect demonstrates, information availability is extremely important at all stages of the supply chain. For example, suppliers need in formation from the retailer on sales, inventory turnover, and feedback on competitors or on the level of customer returns. Information is also needed from consumers on attitudes towards the products, brand loyalty, willingness to pay, etc.

Retailers need, for example, sales forecasts, information on product specifications, advance notice of new models, training materials for complex products, and information from consumers on their shopping needs, where else they shop and their satisfaction level with the retailer and the merchandise. Retailers play a crucial role in collecting information on consumers, because they have direct con tact with the customers at the point of sale and can collect information which goes beyond sales or scanning data and is important for marketing and logistics.

They thus can act as gatekeepers in the supply chain who are able to control information flows. The above examples demonstrate the need for information flows between the different departments of the retailer (*e.g.* marketing and logistics) and also at an inter-organisational level.

In order to guarantee efficient and timely information flows and to reduce errors in information transmission, information technology (IT) plays a vital role. In a pull oriented supply chain, the starting point for information flows is the retail outlet. Thus, store based IT, especially point of sale systems that enable the scanning of bar codes, is of particular importance. Such point of sale systems does not only increase efficiency and productivity in the stores (*e.g.* faster check outs), but, in terms of logistical benefits, enable the immediate recording of sales and a rapid flow of sales and inventory information.

Also, orders can be automatically recommended or triggered (sales based ordering (SBO)). Also important are enterprise software systems such as enterprise resource planning systems (ERP) or merchandise information systems (MIS). ERP systems such as SAP, Oracle or Microsoft Dynamics integrate all data and processes of the retail company into a single unified system. They usually consist of various components such as human resources, finance or logistics. In retail companies, particularly MIS, as integral part of ERP systems, play a central role. MIS such as SAP for Retail or Oracle Retail support all information processes related to product flows in the retail channel, for example, merchandise planning, ordering or inventory processes.

At all stages of the supply chain, data is important for decision support. The information (*e.g.* merchandise information, sales, customer data, or supplier information) is "stored" in huge databases that are referred to as data warehouses. This information can be accessed by different departments within a retail company (*e.g.* marketing, buying, or logistics) and serves as input for the various software systems such as ERP, MIS or data mining systems.

SUPPLIER DEVELOPMENT

The issue of supplier development is not one which has traditionally been well explored in the quality literature, although there has been recent substantial development in the area, particularly following the integration of supplier relationships with the revised ISO 9001:2000 standard. A useful text is Kenneth Lysons's Purchasing and Supply Chain Management, which provides a broad grounding in this area.

Suppliers of both materials and services are critical to the achievement of quality. The quality of material inputs to a manufacturing process are strong determinants of the quality of output. Similarly, the quality of bought-in services, such as distribution and logistics, accounting, information technology support and building or machine maintenance, affects either the production process or the interface with the customer - for example, through deliveries or invoicing. Clearly, a part of being a quality organization is ensuring that the external factors affecting the input and output ends of the internal processes meet the requisite quality standard.

WHAT IS SUPPLIER DEVELOPMENT?

Supplier development is best thought of as a business policy espoused by a company which is serious about achieving quality. It involves a commitment by that company to set and attain internal quality standards which meet the requirements of its customers, and to support its suppliers in enabling them to meet those same requirements.

Traditionally, companies wishing to exercise a degree of control of the upstream or down-stream elements of the value chain have followed the route of vertical integration, either through development of their own services or through acquisition. However, these traditional routes have usually proven less than fully successful. The company loses the focus on its core business, often operating the other parts of the business less successfully and at greater cost than specialists, so that instead of excelling at one task it becomes mediocre at many. Equally, it is frequently the case that overall profitability is adversely affected. Supplier development moves away from this strategy, recognizing its inherent difficulties and limitations, and respecting the expertise and knowledge specific to the fulfilment of a particular need.

Supplier development requires that the company change its posture in relation to its suppliers. Traditionally, the buyer-supplier relationship is adversarial, each party seeking to maximize its own benefit from the relationship. Supplier development requires that this relationship become co-operative or collaborative, such that buyer and supplier work together to maximize their mutual interests. Forming the new relationship demands a change in buying processes. The placing of orders based on lowest price and sealed tenders has to cease, with a change to open exchange of information and negotiations based on a willingness to achieve an equitable outcome for both parties. For example, the need of each party to generate an adequate return on its efforts must be respected.

A move towards using a single supplier is also advocated by some writers, including Deming (1986:35-40). This policy has both advantages and drawbacks. Positively, utilizing a single source of supply should ensure greater reliability of inputs in terms of consistency, lack of variability (that is, closer adherence to standards) and the potential for continually improving standards and reduced paperwork. From the supplier's perspective, it is perhaps assured of a particular level of order, potentially higher-order values, greater certainty in its business planning and longer production runs with bigger batch sizes (with reductions in down-time and set-up time, which in both cases increases productivity), more reliable payment and availability of additional expertise (from their customer).

However, there are drawbacks; the buying organization may close itself off to other options, reducing the opportunity for speculative or spot purchases of materials (which meet requirements), and may reduce its leverage in price negotiations with the supplier, particularly when supplier power is high (Porter, 1980). The organization becomes vulnerable to changes in strategy, tactics or performance by its supplier. This is particularly important when the product or service purchased is critical to the process.

An example of this would be when distribution is contracted out to a dedicated haulage firm, which then, for reasons unrelated to the particular contract, experiences financial or other difficulties such as a strike or limitation on the availability of vehicles. From the supplier's perspective, becoming the sole source of supply to a particular organization may involve the dedication of a significant proportion of its resources to fulfilling that order. In this case, it in turn may become vulnerable to any difficulties experienced by its customer or any change of product or strategy on the customer's part.

For example, if the buyer ceases to produce a particular product, or suffers from extensive competition, leading to falling volumes, the fortunes of the supplier are similarly affected. This is a particular issue for small businesses acting as specialist suppliers to large organizations. The maintenance of the relationship and the volume of resources required to maintain the supply can swamp the small company.

The foregoing comments are general considerations which must be addressed before any sole supplier relationship is agreed. It may be that both parties feel that the advantages outweigh the disadvantages and associated risks in the particular case and choose to proceed. On the other hand, one or the other may find that the relationship would make it especially vulnerable, in which case it should instead seek alternative arrangements.

Clearly, there is a significant degree of risk to a supplier if the agreement with a buyer constitutes a significant proportion of the total business and limits, for whatever reason, the supplier's ability to undertake business with other parties. That said, there is also significant potential advantage to the buying organization in successfully pursuing the strategy of supplier development, particularly in the creation of a long-term and stable relationship.

HOW IS SUPPLIER DEVELOPMENT UNDERTAKEN?

The decision to pursue a policy of supplier development can reasonably be undertaken only by an organization already fully committed to quality and which recognizes that improved input quality is necessary to support its implementation programme. To pursue this policy when the organization is not already achieving high standards may well be seen by the supplier as an attempt to shift the blame for quality failure. Such an approach is unlikely to be well received. Supplier development takes place in seven stages. The first stage is, like the first stage in a quality programme, crucial. If the senior management are not committed to the process and its outcomes (including the need to provide short-term financial support and to commit workforce resources to the strategy), it will fail.

SEVEN STAGES OF SUPPLIER DEVELOPMENT

Stage 1: Make a commitment (at senior management level) to supplier development
Stage 2: Audit and evaluate internal standards
Stage 3: Define and quantify the desirable or necessary changes
Stage 4: Develop agreement with identified suppliers
Stage 5: Form joint teams and develop a training programme (if necessary)
Stage 6: Teams define precise objectives, deliverables and timescale
Stage7: Implement changes and monitor impacts

The second stage is to audit and evaluate the processes in which the supplier's inputs are used, to ensure that these meet the current internal expectations. Similarly, the inputs themselves must be formally evaluated. If a process is failing because of internal factors, then no amount of supplier development will cure it. Similarly, if suppliers are to be approached to improve their performance, it is vital that the buyer can precisely demonstrate the need by showing the impact on the buyer's own output.

Stage 3 is for the buying organization to determine what standards it expects its suppliers to achieve and, consequently, what changes are necessary and which desirable. It is important to discriminate between those aspects which are essential to acceptable performance - that is, meeting requirements - and those which would be beneficial in the longer term but are not currently essential. This stage, taken together with stage 2, defines the gap between the current

CO-OPERATION OR COMPETITION?

As the public face of the food industry, the large supermarket chains adopt what might be regarded as supplier development strategies. They are committed to continuously enhancing the quality (by their measures) of the foodstuffs they sell, and make use of this commitment in their advertising.

These organizations work closely with their suppliers through the buying process, evaluating not just the goods themselves, but the factories, farms and delivery systems. They agree exacting standards with the suppliers for all aspects of the product and reserve the right to refuse deliveries which do not meet those standards. Pricing is a difficult issue in this area, with strong competition between the supermarket chains and consequent pressure on suppliers to reduce costs. They do not always, however, adhere to the supplier development strategy outlined. While the first three phases are usually completed, thereafter the process often breaks down. The agreement is often rather one-sided.

The buying power of the supermarket chains, coupled to the fragmentation of the food production industry, with its many competing small suppliers, tends to make those suppliers vulnerable to pressure. Similarly, stages 5, 6 and 7 are usually forgone, with the supermarkets expecting the supplier to conform to the new standards and to bear the cost of so doing - and it has been widely reported in the press that they sometimes require the supplier to contribute financially to the allocation of shelf space in the supermarket itself.

While in the short term this appears beneficial to end-consumers, there is a danger in the longer term that the number of suppliers will be significantly reduced. In this circumstance, choice and variety will fall and prices will rise, reflecting the greater strength of those suppliers in their relationships with the supermarkets.

The idea of 'partnership' between buyers and suppliers, which supplier development strategies imply, would probably be most beneficial to all parties in the long run. Variety would be maintained, prices would be relatively stable as a result of continuing competition, and food quality would continually improve. This beneficial outcome can be achieved only under co-operative rather than combative conditions. Performance of the supplier and the necessary performance.

This defines the initial scope for the supplier development strategy and provides a basis for measuring subsequent performance improvement. The first three stages simply prepare the ground for approaching suppliers. The buying organization is now equipped with the information necessary to engage in meaningful discussions.

Stage 4 is the development of agreement with the identified suppliers. Clearly, if the suppliers are not willing to join in with the programme, then nothing is lost, since the organization is fully prepared to approach alternative sources with a clear idea of its expectations. The supplying organization must be prepared to make the same commitment to improving performance as the buying organization. The basis of moving forwards should be a written agreement setting out the aims and objectives of the programme and the benefits to be delivered.

Stage 5 is the formation of joint problem-solving teams tasked with pursuing the various benefits. These should take the form of quality circles and may require training or development input in order to function effectively. Ideally, these teams should include representatives of all relevant functions in the two organizations.

For example, a team made up exclusively of product buyers and sales staff would not be effective, since they are likely to have only limited knowledge of the problems in use of the particular product or service. Operational staff must be regarded as fundamental to such a team, which should have the authority to draw on other resources when appropriate - for example, accounting staff (for costings), statisticians (for the development of process control measurement), and so on.

Stage 6 is the implementation phase, when the designated teams should initially define precise objectives, tasks and timescales in the light of the current performance gap. Implementation itself should more or less follow the pattern of quality circle operation, using the same quality tools and techniques. Finally, stage 7 is concerned with implementing any changes arising, and monitoring the impacts against the expected benefits. It may be that for very large organizations a supervisory or steering board is required to oversee the implementation programme (particularly if a part of the strategy is to transfer the learning which takes place to other parts of the respective operations). For smaller organizations, this should not be necessary. Like most other aspects of a quality programme, supplier development can never be considered complete. It is an ongoing, iterative process which aims to continually improve performance for the benefit of both parties.

CRITIQUE OF SUPPLIER DEVELOPMENT

There is clearly significant benefit to be gained by organizations working together to improve performance. They can streamline processes, reduce costs, enhance productivity and more adequately satisfy their customers' expectations. The drawbacks to this strategy principally surround the issue of vulnerability of either the supplier or buyer through dependence on a single source. This vulnerability relates to financial leverage and to the risks of failure to supply.

To be successful, a supplier development strategy relies upon absolute commitment by both parties to making the arrangement work and a willingness and intent to act in the utmost good faith at all times.

2

Issues of Supply Chain Management in a Global Setting

A month before year 2006 Christmas, I visited a shopping mall in the southern Virginia area. A majority of all their merchandise was being manufactured offshore. In the same month in Ha Noi, Viet Nam on November 19, 2006, 21 Asian-Pacific Economic Cooperation countries had the 14th APEC Economic Leaders' Meeting. The APEC leaders acknowledged the role of comprehensive Regional Trade Agreements/Free Trade Agreements in advancing trade liberalization. They also agreed RTAs/FTAs lead to greater trade liberalization and genuine reductions in trade transaction costs. Globalization is inevitable. As we are looking five to ten years down the road, we are sure about one thing that is the continual liberalization of trade. As more and more countries get opened up to world trade, more and more companies are seeking for the most cost effective way to produce and deliver products. Companies of various sizes realise that they have to be part of the global supply chain in order to stay competitive and remain in business.

SCM ISSUES IN THE US

In the past 20 years, the United States has been at the forefront of developing new supply chain management models, reengineering operations processes, and advancing technologies for supply chain management. Wal-Mart, Dell Inc., and HP as well as many other companies have already demonstrated their ability in managing supply chain under the electronic commerce environment. As one of the world's largest consumer, producer, and trader, the US has a number of advantages in advancing supply chain management. First, the US citizens use the same official language, currency, and technology.

Additionally, the culture is much more similar than that in the other parts of the world, although there are some variations from region to region within the country. Second, it has a well-developed transportation infrastructure. Its sea and airport facilities are adequate to handle the flow of imports and exports. As far as intra-country transportation, its freight rail system is very productive and its highway system is more than sufficient to connect all activities within the supply chain. Third, its technology is readily available to all participants in the supply chain. Convenient access to the Internet and telecommunication is a feature of U.S. supply chains. From the aspect of technology, the U.S. leads both Europe and Japan in the deployment of e-commerce systems.

SCM ISSUES IN EUROPE

In recent years, the European Union has done much to unify the continent but there are still major differences in local markets, culture, legal regulations, politics, taxation requirements, economic development, wealth, and geography. Markets vary greatly from country to country, especially now with the emergence of new democracies in Eastern Europe. Influencing these differences is the widely varying cultures from region to region. Although some standard issues in the areas of quality, health, the environment, and timeliness are emerging, consumer service values vary widely across Europe. The difference in the value system forces manufacturers to focus on customization at the local level. Secondly, transportation infrastructure varies from country to country across Europe.

The geography of a country affects accessibility, which in turn influences both transportation methods as well as distribution networks. For example, Italy chooses a more local distribution network due to its compartmentalized geography. Holland, on the other hand, tends to use a more centralized distribution network with its relatively accessible geography. These transportation and distribution issues have led some firms to establish regional stockholding distribution centres, which may reduce the need and reliance on extensive distribution networks and reduce the dependency on transportation.

A considerable disadvantage of localized transportation systems in Europe is its relatively low usage of rail to transport freight. Poorly maintained infrastructure in some Eastern European countries, as well as differences in rail gauge size, technical standards, and height/width allowances between countries within Europe are the issues that slow down the development of supply chain management. Finally, the application of current technology also varies from country to country. Unlike the U.S., the availability of reliable Internet access and current technologies is not always a given in all countries throughout Europe. The variation of Internet access from region to region has a significant impact on the ability of firms to conduct collaborative planning, forecasting and replenishment within the supply chain in order to compete on a global level.

Although the continent and its countries are fighting to overcome some inherent challenges, Europe has made some significant strides forward and has implemented innovations to overcome some of these challenges. Mobile commerce, vehicle tracking and dispatching, radio frequency identification tags, silent commerce applications, and collaboration are few examples of recent development in Europe. High cell phone usage level has led to the development of mobile networks that are integrated into back end operations. Expanding on these wireless application advancements, Europe also has an increasing number of vehicle tracking and distribution systems. Nevertheless, cross-border and cross-culture issues are still the areas that need to be improved upon. The European Union has initiated to bring the whole of Europe to a single accepted standard, which may include the development of "freight corridors" via road, rail, and water to address distribution both within countries and regions as well as the continent as a whole.

SCM ISSUES IN ASIA

Supply chain management in Asia is considered more fragmented and less competitive than those in the United States and Europe, but the gap between these regions is closing. First, the Asian market is made up of many countries varying in culture, religion, political system, language, legal system, and stages of economic development. Some of the major countries include Japan, China, India, Australia, Indonesia, South Korea, and Thailand. This list of countries presents an obvious diversity in various aspects. Culturally speaking, most Asian cultures differ greatly from Europe and the United States. As an example, Asian culture values relationships greatly, and they are established over time and past dealings. This precludes the establishment of quick business deals. The focus tends to be on the establishment of respectful relationships over time. Second, the transportation infrastructure in many developing countries in Asia is less developed as compared to that of the US and Europe. Traditionally, rail transportation was a dominant public transportation in countries such as India, China, and Japan.

Air transportation is undergoing fast development in recent years, and highway construction is advancing at a rapid pace. For example, China is aggressively developing its highway system as well as improving the efficiency of its rail freight industry. In 2000, 50,000 kilometers of new highway was added in China. Finally, technology is also a major concern to developing efficient supply chains in Asia. There is weak availability of information technology in many developing Asian countries. Lowering production costs has been prevalent in Asia. However, the opportunity to reduce costs now lies in developing efficient logistics and distribution, which is a weak area in Asia. The use of information technology can assist greatly in this regard. Collaboration is an area of opportunity in Asia. Currently many of the collaborative efforts have been informal. As a more formal form of collaboration develops, especially at the industry level, greater efficiency can be achieved and savings will occur.

One of the main areas that need to be developed to enable this increased collaboration is information technology. Data integrity needs to be increased and information needs to be available upon request. This may require some companies to undergo a certain amount of re-engineering of their supply chains. In the near future, the outsourcing of logistics and supply chain functions will pay great dividends in the Asian market. As manufacturing companies begin to compete for a larger piece of the global market, they will need to compete on more than just low cost labour. Quality and cycle time management will be essential. To capitalize on the supply chain efficiency many small manufacturing companies, who lack the capability, have the need to turn to third party logistics providers to attain a competitive efficiency.

SCM ISSUES IN LATIN AMERICA

Latin American countries can offer U.S.-based firms an opportunity to expand their list of suppliers and cut down on costs. The NAFTA agreements give the US access to Mexico's low labour market. However, the differences in currency, transportation, infrastructure, political systems, and laws are just some of the hurdles facing businesses looking to take advantage of the opportunity in Latin America. Technology is also a major concern to developing efficient supply chains in Latin America. While computers are common in Mexico and other Latin American countries, high-tech communications aren't as reliable as they are in the U.S. Fewer people are networked via the Internet than those in the US, which makes it difficult to automate supply chains and reliably monitor inventory as it passes from one link to another.

In the rural area, technology is old or even not available. Because of Latin America's technology disparities, a company looking to connect with suppliers there will either have to invest in a mixed infrastructure involving electronic data interchange, Web, phone and fax systems or link up with third-party logistics providers that offer the necessary interfaces. For example, Ryder transports 3,000 different parts from Latin America for an automotive manufacturer that assembles trucks in Indiana. To keep track of inventories, Ryder uses a mixed radio, cell phone and EDI communications system. Each Sunday, Ryder gets e-mail with the plant's requirements. Half of the parts makers are either online or have EDI capabilities; the other half requires phone or fax-based transactions. The company had to build a considerable infrastructure to facilitate various communication devises.

SUPPLY CHAIN MANAGEMENT MODELS

COMPETITIVE PRIORITIES AND MANUFACTURING STRATEGY

The ability of a supply chain to compete based on cost, quality, time, flexibility, and new products is shaped by the strategic focus of the supply chain members. A firm's position on the competitive priorities is determined by its four long-term structural decisions: facility, capacity, technology, and vertical integration, as well as by its four infrastructural decisions: workforce, quality, production planning and control, and organization. The cumulative impact of infrastructural decisions on a firm's competitiveness is as important as long-term structural decisions. Manufacturing strategy focuses on a set of competitive priorities such as cost, quality, time, flexibility, and new product introduction.

It classifies production processes to five major types: project, job shop, batch, line, and continuous flow. "Make-to-stock", "assemble-to-order", "build-to-order" and "engineer-to-order" are a few of the manufacturing strategies used to address competitive priorities to compete on the market place. Make-to-stock involves holding products in inventory for immediate delivery, so as to minimize customer delivery times. This is in the category of push system. Demand is forecasted and production is scheduled before demand is there. Assemble-to-order is the strategy to handle numerous end-item configurations and is an option for mass-customization. Assemble-to-order items use standardized parts and components.

They require efficient and low cost production in the fabrication process and flexibility in the assembly or configuration stage to satisfy individualized demand from customers. Build-to-order, on the other hand, produces customised products in low volume after the manufacturer receives the orders. Build-to-order items are usually in very small volumes and require high technical competency, high product performance design, and effective due date management. Engineer-to-order produces products that are with unique parts and drawings required by customers. Product volume is very small and typically is one-of-a-kind in a job-shop environment. The cycle time from order to delivery is usually long because of the unique customization nature. MRP planning is extremely important for engineer-to-order.

Efficient Supply Chain and Responsive Supply Chain

One of the causes of supply chain failure is due to the lack of understanding of the nature of demand. The lack of understanding often leads mismatched supply chain design. Fisher suggested two distinctive approaches, efficient supply chain and responsive supply chain, to design a firm's supply chain. The purpose of responsive supply chain is to react quickly to market demand. This supply chain model best suites the environment in which demand predictability is low, forecasting error is high, product life cycle is short, new product introductions are frequent, and product variety is high. The responsive supply chain design matches competitive priority emphasizing on quick reaction time, development speed, fast delivery times, customization, and volume flexibility.

The design features of responsive supply chains include flexible or intermediate flows, high-capacity cushions, low inventory levels, and short cycle time. The purpose of an efficient supply chain is to coordinate the material flow and services to minimize inventories and maximize the efficiency of the manufacturers and service providers in the chain. This supply chain model best fits the environment in which demands are highly predictable, forecasting error is low, product life cycle is long, new product introductions are infrequent, product variety is minimal, production lead-time is long and order fulfillment lead-time is short. The efficient supply chain design matches competitive priority emphasizing on lowcost operations and on-time delivery. The design features of efficient supply chain include line flows, large volume production, and low-capacity cushions.

Table. Efficient Supply Chain and Responsive Supply Chain

	Efficient Supply Chain	**Responsive Supply Chain**
Demand Customer Order	Constant, Based on	Fluctuate, based on Forecasting
Product life cycle	Long	Short
Product variety	Low	High
Contribution margin	Low	High
Order fulfill lead time cycle	Long-term	According to product life
Supplier cycle	Long-term	According to product life
Production	Make-to-stock	Assemble-to-order Make-to-order Build-to-order
Capacity cushion	Low	High
Inventory	Finished goods inventory	Parts, components, subassembly
Supply selection	Low cost, consistent quality, and on-time delivery	Flexibility, fast-delivery, high-performance design quality

Clock-speed of Product, Process, and Organization Life Cycles

Fine suggests that each industry evolves at a different rate, depending in some way on its product clock-speed, process clock-speed, and organization clock-speed. For example, informationentertainment industry is one of the fast-clock-speed industries. Motion pictures can have product life measured in hours. Christmas time is the best season to introduce new movies when the number of viewers is greatest. The process for information-entertainment industry changes rapidly. New processes for delivering information-entertainment products and services to our home, public centres, and offices evolve daily. CD players, DVD are just a couple of examples. Organization structure is dynamic as well. Relationship among media giants such as Time- Warner, Disney, and

Viacom are negotiated, signed, and re-negotiated constantly to accommodate the changes in product and process design.

Aircraft industry is an example of slow clock-speed product industry. The Boeing Company measures its product's clock-speed in decades. Thirty years after Boeing 747 was first introduced, the profit generated from selling Boeing 747 is still flowing in. Boeing 747 produced and sold in 2000 has the same manufacturing plant as it had for the first of these aircraft. Somewhere in the middle is automobile industry. The product does not change as fast as information-entertainment industry, nor does it as slow as aircraft industry. Passenger cars, for example, have a product life of three to five years. As for its process clock-speed, each time automaker makes a new design, it expects much of that investment to be obsolete in four to five years. Supply chain design should reflect the nature of the product clockspeed; understanding what requirements would make it more likely for one to have an effective supply chain or *vice versa*. Analyzing the clockspeed of product, process and organization enables us to see with greater clarity and accuracy of the future needs from our customers.

Pull and Push Processes

All processes in a supply chain fall into one of two categories: push or pull. In the push process, production of a product is authorized based on forecasting which is in advance of customer orders. In the pull process, on the other hand, the final assembly is triggered by customer orders. In a pure push process, make-to-stock is the primary production approach. Demand is forecasted based on historical sales data. The need from the end users is satisfied from inventory. Production lead-time is relatively long and finished goods inventory is more than that of the pull system.

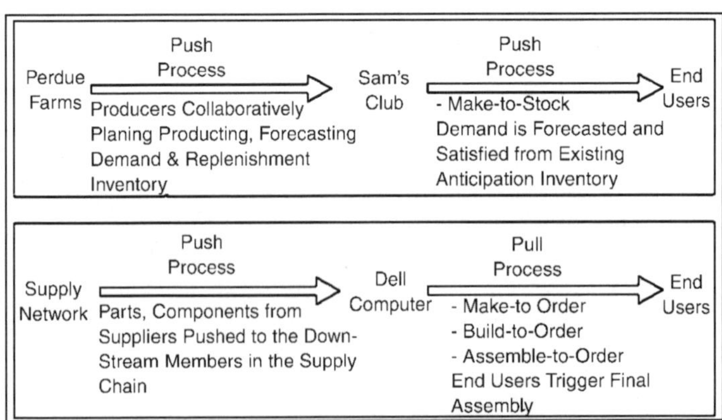

Fig. Pull *vs.* Push Process

The major technical sophistication that has been applied in the supply chain is Perdue Farms' vertical integration, which focuses on "We do it all for you."

In the pull approach, end users trigger the production of computers at Dell's manufacturing factory. The major production strategy is make-to-order, assemble-to-order, and build-toorder. In a pull scenario, demand uncertainty is higher and cycle time is shorter than that of the push approach. Finished goods inventory is minimal. Dell is an obvious captain of the supply chain. The major technical sophistication that has been applied in the supply chain is Dell's direct model, which focuses on "Have it your way."

The push/pull approach is important in designing supply chain. Demand uncertainty and variations are treated differently in these two systems. In a push system, safety stock is used to manage demand variability; while in a pull system, flexible capacity is required to meet the demand variability. Both inventory and capacity represent financial expenditure. Therefore, developing effective supply chains is crucial to achieve the cost-effective goal as well as delivering what the customer needs at the right time, right place, and in the right quantity.

SUPPLY CHAIN MANAGEMENT IN AN E-BIZ ENVIRONMENT: VIRTUAL INTEGRATION

Virtual integration is to use technology and information to blur the traditional boundaries among suppliers, manufacturers, distributors, and end users in a supply chain. Today, the virtual corporation of various firms in a supply chain is a reality with suppliers and customer trading over the Internet in real-time to create maximum value. Virtual integration offers the advantage of tightly coordinated supply chain that has traditionally come through vertical integration. In the age of virtual organizations, managers, engineers, professional staff, and technical workers are no longer the lone custodians of the corporate knowledge base. Knowledge is shared across cultural-boundaries, time-boundaries, and space-boundaries to create strategic frontiers in global and virtual enterprises.

A seamless virtual integration of firms within a supply chain requires real-time automation of inter-organization business processes that span across trading partners. In the last decade, organizations involved in a supply chain use e-mail, faxes, and voice mail. These practices introduce delays and often require data to be re-entered multiple times. In 1997, American companies spent ₹ 862 billion, or approximately 10 per cent of GNP, on supply related activities.

This includes the movement of materials, storage, and control of products across the supply chain. During the late 90s of last century, productivity surged from 1.5 per cent in earlier years to 2.5 per cent. The increase in productivity in the late 90s is a direct result of computer technology. The traditional arm's length transaction from one stage of supply chain to the next is showed in Figure. Organizations view their suppliers and customers as adversaries who are not to be trusted. This prevents entry into successful long-term relationships.

Performance is often narrowly viewed and procurement decisions are often based solely on price. Relationships are viewed in terms of a zero-sum game where there is a clear winner and a clear loser.

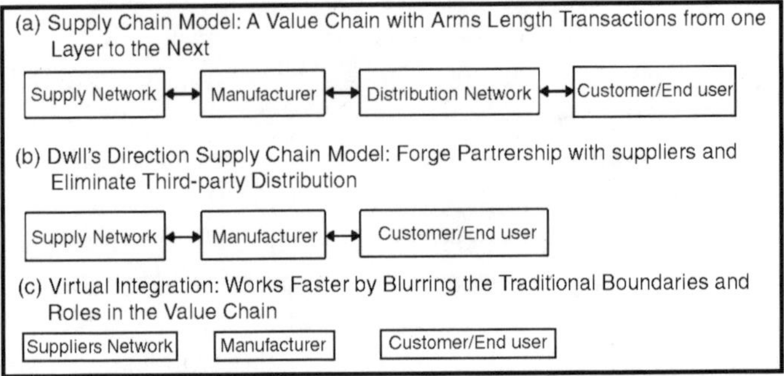

Fig. Supply Chain in e-Biz Environment

This model focuses on mutual trust and respect of supply chain members, just-in-time manufacturing, and eliminating third-party retailers. With this integrated supply chain, Dell only holds five days of inventory, and has a build cycle of two days on most systems. The integrated supply chain includes joint improvement projects, training seminars, workshops, and meetings between organizations' top management. As the degree of communication increases between customers and suppliers, higher levels of informal information sharing are witnessed.

THE TREND OF MASS-CUSTOMIZATION FORCES MANY COMPANIES TO FOCUS ON

Their core competences, and outsource a wide range of functions including design, manufacturing, and distribution. This trend drives the need for a virtually integrated supply chain.

AN EVOLUTION: FROM MATERIAL MANAGEMENT TO SUPPLY CHAIN MANAGEMENT

Information technology is the key driving force for moving material management to supply chain management in the second half of the 20th century. In 1970, the cost of one megahertz of computing power was ₹ 7,600. By the end of the century, it was 17 cents. The cost of storing one megabit of data was ₹ 5,256 in 1970. It is less than 17 cents now. Ever since the 1960s, technology has enabled business to create tools to ease the management of materials. The stages of the business model evolution with Bill of Materials processor in the early 60s, Material Requirement Planning in the 70s, Manufacturing Resource Planning in the 80s, Enterprise Resource Planning in the 90s, and supply chain management packages in the early twenty-first century. The impact in the evolution of advanced technology and computer power on materials and supply chain management is phenomenal.

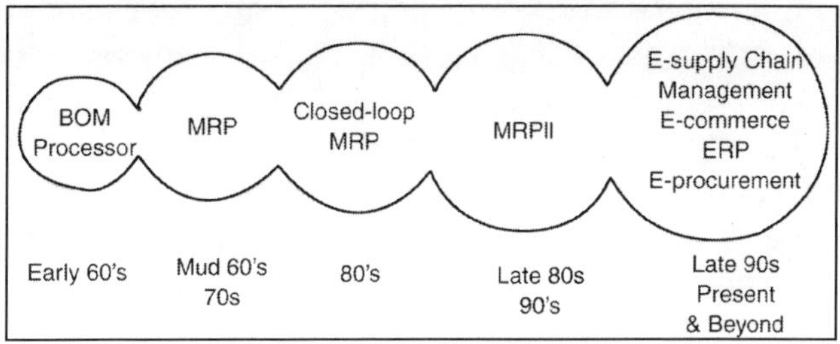

Fig. Evolution of e-supply Chain

In the early 1960s, a BOM processor was written on a 1400 disk computer in Milwaukee. In mid 1960, the first use of the computer for planning material was introduced and was named MRP. IBM was the first to introduce MRP software to the market. The significance of MRP is that it identifies what product is required by the customer; compares the requirement to the on-hand inventory level and calculates what items need to be procured and when. By itself, MRP does not recognize the capacity limitation. It will schedule order release even when the capacity is not available.

Closed loop MRP was then introduced to include capacity requirement planning as a part of material requirement planning. Advancement of computer capacity makes the extra mathematical computations for capacity planning available and affordable. In the mid 80s, Manufacturing Resource Planning evolved out of MRP and closed loop MRP. MRPII is a method for the effective planning of all resources of a manufacturing company. MRPII closed the loop not only with the capacity planning and accounting systems but also with the financial management systems. Consequently, all the resource of a manufacturing company could be planned and controlled as the information became more accessible using MRPII.

In the 1980s, labour cost decreased and material cost increased due to the automation of production process. Reducing inventory and shortening lead-time became inevitable to survive the competition. Companies searched for new business paradigms that would lead to competitive advantage. Just in Time, Theory of Constraints and Total Quality Management are examples of strategies that helped companies to improve production processes, reduce costs and successfully compete in a variety of business environments. The late 80s and early 90s witnessed the shift of 'time to market'. Customers demanded to have their products delivered when, where, and how they wanted them.

JIT requires cooperation along the entire supply chain with the ultimate goal of maximizing the profit of the supply chain. The beginning of JIT started along the assembly line and was not necessarily controlled by a computer but by a Kanban card using pull tags to suppliers. Sending a Kanban card or an empty container upstream along the assembly line was the signal to replenish inventory. A phone call to the supplier with an order was the trigger to deliver the next order. Companies world-wide began to embrace the philosophy of JIT and supplier partnership as a way to remain competitiveness. The 1990s caught sight of increased globalization and the Internet. In order to improve competitiveness, companies began realise the potential of information technology to dramatically transform their business. Instead of automating old, inefficient processes, companies began to reengineer business processes using technology as the enabler. This led to the development of ERP systems that give complete visibility to the organization, integrating previously stand-alone systems.

ERP became more acceptable during the mid- and late 1990s. ERP is not just MRPII with a new name. ERP is the next logical sophistication level in an evolutionary series of computer tools for material and supply chain management. ERP systems provide an integrated view of information across functions within a company and with the potential to go across companies. In late 90s and the beginning of 21st century, electronic communications as opposed to paper transactions allow for a decrease in amount of lead-time required to replenish inventory. Cutting lead-time minimizes the risk of uncertainty in demand and decreases the probability of over or under-stocking inventory. The 90s marked the wide use of the Internet.

This provided great opportunity for companies to integrate E-commerce into their business models. The primary emphasis during that period was business-to-customer. Today, the emphasis expands to include business-to-business or B2B. Back-end system integration, especially supply chain management provides greater visibility and more strategic capability for companies to improve profitability and competitiveness. Supply chain management models emerged. A supply chain consists of all stages involved, either directly or indirectly, in fulfilling a customer request. A supply chain includes manufacturer, supplier, transporters, warehouses, retailer, third-party logistic provider, and customer. The objective of supply chain management is to maximize the overall value generated rather than profit generated in a particular supply chain.

SUPPLY CHAIN ALIGNMENT WITH INTERNATIONAL REQUIREMENTS

The supply chain needs to be aligned with the requirements of importing countries which require control and monitoring of quality standards of the raw material and processed products. The specific action steps to facilitate this are:

- Enable direct farmer-processor linkages by amendment of the APMC Act
- Set-up independent world-class food testing and inspection infrastructure, particularly in clusters with significant presence of exporters

- Devise an alternate system of processing-grade product specifications based on internationally accepted norms, delinked from fair average quality of table grade products.
- Encourage investment in infrastructure to improve product quality, through part-funding these investments, such as financing of bulk coolers
- Support private sector initiatives for investing in specialized transport infrastructure such as reefer vans through specific financing schemes for this purpose

INTEGRATION OF GOVERNMENT SCHEMES

The Government, through various Ministries and allied agencies, offers support to exporters through various schemes to part-finance specific investment requirements.The Ministries/allied agencies include Ministry of Agriculture, Ministry of Food Processing, APEDA, MPEDA, Coffee Board, Tea Board, Export Inspection Council etc. It is essential to align the various offerings of the Government, to address various requirements of exporters and avoid duplication of efforts.

Supply chain issues have been identified as a key constraining factor for exports. The current approach to supporting food/agri exports, through isolated schemes operated by various Ministries/Departments of the Government has not been able to address bottlenecks to exports in an effective manner. There are significant overlaps, while at the same time several need gaps which have not been addressed. Further, the quantum of assistance has a low ceiling, which is one of the factors which contributes to small scale of operations of exporters.

The action plan is stated below:

- Integrate all schemes offered for export promotion through various Ministries and allied agencies such as APEDA, MPEDA, Coffee Board, Tea Board, Export Inspection Council, Ministry of Agriculture, Ministry of Food Processing etc. under one body.
- Strengthen food processing infrastructure in AEZs
- Encourage food testing laboratories in India to get accreditation from international agencies.
- Set-up independent world-class food testing and inspection infrastructure, particularly in clusters, with significant presence of exporters
- Devise an alternate system of processing grade product specifications based on internationally accepted norms.
- Promote aggregation of exports to meet the minimum order requirement of importers
- Expand the list of export products for certification by EIC

- Develop a strong market intelligence system to aid exporters to take rational decisions.
- Introduce certification zoning systems pesticide-free zones, organic production zones, disease free zones to facilitate high value exports from India
- Promote certification for organic farming for different crops
- Build global brands on the back of India's strengths (Darjeeling tea, Basmati rice, Durum wheat, Alphonso mango)

3

Supply Chain Stores and Voluntary Chain Management

Despite abundant literature on the subject, no clear-cut and universally acceptable definitions of the terms chain, chain store, or chain system have been developed. Common usage seems to relate the term chain to retail store operations and tends to neglect the existence of many chains of public utilities, banks, hotels, motion picture theatres, finance company offices, and other types which are an integral part of marketing.

Most of the best known so-called *retail* chains also operate chains of warehouses for the performance of the wholesaling functions and many also are extensively engaged in manufacturing activities. It is important, therefore, that one get an overview of the structure of chain store organizations, including the various levels on which they operate, before delving into an analysis of their competitive position and performance on the plane of retailing. Another matter of great importance is the manner in which various independent merchants have achieved certain advantages of chain operation by voluntarily integrating their interests and activities with those of other firms, both on the retail level and on other levels of the distribution channel as well.

DEFINITION

Several criteria are useful in differentiating chain store organizations from other types which tend to resemble them in some respects. These include

- Number of establishments,
- Type of merchandise handled,
- Plane or level of operation,
- Ownership of the units, and
- Management control.

On the basis of these factors, *a chain or chain store system or organization may be said to consist of two or more centrally owned units, handling, on the same plane of distribution, substantially similar lines of merchandise.* This definition is in line with that used by the Federal Trade Commission in various of its studies of chain stores and it is also in accord with Census of Business classification procedures.

While avoiding use of the term chain, the Census considers a store as a member of a *multiunit* organization "if it is one of two or more stores in the same general kind of business operated by the same firm." Thus, for example, a firm is classified as a *multiunit* if it operates two or more food stores, or if it operates two or more apparel stores; but a firm operating one drugstore, a hardware store, and a furniture store would not be so classified, and all the individual stores in this case would be regarded as *single units.*

Emphasis is placed on central ownership rather than management control, and to that extent at least, chains are to be distinguished from the so-called cooperative or voluntary chains in which the retailer members preserve individual ownership. The regular chain has full control over its retail units, assumes full financial responsibility for such units, bears all loss when a unit is closed and retains all profit made by each store. In a voluntary chain, on the other hand, cooperation with the central organization is contractual; the individual store assumes full financial responsibility for its acts; all profit earned by the store is retained by its owner; when a store is forced to close its doors it is considered commercially and legally a failure and the total loss is borne by the owner and his creditors.

CLASSES OF CHAINS

Two important ways of classifying regular chains are according to the extent of area served and according to the degree to which the organization has integrated retailing with other kinds of business activities.

GEOGRAPHIC BASIS

In terms of radius of operation, chains are generally classified as local, sectional, and national. Substantially all of the stores in *local chains* are located in or near the same metropolitan area. In almost all major cities, there are to be found local multiunit organizations in the food and drug fields. Such organizations are also rather common among department stores, clothing stores, furniture and appliance establishments, gasoline service stations, and liquor stores.

Chains are classified as *sectional* if their stores are located in some one major part of the country, such as New England, the Pacific Coast states, or any other recognized broad geographic division. Many of these are very large and are as well known to consumers within their area of operation as are the still larger national organizations.

Integration

Another useful classification is that based upon the degree of vertical integration. One group consists of retail chains *without wholesale distribution or manufacturing facilities,* thereby confining their activities to retailing. They procure merchandise through wholesalers or purchase directly from manufacturers, without special facilities for performing wholesaling functions within the company. In this group belong many local chains of only a limited number of units, also a substantial number of large organizations in the shoe, millinery, and apparel fields. A second group consists of chains with *warehouses or wholesale distribution centers.* This is typical in all convenience goods lines where regular wholesalers are of importance in serving independent merchants. As such chains grow in size and circumvent the wholesaler, they find it necessary to provide somewhat comparable physical facilities in which wholesaling activities are performed for the organization. In fact, there is no stronger evidence of the indispensable nature of the functions of the wholesaler than the existence of chain store wholesale warehouses.

The third type consists of chains that have integrated still farther by *the performance of manufacturing activities.* This group overlaps with the second in that its members ordinarily also operate wholesale distribution centers in addition to manufacturing establishments. Outright or partial ownership of subsidiary manufacturing companies, or strong control over the activities of supplying manufacturers by furnishing specifications and taking all or a substantial part of their output is common among the mail order companies that also operate large numbers of retail stores.

In the grocery trade, 63 major chains reported that they were engaged in some forms of manufacturing in 1958, and this group operated 340 manufacturing establishments, primarily to supply private brand merchandise to company stores. Sometimes integration has proceeded *forward* from manufacturing towards retailing, rather than *backward* from retailing towards manufacturing. Illustrative is the practice of certain major oil-producing companies whose principal business is done through bulk tank stations but which also operate some gasoline service stations. Several large shoe manufacturers have acquired chains of stores and operate them as controlled outlets. A well-known example is Genesco (formerly General Shoe Corp.). While long known as a leading shoe manufacturer, this company also diversified by acquiring firms manufacturing apparel and apparel accessory items. It operates a number of separately identified shoe chains and apparel stores.

It is thus apparent that to regard chains as purely retailing institutions is erroneous. Almost all of the medium-sized and larger organizations possess most of the characteristics of both retailing and wholesaling enterprises, and many are manufacturing as well as merchandising concerns.

ORIGIN AND DEVELOPMENT OF RETAIL CHAINS

The modern chain store is of comparatively recent origin. The chain idea of distribution, however, has many forerunners and prototypes. As early as 200 B.C., a certain Chinese businessman owned a chain of a great many units. A poster found in Pompeii, destroyed in A.D. 79, advertised for lease a certain property consisting of 900 retail shops. The Mitsui system of apothecary shops in Japan dates from 1643, and the company has been one of the wealthiest and most powerful businesses in that country. In the Americas, the Hudson's Bay Company operated a chain of trading posts prior to 1750. But in the United States the development of the modern chain was not started until the Great Atlantic and Pacific Tea Company was founded in 1858, although the second store was not opened until a year later. The second of existing chains is Park and Tilford, which began business in 1840 but did not open a second store until 1860.

The Jones Brothers Tea Company came into being in 1872, and the F. W. Woolworth Company proved the validity of the chain principle in the variety business about 1880.

While a number of chains were established during the latter half of the nineteenth century, their real growth occurred during the present century. It is estimated that in 1900 there were but 700 chains with 4,500 stores. Each succeeding year showed an increase in the number of chains and in chain stores. At first the number of chain systems increased faster than store units, but the reverse was true during the latter half of the period, indicating a possible absorption of smaller chains by larger ones and a more rapid expansion within large chain systems.

Growth in chain store volume of sales was spectacular. As late as 1919 the estimated volume of chains was less than 5 per cent of total retail sales, but by 1929 this proportion had increased six fold to about 30 per cent. The almost phenomenal development of chain organizations during the 1920's is explained by economic and social factors. The time was ripe to apply mass methods on a more widespread basis in retail distribution where efficiency had not generally kept pace with mass production techniques in industry.

The number of people living in cities was about twice that at the beginning of the century, with a large amount of the city growth coming during the 1920's. City locations are particularly desirable from the standpoint of chain store organizations, for the cost of advertising, supervision, and distribution from wholesale warehouses is low when units are highly concentrated. The development of the automobile and the improvement of roads made it possible for rural residents to shop in cities more frequently.

Between 1914 and 1920 retail prices almost doubled, with the result that most consumers became extremely price conscious. Because certain operating economies were effected, in part by a transfer of marketing functions to consumers, and because chains were able to purchase merchandise on very favorable terms in a prevailing buyers' market, they were usually able to undersell independents. It is doubtful if there was any period in our previous history when price appeals were any more in harmony with the interests of consumers.

LATER DEVELOPMENT AND CURRENT STATUS

The number of retail store units and sales volume importance of chains in recent decades is indicated by the following data:

Census of Business Year	Number of Stores in Multiunit Firms	% of Total Retail Sales
1968	326,524 ,43	29.6%
1979	291,040 ,48	30.6
1988	312,655 ,69	29.6
1994	257,027 ,71,	30.1
2005	252,735 ,52	33.7

From the standpoint of number of stores, chains had reached an apparent saturation point by 1929, followed by a decline until after 1948 when the downward trend was reversed. The volume of business transacted is, however, a much more important criterion of relative significance. During the 1930's and 1940's, chain store sales were stable at about 30 per cent of retail trade. During the latter 1950's, however, chains forged ahead, increasing their share to 33.7 per cent. Most of this increase was accounted for by chains of 11 or more stores.

The decline in the number of chain stores in the period 1929-48 is explained by several factors. One relates to a trend towards complete food stores, as opposed to earlier greater relative importance of specialized stores such as meat markets and produce stores (once known as "green grocers"). In the 1920's, grocers tended to add meats and fruits and vegetables to their stock and thus became combination grocery stores. This trend was greatly accelerated after 1929. A second reason has been the need for grocery chains to meet the competition of supermarkets which developed in the early 1930's, by operating fewer but larger units. Third, during the 1930's many oil refineries adopted a policy of turning over the operation of company-owned stations to independent merchants. Fourth, all of these trends and policies were stimulated by special taxes levied by some states on the stores operated by chain organizations, thus encouraging the closing of small and marginal units.

In some fields, however, the number of chain stores actually increased during this period. As experience proved their worth, the number of such stores was increased in the retailing of shoes, apparel, and other kinds of business.

Small Versus Large Chains

Multiunit firms that operate only a few stores are usually local organizations. Their interests, competitive situation, and methods of operation are often closer to those of independent merchants than they are to major chain store systems. Companies operating two to ten stores accounted for slightly more than one-half of all chain store units and about one-third of chain store sales volume in 1958.

This is a lower proportion of total chain store sales than achieved by this group in 1948. Among the explanations for this decline are the acquisition of some small chains by larger organizations, expansion of some small chains resulting in reclassification, and greater sales volume expansion by chains of larger size.

Chains of 11 or more stores tend to operate establishments of greater sales volume size. They account for about two-thirds of chain store sales but operate slightly less than one-half of the chain store units. Especially significant are chains with more than 100 stores. This group, with about 27 per cent of chain store units, does about 42 per cent of chain store sales.

Kind of Business

In some lines of business, chains dominate the trade, in others their position is not greatly different than their average share of market for total retail trade, and in still others they are of negligible importance. Chains account for more than 80 per cent of sales in the department and variety store classifications, for more than 50 per cent of the sales of grocery and food stores, and for more than 40 per cent of sales of women's ready-to-wear and tire, battery, and automotive accessory stores. By way of contrast, they do less than 20 per cent of the volume in the hardware trade, gasoline service stations, eating and drinking places, and less than 10 per cent of the business of automobile dealers.

The lines of business which are dominated to the greatest extent by chains tend also to be lines in which large chains have a much greater share of the market than do smaller companies (two to ten stores). On the other hand, small chains tend to be of as great or greater importance than large chains in lines where the per cent of sales done by all chains is low.

Between 1948 and 1958 large chains (11 or more stores) made strong advances in share of total sales in the following lines of trade: department stores, grocery stores, and women's ready-to-wear stores. These lines of trade have been affected both by acquisition of smaller companies by large organizations and by substantial expansion of chain store units in new shopping centers.

Urban Concentration

During the early periods of development, chains tended to concentrate in large urban areas and in the most heavily populated sections of the country. While some chains are to be found in cities of any significant size, marked concentration in the largest population centers continues to be the rule. Heavy concentration in large cities is explained in part because certain prominent chains, especially in shopping goods lines, operate only in such cities; also, in convenience lines, the number of different chains competing with each other tends to be much larger than in smaller markets. The smaller the size of city, the easier it is for independents to compete with chains, especially in regard to advertising and other forms of promotional activity.

COMPETITIVE POSITION OF LARGE, CENTRALLY MANAGED CHAINS

Since some chains operate in almost every kind of business and since almost every method of store operation or merchandising technique is used by them, no competitive advantages or disadvantages are common to all multiunit organizations. Certain competitive circumstances are, however, so widespread among large, centrally managed chains that they are characteristic of this segment of trade. Most chain store advantages are basically those of large-scale retailing. Some advantages of scale nevertheless take on a distinctive form within the chain store field, and some others are peculiar to all multiunit organizations.

BUYING POWER

By channeling the merchandise requirements of many retail units through a central office that negotiates with resources, the large chain is able to buy on more favorable terms than is the single-unit store in the same line of business. Since the manufacturer's selling expenses are relatively low when disposing of large quantities to one customer, the chain is able to obtain the lowest prices and to secure other allowances related to quantity buying as, for example, advertising funds, and compensation for store displays.

While this advantage is important, it can be overemphasized. Ability to obtain lower net prices is significant only when comparing such prices with the prices paid by a competitor who performs similar functions in the channel of distribution. There is no question but that chains generally pay lower prices than independent retailers. However, most chains are integrated, at least to some extent, and must incur costs in performing wholesaling activities. It is more meaningful, therefore, to compare the prices paid by chains with those ordinarily paid by wholesalers that serve independent merchants. Most large wholesalers operate on such a scale that they are able to take advantage of the maximum quantity discounts offered by well-known manufacturers selling branded goods.

The chain's buying power may result in prices slightly more favorable than those paid by some wholesalers, but as a practical matter it is largely confined to situations where manufacturers are small and sell the entire output to the chain or produce only private brands of merchandise to the chain's specifications.

There is no doubt that the larger chains have significant advantages in instances where they are able to contract for all of the output of manufacturers—something that cannot very well be done by the typical independent wholesaler.

Buying Skill

Large chains also have the benefit of considerable *buying skill,* a natural result of specialization of labour. At the central or district headquarters are to be found merchandising experts who spend all of their time maintaining market contacts, collecting and interpreting marketing information, viewing offerings of vendors, determining the suitability of merchandise for sale by the company, and conducting negotiations.

Unlike the manager of the independent store, the chain buyer specializes in a narrow range of merchandise and becomes thoroughly acquainted with sources of supply and current supply and demand conditions.

Unlike the "buyer" in a regular department store, the chain buyer spends practically all of his time performing the buying function; he does not have the problems of managing a retail department, preparing advertising, supervising salespeople, and other similar activities of the department manager in the large department store. Here, too, the chain's advantage is largely dissipated when compared with the wholesaler's buying organization and skill, which is similar to that of the chain.

Low Operating Costs

Certain economies, attributable to characteristic practices among large chains, result in relatively low operating costs. One of the most significant economies among chains with warehouses is derived from the *integration of wholesaling* with retailing. A better coordination between these functions is secured, stores are supplied from or through a single chain store warehouse, no salesmen need call upon store managers to solicit business, credit *problems* are eliminated, and deliveries can be effectively scheduled.

On the other hand, chain store home office and district executives must supply more supervision and assistance than is normally given to retailers by independent wholesalers. In any event, it is often possible for the chain to save part of the wholesaler's margin, particularly in lines of business where wholesalers have appreciable costs of selling to retailers and the latter do not concentrate their purchases with a single source of supply.

Another economy is *curtailment of consumer services.* As compared with its typical independent competitor, the large, centrally managed chain tends to sell to a greater extent on a cash basis; to render delivery service only for bulky or expensive items, or to make a charge for delivery when provided; and to emphasize self-service or self-selection merchandising techniques, thus limiting the assistance the consumer receives from salespeople. All of these service limitations, while making possible operating economies, may be viewed in another light, namely, that they represent successful attempts to shift performance of some marketing functions to the consumer.

Many chains secure economies by *limiting the composition of their stocks.* By concentrating offerings on those items for which there is a widespread and ready demand, higher than typical rates of stock turnover are attained. As long as this is accomplished without risking loss of business on account of out-of-stock conditions, several advantages are realized. These include less risk due to merchandise deterioration or style obsolescence, less storage space required per unit of sales, lower capital costs for merchandise inventories, and lower insurance costs on inventories.

Price Appeal

Low merchandise costs stemming from large purchasing power and the relatively low operating costs of chains, when combined with a prevalent chain store philosophy that a small percentage of net profit will maximize sales and yield large *total* dollar profits, results in a third important competitive characteristic, namely, the ability to feature price appeal. This has been an historic advantage of chainsone which accounted for significant diversion of patronage from independent to chain store in the period of rapid early growth of chains.

While chains, as a general rule, tend to continue emphasis upon "low prices," the effectiveness of this appeal as a patronage-attracting device has been limited by two major factors. The buying advantages and pricing freedom of chains has been limited to some extent by the trade legislation of the 1930's. Second, and undoubtedly more important, is a tendency which became much more prominent in the latter 1950's, namely, the willingness of many different types of retailers to meet the lowest prices prevailing in a given local market, particularly in the case of easily identified, fast-selling, standard items.

Thus, something approaching price uniformity is commonplace for such merchandise. This tendency has become more pronounced with increased inter trade competition, as illustrated by cut-rate drugstores, supermarkets, discount houses, and variety stores, all selling similar merchandise. While the appeal of price is commonly stressed in chain store advertising and store displays, most volume-conscious independents price their merchandise at similar levels, and both groups attempt to differentiate their establishments to a greater degree through various forms of non-price competition, such as location, character of merchandise assortments, store atmosphere, and special promotional devices.

Advertising Advantages

Where chain stores are in competition with neighbourhood unit stores, they have marked advertising advantages. For example, a grocery chain with stores in all sections of a city can afford to use newspaper advertising space or radio and television. Neighbourhood unit stores, with localized markets, cannot afford newspaper or broadcast advertising since their places of business are relatively inaccessible to most readers or listeners. Where voluntary chains have been formed, independent grocers have combined their efforts and used citywide advertising effectively. In the main, however, the chain occupies a preferred position with reference to local advertising.

Experimentation

Chains can often undertake experiments which cannot be made without great risk by their competitors. For example, lines of merchandise can be added to or dropped from the stock at one retail unit, and the results can be used in formulating the practices and policies of all of the stores. Similar experiments can be made with respect to services, displays, stock arrangement, store layout, and other matters.

Risk Distribution and Competitive Superiority

The wide territorial coverage of many chains reduces their risks, since a lack of local prosperity and a decline in sales or profits in one store may be offset by profits in other areas or stores. This same width of their market enables chains to transfer slow-moving stocks from some of their stores to units in which the demand for such goods is greater.

By varying prices charged to consumers between different cities and sections of the country, the chain is able to average its profits and meet whatever competition may arise locally. This is an advantage which the voluntary chains cannot emulate, for a price war affects the total business of a retailer member which cannot be offset, as in the case of chains, by the profits earned in the other stores of the group.

Location Advantage

As a form of large-scale retailing, chains are in an enviable position with respect to their ability to command the most favorable merchandising sites in established business districts and in new shopping centers. So it is adequate to note at this point that the competitive position of chains was considerably enhanced during the 1950's by the preference accorded to them as the dominant tenants in most planned centers.

Competitive Limitations

As in the case of the favorable factors discussed above, no single disadvantage applies to each and every chain in every line of trade. A number of unfavorable factors do, however, exert a restrictive influence upon most large, centrally managed chains.

Standardization of Operating Procedures

While standardization of merchandising and operating policies and procedures is a feature which makes it possible to operate a large chain from a central or regional headquarters office, it is also a factor which has limited chain development in certain fields where individualized management attention is of unusual importance. Large national chains are non-existent in the hardware trade, for example, partly because of the great diversity of items which must be handled and the minute supervision and care necessary to maintain balanced stocks. Carelessness on the part of the local manager may result in a serious lack of necessary items or in excessive inventories of unsalable or slow-moving stocks.

Further difficulties are found in the multiple price system which prevails in the sale of such lines as builders' hardware. Price concessions to builders often vary roughly with the volume of purchases and the bargaining power of buyer and seller. Under such circumstances chains find it particularly difficult to operate, since they may be unwilling or unable to entrust such responsibilities to local managers. In any trade in which contract work appears, chains are at a disadvantage, because each contract presents a particularized pricing problem and the need for outside sales promotion and installation introduce complications.

Limited Service

The common practice of restricting consumer services and the limitation of stocks to articles in large demand, while reducing expenses of operation, limits the appeal of many chains. There still are and are likely to be large numbers of consumers who insist upon and are willing to pay for the wider range of services and facilities which many independent stores offer.

Limited service is not a policy inherent in chain store operation. At least some large chains provide every kind of common consumer service. Variety stores found it necessary to introduce various forms of service, such as credit, delivery, and "lay-away" plans, as they diversified their merchandise offerings by expanding into shopping goods lines. The well-managed independent store nevertheless has a distinct advantage in adjusting its own programme of services to meet the particular needs of the clientele it seeks to serve within its trading area.

Imitative Innovation

Within and between the various lines of trade in which chains are of greatest relative importance, many companies are only weakly differentiated from each other. In spite of excellent opportunities for research and experimentation in the chain store field, innovations have tended to be imitative rather than imaginative. Many chains have copied operating methods and techniques that have apparently worked well for other companies, thus contributing to a type of monotonous uniformity and a lack of exciting and dynamic merchandising. One critic has described the store units of most large chains as being characterized by bowling alley aisles with little or no interrupting note, uniformity of display, warehouse atmosphere in interior layouts, display of specialty goods as though they were staples, absence of printed selling other than manufacturers' package and price tags, and discouraging merchandise assortments. Many chains have apparently assumed a role of mere "distributor" of merchandise which is in ready demand either because of its necessary character or habitual use, or because of advance intensive demand creation activity on the part of manufacturers. This tendency among many large chains, especially in their larger and newer stores, again affords the independent an excellent opportunity to do a more outstanding promotional and personal selling job and otherwise to create a distinctive and appealing store personality.

Public Opinion. Particularly during the 1920's and 1930's and, to some extent, continuing until the present time, there have been many attempts to limit the growth of chains by arousing consumer sentiment against them. Led by some so-called representative organizations of independents and by a few individuals who perhaps saw an opportunity to further their own interests, many arguments have been made to the effect that the independent merchant, who lives and does business in the home city, deserves patronage rather than the customarily "foreign-owned" chain.

It has been alleged that chains take money out of town, fail to patronize local business, pay low wages, destroy opportunities for young men to enter business for themselves, do not bear their share of the local tax burden, destroy small business, resort to unethical or unfair practices, and tend towards monopoly. Some such allegations are obviously unfounded or exaggerated. All of them have nevertheless influenced public opinion to some degree and probably contributed to the passage of chain store tax laws and to other legal limitations.

To some extent they have also doubtless contributed support to governmental policies that favour private enterprise of the small, local business firm type, as witnessed by the creation of the U.S. Small Business Administration in 1953. It is not likely, however, that such pressures upon public opinion have seriously restricted chain store patronage. While some consumers prefer independent merchants, the vast majority patronize retail stores for other kinds of reasons.

Legal Limitations

Most of the legal limitations, in connection with large-scale retailing, were originally enacted as an aspect of the anti-chain store movement of the late 1920's and the 1930's. The chain's ability to induce discriminatory advantages in purchasing was limited by the Robinson-Patman Act, and its freedom to engage in loss-leader pricing was curtailed to some extent by the state pricing legislation discussed at that point.

In addition, many states have taxed chain store organizations in some special manner, with the intent, at least in part, of restricting the growth of chains and the multiplication of their store units. At one time chain store tax laws were in effect in 29 states. Original impetus to such laws was the Indiana statute, approved by the U.S. Supreme Court in 1931. In that decision chain stores were recognized for the first time as differing sufficiently from other types of retailing to justify a separate classification for license or occupation tax purposes. A classification for graduated license fees according to the number of stores in the state was thus held to be a valid classification based on substantial differences.

In all cases the tax is levied only on stores operated in the state in question, but the *rate of tax* is determined in two different ways. Most common is the Indiana-type law providing a graduated license fee based on a schedule of the number of stores in the same company *located within the state* and levying, for example, a fee 50 times greater for each store in a company operating more than 20 stores in the state than would apply in the case of a single unit store. Louisiana and several other states departed from this principle and based the rate on the total number of stores in the company *wherever located*—for example, a company with more than 500 stores no matter where located would pay a tax on each of its stores in Louisiana some 55 times greater than the tax applicable to a store in a company that operated not more than 10 stores.

One effect of these laws was to discourage the multiplication of chain stores in the states where rates were the highest. Another was to encourage chains to close marginal and small units, and to plan newer stores of larger sales capacity. With the passage of time, chains tended to be regarded as better neighbours. It became more widely recognized that they brought new business into many communities in which they located new and modern stores, that they employed local people, and that they purchased supplies and merchandise from all segments of the economy. As a consequence, many of the laws have been allowed to lapse or have been repealed. In 1960 there were only 12 states with chain store taxes based upon graduated license fees.

Increasing Efficiency of Independents

One of the major limits to the expansion of chains is the increasing efficiency of many of their independent competitors. Independents as a whole are carrying on their business much more efficiently than was formerly the case. This is due to at least two causes. The increased business of the chains has driven out many of the least efficient merchants. The better independents are the ones who have survived. Hence, the general level of merchandising ability is higher. A second reason is that many independents have learned much from the chains. Such merchandising practice as the use of open display in grocery, drug, and hardware stores, better lighting, and better entrances and fixtures have been copied, in part at least, from chains. Superfluous brands, price lines, and sizes have all been reduced. Better display and advertising practices have been adopted, and in other ways the level of independent merchandising has been raised. All of this has been accelerated through the voluntary chain movement. This fact will make it increasingly hard for chains to displace existing independents in the future. If expansion is made it will be at the expense of the type of merchant who is too old, too indifferent, or too independent and limited in ability to learn the lessons of modern merchandising. Unfortunately, there are still many such merchants, or rather, storekeepers.

Future of Chain Stores

The chain store type of retailing had a phenomenal development in the 1920's. In this period many new chain organizations were brought into being and additional units were added to existing chains with the result that the chain had become a fairly mature form of retailing institution by 1929. Throughout the next two decades, the sales volume importance of chains was relatively stable at about 30 per cent of total retail trade. During the 1950's, however, chains expanded their share of total retail sales to about 33.7 per cent—a significant gain in relative competitive position. Moreover, this increase has come about principally by growth of large chain organizations, both through internal expansion and acquisition of other companies. Thus, within the chain store field, the tendency has been for a larger share of total business to be concentrated among a small number of very large firms.

Among the various factors that accounted for significant growth of chains in the 1950's, several stand out as being of unusual importance. First, the scale of operations in individual retail establishments has continued to increase, thus raising the capital requirements and level of managerial skill essential for effective competition.

This, in turn, has made it somewhat more difficult for new independents to enter retailing on a level of competitive equality. Second, the 1950's were characterized by various newer forms of competition, including expansion of discount houses, branches of department stores, and the advent of the variety department store. Such inter trade rivalry resulted in intense price competition, with a tendency towards price uniformity at low margins for most types of standard, easily identified items. Large chains, possessing the advantages of financial strength and risk distribution, have been able to withstand the onslaught of new types of rivals much better than many independents, particularly those who were weakly financed and who lacked the ability or willingness to adjust dynamically to changing times. Third, a large proportion of the total retail trade expansion in the 1950's took place in planned suburban shopping centers where chains have benefited from their status as preferred tenants. This has been especially noteworthy in the case of department stores, variety stores, apparel stores, and supermarkets—all lines in which chains have long been of high relative importance.

In the foreseeable future, it is expected that the factors just outlined will continue to favour the growth of chains. On the other hand, further expansion is restricted by a number of countervailing influences. One consists of various forms of voluntary chain and cooperative activities within the field of small scale retailing, as discussed in the following major. Second, it must be remembered that the total competitive position of chains is a result of their status in specific lines of trade. In some lines, notably department stores and variety stores, chains have reached a point of near saturation. In other lines where managerial flexibility and individualized attention to customer problems is of unusual importance, the chain method of operation is not well suited. Third, loss of share of market among independent stores has been highly concentrated among the less efficient or marginal types of stores. Further inroads by chains become increasingly difficult due to a strong survival tendency among more capable independent store operators.

When such opposing tendencies are carefully weighed, it is concluded that the growth outlook for chains, while favorable, is also likely to be limited to slow and gradual expansion. Such growth as does occur is, moreover, likely to be concentrated within the lines of trade where chains are already strongly entrenched. Within most such lines, the major rivals of an individual centrally managed chain are other similarly managed companies. Thus, to an increasing degree the competition of chains is with other chains, within and between lines of trade, and to a lesser extent with independent merchants, set apart as a different class of organizations.

VOLUNTARY CHAINS

Independent merchants and their suppliers have resorted to a variety of competitive devices in combating chain store companies. Within lines of trade where chains have been of greatest importance, the outstanding instrument of survival has consisted of various forms of horizontal and vertical cooperation, with the objective of preserving independence while at the same time achieving certain advantages of chain operation.

TYPES OF VOLUNTARY ASSOCIATIONS

Voluntary chains or cooperative associations of retailers assume a variety of specific forms. First, there are buying-and-advertising groups in which a small number of independent merchants combine their purchases and engage in advertising on a cooperative basis. Second, there are retailer-cooperative warehouse groups in which a number of independent merchants mutually own and buy through a common wholesaling facility. A third form consists of voluntary chains which are sponsored by a regular wholesaling organization that has assumed the initiative for cooperative action. Fourth, some of the corporate retailing chains have expanded their area of merchandising influence by licensing or franchising "associate" stores. Finally, the franchised retail outlets of certain manufacturers, who pursue an exclusive agency or selective distribution policy, often result in such a high degree of uniformity of operations on the retail level that this may be properly regarded as an aspect of the voluntary chain idea.

Pooled Buying and Advertising Groups

An early example of voluntary horizontal cooperation was the development of informal buying pools. Basing their action on the assumption that buying power was the principal if not the sole advantage of the chains, certain independent merchants, primarily grocers, druggists, and hardware dealers, developed plans for informal pooling of orders. They thus succeeded in gaining certain price concessions which, when combined with pool-cars as they often were, resulted in substantial reductions in the delivered cost of the merchandise. So long as they failed to attack the problem of effective competition with chains in other than the buying area, such groups were never very significant.

Group operations of small numbers of retailers located in the same metropolitan area became very important in the 1950's when greater emphasis was given to selling and promotion. Under the prevailing arrangement, several independent supermarket-type concerns cooperate in the use of a common name such as "Food town" or "Market Basket." By pooling their advertising budgets, they have been able to develop impressive advertising programmes, rivaling those of major corporate chains. Such firms have also set high standards in store appearance and merchandising. They often maintain the same prices in all stores in the cooperating group. In contrast with the forms of voluntary chains discussed below, the initiative comes from the cooperating retailers rather than from wholesalers, but the retailers do not own or operate any wholesale establishment. They usually pool certain of their buying requirements and often enter into a form of buying contract with some large independent wholesaling organization that serves them on a special cost-of service basis.

Retailer-Cooperative Voluntary Groups

Many early informal buying groups found that a logical step in their development was to purchase an existing wholesale house or to form a new one. In other cases, groups of merchants were organized for the express purpose of operating their own wholesale house. In either case, a paid manager and paid employees conduct the house just about as they would if it were owned by a private corporation. Stocks of goods are purchased, stored, sold, and delivered. Stores operated by members of retailer cooperative voluntary groups do not account for a large proportion of total retail trade but are especially noteworthy due to their substantial influence in the grocery trade and because of their unusual significance in certain geographic areas. Some cooperatively-owned wholesale grocery facilities were established by groups of retailers prior to 1900, but the principal impetus for the movement came from increasing competition from corporate chains at a later date.

About 150 retailer cooperative warehouses were in operation in 1958 and more than one-half of them were organized in the 1930's and 1940's. Between 1948 and 1958, the number of member retail stores in such organizations increased from 25,710 to 33,007, or from about 8 per cent to about 15 per cent of all grocery stores. Sales volume of member stores in the same period increased from about 11 per cent to about 15 per cent of all grocery store sales. In dollar amount, the sales increase of such member stores was 231 per cent over the 1948-58 period, a rate of gain far outstripping that of corporate chains or of wholesaler-sponsored voluntary groups. Retailer cooperatives are of greatest relative importance in the Pacific Coast States, with estimated sales of member stores amounting to more than 40 per cent of grocery trade sales in California and Arizona. Such organizations are, however, to be found in practically all sections.

Most grocery trade retailer cooperatives have from 50 to 500 members each, but a few have more than 1,000. The organization is usually of the corporate form with required minimum investment per member ranging from about $250 in some cases to several thousand dollars in others. Typically, such cooperatives are operated on the basis of one vote per member, regardless of the amount of stock ownership. Profits accruing from operations at the wholesale level are passed back to members in the form of patronage refunds. Members are usually expected or required to concentrate their purchases with the retailer-owned warehouse, thus making possible the elimination of salesmen. In some cases, individual stores are *identified* as members of a voluntary group and carry on cooperative advertising; in many instances, however, members retain a strong individual identity, engaging in no group promotional efforts, thus using the cooperative facilities solely as an economical source of supply.

In former years retailer cooperatives limited their offerings largely to staple grocery products and performed few other services for members. During the 1950's many organizations expanded their procurement services and provided a more complete source of supply. It is common for such cooperatives to supply non-food items, frozen foods, dairy items, and in numerous instances, even perishable produce and meats. Retailer cooperatives are stronger in this regard than wholesalers who sponsor voluntary chains, but they do not engage in as extensive a range of promotional, record keeping, and management advisory services as do members of the latter type.

While retailer-cooperative warehouses are predominantly associated with the grocery trade, some such organizations are encountered occasionally in other lines, notably drugs, hardware, and office supplies and stationery. In most such cases, the emphasis is primarily upon the presumed economies of group buying through an owned wholesaling facility. Outside the grocery trade, such organizations have made little effort to operate according to the voluntary chain principle by common store identification or group advertising.

WHOLESALER-SPONSORED VOLUNTARY CHAINS

Many wholesalers attempted to offset declines in their sales volume incident to the growth of corporate chains by organizing groups of independent merchants who, in return for special services rendered to them by the sponsoring wholesaler, agree to buy a major part of their merchandise requirements from him. Such groups constitute what are known as *wholesaler-sponsored voluntary chains.* They differ from retailer-cooperatives in two ways. First, the initiative for organizing comes from the wholesaler rather than from the retailers themselves. Second, the wholesale house remains under private rather than cooperative ownership.

Although wholesaler-sponsored chains vary in many details, the essential basis of operation is one of mutual cooperation. Retailers agree to concentrate their purchases with the sponsoring wholesaler. While not all retail prices are uniform, advertised articles must be sold at the same price in every member store. The wholesaler in turn agrees to furnish certain merchandising advice and to be alert in his search for favorable opportunities to buy merchandise, the sale of which can be promoted by the group. Moreover, because there is some degree of concentration, the buying power of the wholesaler is usually increased through the sponsorship of a voluntary chain. Resulting savings are passed on to member stores as an aid to them in meeting the competition of the corporate chain.

In 1958 some 330 grocery wholesaling companies were reported as sponsoring voluntary chains. Member stores are estimated at about 36,000 and account for some 15 per cent of total grocery trade sales. Between 1948 and 1958 the rate of sales increase for such member stores was considerably less than for retailer cooperatives, but it was just about the same as that for corporate chains in the food trade. The importance of wholesaler-sponsored groups varies considerably in different geographic areas, with approximately one-half of the affiliated stores located in a group of eight contiguous states in the Middle Atlantic and East North Central divisions of the country.

Operating costs of voluntary group wholesalers have been traditionally somewhat higher than those incurred by retailer-owned warehouses because a larger part of total sales volume is made to small independent stores not members of the sponsored voluntary group, regular salesmen or "store supervisors" are employed to call on and assist members with operational and merchandising problems, credit accommodations are sometimes provided, and because a wider range of advertising, display, store planning, and managerial services is offered to members of the voluntaries than is received from retailer cooperative warehouses by their owners.

While wholesaler-sponsored voluntary chains have attained the highest form of development in the grocery business, they are not limited to this field. Butler Brothers, the leading wholesaler of variety goods, sponsors a voluntary chain of Ben Franklin variety stores located in all sections of the United States. Such stores are operated under a franchise agreement which calls for a payment by the retailer of a yearly fee which depends on store size. In return for this fee, the wholesaler provides: a complete warehouse service for all merchandise items needed to operate a variety store; a detailed stock control system; automatic store shipments of new merchandise items; a planned promotional programme tied to the seasonal requirements of each month of the year; professionally prepared sales plans, display signs, price tags, and store decorations; assistance from specially trained field advisors; cooperative rebates on store purchases based on the annual volume of buying from the wholesaler; and permission to use the Ben Franklin name.

Another example of a wholesaler-sponsored voluntary consists of Rexall Drug Stores that are to be found in almost all communities. They are supplied with merchandise items from wholesale warehouses operated by the Rexall Drug and Chemical Company, are identified to the public as Rexall stores by the familiar orange and blue signs of the company, and participate in a variety of special promotional events, including the nationally advertised Rexall 1-cent sales. Through a subsidiary corporation, Rexall Realty Corp., assistance is given to franchise Rexall merchants in obtaining leases in planned shopping centers.

In the restaurant and motel field, another application of the same idea consists of Howard Johnson establishments. Such units are predominately independently owned, have a uniform appearance, and are under franchise to a central wholesaling organization which furnishes equipment, supplies, and food to individual operators who agree to maintain uniform standards of quality and service.

COORDINATED GROUPS OF VOLUNTARIES

A majority of the wholesale grocers who sponsor voluntary chains are members of a national federation of such wholesalers. In order to secure certain advantages of group action, such as large-scale buying and promotion of private brands, it became necessary for voluntary group wholesalers to operate jointly. One of the best known of these central organizations is the Independent Grocers

Alliance of Chicago. More than 50 wholesaler members serve about 4,500 stores in all parts of the country. It assigns a franchise to a wholesaler who in turn grants the retailer the right to display the I.G.A. sign, carry the private brands of the organization, and receive merchandising aids. The central office buys goods to be packed under the I.G.A. labels and advertises such brands nationally. Red and White Stores, Clover Farm Stores, Food Merchandisers of America, and United Buyers Corp. are other well-known groups providing similar services.

Some 85 retailer cooperative groups are linked together through indirect ownership of National Retailer-Owned Grocers, Inc. (NROG). Three large regional affiliates of this organization carry on large-scale buying and promotional activities. Another affiliate, Shurfine, Inc., owns some 30 registered trademarks for various food product lines which are purchased by the three regional affiliates for exclusive sale in member stores.

Voluntary Affiliates of Corporate Chains

The forms of voluntary chains discussed up to this point may be viewed as defensive measures undertaken by independent merchants or their suppliers in order to compete with corporate chains more effectively. A third form consists of companies that own and operate chains of retail stores and also serve as headquarters for a similarly identified group of independent "associate" stores. When a corporate chain undertakes such action, its motive is not to promote competition with itself. Quite to the contrary, independent affiliates are usually selected from merchants located in places that do not offer sufficient volume potential to be attractive from the standpoint of chain ownership. By selling through associate stores, the chain can add substantially to its purchasing power, increase the volume of its wholesaling facilities, reduce costs or expand the extent of advertising, spread the costs of corporate administration over a broader base, and realise a profit on wholesale sales to affiliated stores.

Probably the best known example is the Western Auto Supply Company which operates 16 wholesale houses, a chain of 376 completely owned retail stores located in medium-sized and large cities, and has some 3,600 affiliated independent merchants who are identified to the public as "Western Auto Associate Stores." For the most part these independents are located in smaller communities, and the typical establishment is considerably smaller than that of the company-owned stores. The independents concentrate their purchases with Western Auto wholesale houses, participate in company advertising, and benefit from the company's merchandising advice and physical assistance in store operation. Additional examples of the same method of operation in the automotive accessory business are provided by numerous independent merchants affiliated with tire manufacturers, such as Firestone, Goodyear, and Goodrich. Each of these companies operates a chain of company-owned stores, performs wholesaling functions, buys and resells merchandise that it does not manufacture, and engages in voluntary chain activities with independent merchants whose stores resemble the company-owned retail outlets insofar as appearance, layout, operating policies, and advertising are concerned.

Examples in other lines of trade include some 1,800 "Walgreen Agencies" which supplement over 400 company-owned stores operated by the Walgreen Drug Company, and some 30 small-town men's clothing merchants who have been licensed by Bond Stores, Inc. to sell suits and coats merchandised in that company's chain of about 100 stores which are located, for the most part, in large cities.

Franchised Retail Outlets of Manufacturers

The similarity among the operations of individual retail outlets that are franchised by certain manufacturing companies places them at least on the fringe of the voluntary chain movement. The merchandising advice and assistance provided by some of the large shoe manufacturing companies, such as the Brown Shoe Company, Inc. and the various divisions of the International Shoe Company, together with the close working relationship maintained with merchants who buy substantially from one source is one good illustration. Certain paint manufacturing companies, especially those that are local or regional in character, distribute through carefully selected retail paint stores, provide them with store signs and other store equipment, plan and carry out sales promotion programmes for the whole group of such dealers, and in general function in accordance with the procedures followed by other classes of voluntary chains. Some manufacturers of men's clothing and men's furnishings enjoy similarly close working relationships with many of their dealers who are identified to the public primarily as outlets for the manufacturer's line of goods.

Similar arrangements are to be found in the gasoline service station trade. It is common for major petroleum refining companies to develop new locations under lease arrangements with property owners, thus permitting the construction and equipping of station facilities. Stations are then commonly subleased to independent businessmen who operate their stations in accordance with the terms of a franchise. This affords the petroleum company a "chain" of independently owned outlets for its products. All gasoline service stations, of course, are not operated in this manner, as some are company-owned stations and some are owned outright by the operator or by a wholesale distributor.

Appraisal of Voluntary Associations

That the various forms of voluntary chains or franchise systems have inherent strength is indicated by a long period of experience, considerable recent growth of many well-established organizations, and the emergence of new voluntary groups and franchising organizations. Enough has been accomplished to establish the principle that groups of merchants working together and with their suppliers can effectively attain many of the buying, advertising, and merchandising advantages of regular chains. Perhaps the strongest advantage is the fact that the superior planning of the sponsoring organization has raised the level of merchandising in member stores. Reference has been made to the establishment of physical standards of store operation. Some plans allow the sponsor to cancel the membership of any retailer who fails to operate his store in such a manner as to reflect credit upon the group as a whole. Possibility of such action stimulates indifferent merchants to greater endeavor.

Certain weaknesses exist, however. Lack of strong central control is perhaps most important. The sponsor or a committee of the members can go only so far in encouragement or instruction in better merchandising methods. In many voluntary plans, the sponsor has field supervisors who work with and provide counsel for affiliated retailers, thus performing essentially the same functions as a district supervisor in a regular chain.

Two fundamental differences are, however, especially significant. First, the supervisor in a corporate chain has disciplinary powers whereas his counterpart in the voluntary group lacks authority to alter undesirable situations in member stores. Second, the chain store supervisor has higher organizational status and rank than the store managers working under his direction whereas the successful operator of an independent retail store often regards the supervisor as a person of inferior status. Whereas the chain company supervisor has but one loyalty, to the firm that employs him, the voluntary group counselor has two—the group sponsor and the retailer and must devote considerable time and energy to winning and maintaining acceptance of merchandising programmes by the latter.

Such weaknesses have not seriously handicapped the expansion of voluntary groups. As previously indicated, voluntary chains in the grocery trade account for a majority of the business done by independent stores and the growth of retailer cooperatives, in particular, outstripped that of corporate chains in the 1950's. Significant expansions have occurred in other lines of trade as well.

Voluntary cooperation within the framework of a franchising system is attractive to a sponsor because it provides a semicontrolled network of outlets for his products or services and because administrative problems and capital investment are substantially less than would be the case if the franchiser owned and operated all outlets.

It is attractive to the retailer since it gives him a national or regional identity, provides him with training and guidance in business management, supplies a merchandising programme based on the successful experience of similar stores, and often affords him an opportunity to establish an enterprise which could hardly be started without the sponsor's aid. It appears that the concept of voluntary association has wide application, that it has strengthened the position of independent merchants who have taken advantage of the opportunities thus offered, and that future expansion is limited almost solely by the number of qualified leaders and merchants who develop an appreciation for the benefits that such group activities may hold for them. As is evident from the context of this discussion, voluntary chains have developed primarily in lines of merchandise where merchants can utilize one principal source of supply on the wholesale level. Up to this time, little voluntary chain activity, other than group buying, has been observed in the case of fashion merchandising which involves assembling from numerous sources located in markets at a distance from the typical dealer.

4

Purchasing and Supply Management

Over the last six years, the Air Force has adopted an operational concept built on being expeditious. The Air Force has restructured and transformed its combat forces to provide quick response to operational demands anywhere in the world using a concept called the Expeditionary Aerospace Force (EAF). Several RAND studies have helped to frame policy and support structure changes needed to meet the demands of an EAF.

The RAND analysis calls for a support infrastructure consisting of Forward Operating Locations (FOLs), Forward Support Locations (FSLs) and CONUS [Continental United States] Support Locations (CSLs), as well as an integrated distribution system and command and control network. Collectively, the support infrastructure can enable the EAF concept and meet the dynamic operational requirements of an expeditionary force.

Implementing the support infrastructure, however, requires significant changes in current practices. The support system must be proactive rather than reactive. It must be adaptive and responsive, able to expand and contract production as demands change. These needed characteristics are in stark contrast to the current environment where the Air Force's aircraft and missile spares support declined between fiscal year 1991 to 2000 because of funding issues, aging systems, high Ops Tempo, retention/experience levels, and aggressive inventory reductions.

There is hope, however. There is great potential to reduce unprogrammed unbudgeted bills, achieve best readiness capability given dollars and aging, and improve responsiveness to Aerospace Expeditionary Forces (AEF) operations.

In response to the AEF, the rate of ongoing operations, and associated resource constraints, the Air Force Deputy Chief of Staff for Installations and Logistics chartered a complete review of the spare parts supply process. The review was called the "Spares Campaign."

The goal of the campaign was to put more spares into the hands of the maintainers. The Spares Campaign resulted in eight initiatives designed to modernize the spares process to support AEF operations, insert financial management changes into the fiscal year 2004 Programme Objective

Memorandum (POM), provide credible estimates of Air Force spares requirements, provide authority and accountability for spares performance to meet planned weapon systems availability, and exploit relevant commercial capabilities. The last of the eight initiatives approved for implementation was PSM. The goal of the PSM initiative was to adopt improved purchasing and supply management practices to reduce purchase costs and improve product quality and delivery.

In July 2001, the Secretary of the Air Force and Chief of Staff endorsed the initiative. In October 2001, CORONA Fall endorsed the Spares Campaign. Engines were selected as the test candidate because they have been a notoriously high-cost and low-performance driver for the Air Force. Specifically, the candidate system selected for demonstration at Oklahoma City Air Logistics Centre (OC-ALC) was the F100 engine.

DEVELOPING AN ORGANIZATIONAL CONSTRUCT FOR EXECUTING PSM IN THE AIR FORCE

Given Air Force leadership's decision to conduct a PSM implementation demonstration, the organizational structure that will support the demonstration and provide a more strategic focus on purchasing and supply activities must be defined. The organizational structure needs to ensure that supplier relationships, supply chain, and supply base strategies are focused on the strategic goals of the organization. The constructs proposed in this report are entirely focused on the development of a PSM organization and do not address the entire breadth. According to fiscal year 2000 Air Force Total Ownership Cost (AFTOC) data, engines represent 40 per cent of the Material Support Division (MSD) net cost.

The analysis supporting the decision to implement PSM was accomplished during the development of the Spares Campaign and is not summarized or addressed in this report. Although an initial near-term construct is needed for the implementation demonstration, more dramatic changes to the organizational structure are needed to enable full PSM implementation and benefits. Evolving to an Air Force–wide, long-term PSM organizational construct can enable more effective and efficient supply chain integration as well as a higher-quality and more responsive, reliable, and robust supplier base.

Because PSM involves changes in numerous functions and organizations, it is important to consider the sensitivities involved with this controversial subject matter. At the same time, however, it is equally important to recognize that fundamental change is needed to enable EAF objectives.

ANALYTICAL APPROACH

This research on organizational options for implementing PSM uses a process approach to evaluate alternative options against a set of criteria derived from PSM principles and commercial practices. In evaluating organizational options, the existing structure of the targeted demonstration organization for the PSM implementation test must be identified and understood. The next step includes evaluating and defining the objectives for the selection of a PSM organizational structure. After considering different organizational alternatives and evaluating them against the criteria, an approach is chosen for consideration.

Throughout this analysis, we consider research and application of best commercial practices. We conducted extensive literature searches and reviews as the basis for analysis and integrated commercial best practices with applicability to the Air Force into the proposed constructs. Participation from and knowledge-sharing with the F100 PSM demonstration team at OC-ALC was also extremely beneficial to this analysis.

A BRIEF INTRODUCTION TO THE PROPOSED PSM ORGANIZATIONAL CONSTRUCT

The PSM organization discussed in this report is designed to accomplish two primary objectives. The first is to elevate the procurement function of the Air Force supply chain to the level of the supply management function to support a more integrated purchasing and supply process. The second objective sought by the organizational structure is to improve management of the supplier network. Those two issues provide the underlying motivation for the major changes proposed here. Other minor changes in function and roles or responsibilities are tied to cross-functional integration of skills and the need for particular skills or positions to facilitate the cultural change associated with organizational shifts.

Purchasing Decision

Historically, large corporations and minority-business enterprises (MBEs) have encountered many impediments as they have worked together. As a result, the government has adopted public policy to help promote greater interaction between large firms and MBEs. At the same time, the competitive environment has changed in ways that make it important for large corporations and MBEs to work more closely. This chapter presents the results of a study that examined the impediments and approaches to buyer/supplier relationships between Fortune 500 firms that have corporate minority purchasing programmes and MBEs.

In many instances, the objectives of both large corporations and minority-owned business enterprises (MBEs) would be better achieved if the two worked together. Unfortunately, despite efforts by large corporations, MBEs, and government to promote the development of buyer/supplier relationships between large companies and MBEs, the approaches and challenges involved in these relationships continue to be misunderstood. In fact, perceptions regarding these relationships vary greatly, especially between the two groups—

large corporations and MBEs. They key to progressing towards more beneficial buyer/supplier relationships is to recognize the needs and abilities of each group so that the two can mutually strive to overcome barriers to cooperation. Efforts to promote buyer/supplier relationships between large firms and MBEs have emerged from many sources. First, supplier development has long been viewed as a primary function of the purchasing department in larger firms.

Many purchasing departments in large firms have instigated programmes designed specifically to increase the amount of purchases from small or minority-owned firms. This effort is one important aspect of corporate programmes designed to help large firms fulfill their role as socially responsible corporations. Second, MBEs have joined together in many communities to form business development groups to increase their visibility and leverage.

An example of such a group is the National Minority Supplier Development Council (NMSDC). Finally, the development of small minority owned business has become an important objective of both national and state governments.

The Minority Business Development Agency was established in 1969 to direct public policy towards assisting MBE development. Further, because many MBEs also qualify as small business enterprises, they are promoted through the Small Business Administration. In fact, the Small Business Administration provides support for over 650 Small Business Development Centres nationwide.

Unfortunately, these efforts have lacked the necessary resources, scale, and scope to bring about an effective change in attitude and knowledge concerning buyer/supplier relationships involving MBEs. The efforts of the past 20 years have not even been able to get the two sides to consistently agree on the principal impediments to building mutually beneficial relationships.

However, circumstances and competitive pressures are changing, placing more emphasis on the development of successful relationships involving small and minority owned businesses. Two changes in particular are working to change attitudes and to create opportunities for both large corporate buyers and MBEs:

- The enactment of Public Law 99-661 with its contract goal for minority business;
- The increased use of just-in-time purchasing relationships.

The inclusion of the contract goal for MBEs within Public Law 99-661 is the most obvious change and has had considerable impact on the thinking of both large corporate buyers and small "socially and economically disadvantaged" suppliers. This law requires firms that contract with the government to source at least five per cent of each contract from MBEs.

Requiring such set asides has greatly increased the pressure on government contractors to find or develop MBE suppliers. Although this law only applies to government contractors, its enactment has had a noticeable effect on many large companies, increasing their social awareness and, in some instances, awakening them to opportunities they had previously overlooked. Increasing global competition is also creating new opportunities for MBEs. In response to competitive pressure from global manufacturers, many U.S. firms have adopted just-in-time (JIT) production techniques, including JIT purchasing. The cornerstone of JIT purchasing is the development of long-term partnership relationships between buyer and supplier. Within these relationships, the buyer's purchasing organization takes an active role in helping the supplier overcome performance obstacles to achieve "world class" standards.

Likewise, the supplier plays a proactive role in meeting the buyer's needs. Inherent in building this relationship is a reduction in the number of suppliers, with the remaining suppliers being certified with respect to quality and delivery performance. Emphasis is also placed on utilizing local suppliers (co-location of suppliers is often considered to be the ideal) to facilitate physical flows as well as relationship building.

This last point is the most important in the current context—as corporate buyers seek to find or develop local suppliers, MBEs have a unique opportunity to position themselves as dedicated and responsive suppliers. The two environmental changes will create many opportunities for MBEs to increase the amount of business they conduct with large corporations.

Indeed, there are ample opportunities in today's business environment for MBEs if they can properly position themselves as value-added entities. If they cannot promote this position, it is unlikely that individual MBEs will be able to survive the intense competitive pressures of the 1990s and beyond.

Because MBEs are at a crossroads with respect to their future development, the relationship between MBEs and corporate purchasing personnel (CPPs) needs to be better understood. That is, while incentives exist to build relationships between large corporations and MBEs, a relatively scant knowledge-base has emerged to guide the establishment of successful buyer/ supplier relationships between CPPs and MBEs. The objective of this chapter is to extend the current understanding of both the challenges that inhibit the formation of strong relationships between CPPs and MBEs and the approaches that are being developed to overcome the existing challenges. The literature regarding MBE development.

A brief description of the research methodology follows. Study results are then reported—a longitudinal comparison with Dollinger and Daily is also presented.

TYPES OF PURCHASE DECISION BEHAVIOUR

Consumer buying behaviour varies with the type of buying decision. Earlier, we stated that while a decision for buying bread was almost made automatically, the decision for buying a sofa set was more deliberate and time consuming. Similarly, there is a great deal of difference in buying a tube of toothpaste, clothes for yourself and a refrigerator for your home. We shall now distinguish three types of buying behaviour:

- *Routinised response behaviour*: This occurs when the consumer already has some experience of buying and using the product. He is familiar with the various brands available and the attributes of each and has a well established criteria for selecting his own brand. Consumers do not give much thought or time when buying such products and already have a preferred brand. The degree of involvement in buying such products is low. Frequently purchased and low cost products such as razor blades, coffee powder, toothpaste, soap, soft drinks, etc. fall in this category. Marketers dealing in products involving routinised response behaviour must ensure the satisfaction of existing customers by maintaining consistent quality, service and value. Also, they must attempt to attract new customers by introducing novel features, using point-of-purchase promotional material and special displays.
- *Limited Problem Solving*: In this type of buying behaviour, the consumer is familiar with the product and the various brands available, but has no established brand preference. The consumer would like to gather additional information about the brands to arrive at his brand decision. For instance a housewife buys refined vegetable oil for her cooking. She is familiar with the concept of vegetable oil and also knows that Postman, Dalda and Ruby are some of the prominent brands available. But to establish her choice of brand, she would like to check with her friends and regular shopkeeper about the attributes of each. Limited problem solving also takes place when a consumer encounters an unfamiliar brand in a known product category. The housewife who buys refined vegetable oil, on her next visit to the market, sees a new brand of oil, Saffola. Apart from being a new brand, this brand of oil also claims the unique attribute of being low in cholesterol. To arrive at a decision, whether or not to buy this brand, the housewife needs to gather information about the new brand which will allow her to compare it with the known brands. The marketer's task in a situation where he is introducing a new brand in a well known product category is to design a communication strategy that gives complete information on all the attributes of the brand, thus increasing the consumer's confidence and facilitating his or her purchase decision.
- *Extensive Problem Solving*: Extensive problem solving occurs when the consumer is encountering a new product category. He needs information on both the product category as well as the various brands available in it. This kind of decision is by far the most complex. For instance, you are thinking of buying a Flat colour television to replace

your existing black and white TV set. You do not have much idea about how to judge the quality of a, colour TV set. You have heard about the various brands, such as Videocon, BPL, Samsung, LG, Sony, Thomson etc. but you do not know what t heir respective quality ranking is in colour TV. Each brand makes claims of foreign technology, latest features such as flat square tube and channel display. Further, t here is a range of models to choose from within each brand, models with remote control. different cabinet colour finish, vertical monitor styling etc. To arrive at a decision, you have to gather information at three levels and also establish a criteria for evaluating this information. The three levels of information gathering and evaluation are at generic product level, brand level and model level within each brand. The marketing strategy for such buying behaviour must be such that it facilitates the consumer's information gathering and learning process about the product category and his own brand. The marketer must be able to provide his consumer with a very specific and unique set of positive attributes regarding his own brand, so that the purchase decision is made in his favour. The concept of EPS is most applicable to new products. The product may be new at the generic product concept level or it may be an established product concept but new for a particular consumer. In case of a new product concept such as ready to cook instant snack, the entire consumer universe is unfamiliar with the product. The marketer has to spend large amounts of money in educating the consumers about his product. The consumers in turn need a great deal of information before they can take a decision; and the decision process takes a long time. On the other hand, you may have the situation where the product concept is well understood by a majority of the consumers, but it is being bought or used by a particular consumer for the first time. To take a very simple example, a tribal who is exposed to the concept of toothpaste for the first time in his life will seek a lot of information and take a long time to decide. For him, buying a toothpaste is a EPS behaviour, whereas for most of us it simply requires a routinised response behaviour.

Purchasing Organizational Management

Recent studies regarding MBEs focus on three primary themes: discussions of public policy, comparisons between MBE and non-MBE firms, and reviews of corporate purchasing practices. First, regarding discussions of public policy, Levinson used a historical approach to evaluate the evolution of MBE assistance programmes. The transition from administrative programmes based on racial and ethnic standards to statute-based programmes that focus on "social and economic disadvantage" is viewed favorably. Levinson concludes that these new statutory programmes will better assist those MBEs "truly in need of assistance" and lead to the "enhancement of the general economic welfare of the nation."

Interestingly, Bates looked at the impact of preferential procurement policies on MBEs and suggested that efforts to help marginal MBEs are largely ineffective and that more emphasis should be placed on "stronger and better managed minority firms. " Bates further states that preferential policies are beneficial in removing traditional barriers to MBE participation in the economy and reducing the "costs of transition to a less discriminatory economy." Gray and Peery also discuss the costs of preferential policies and examine minority set-aside programmes from the perspective of recent judicial action.

They note that set-aside programmes are warranted when they are used to remedy past discriminatory behaviour. They further emphasize that this judicial standard established via the Croson case "will eliminate costs associated with unwarranted affirmative action provisions in public contract bidding." Overall, preferential policies appear to be viewed in a generally favorable light; however, their efficacy and structure need to be studied further to better understand their true impact on managerial practice. The objective of future research should be to empirically establish guidelines to be used in the setting of preferential policies.

Second, comparisons of MBE and non-MBE firms have been performed to justify preferential policies for MBEs and to understand the competitive environment encountered by MBE firms. Enz, Dollinger, and Daily examined the value orientations of MBE and SBE firms. MBE owners were found to place significantly greater emphasis on six value orientations: collectivism, rationality, materialism, duty, novelty, and power. MBE owners also demonstrated higher levels of value similarity with their primary customers.

Thus, MBEs appear to be aligning their organization-based values to those of their customers as a means of building trust and reducing uncertainty; that is, to overcome the barriers to building strong buyer/supplier relationships. Scott used a large-sample method to compare the financial performance of MBE and non-MBE firms.

Interestingly, study results indicated that there is no pervasive statistical difference in performance between MBEs and non-MBEs in terms of profitability, liquidity, or indebtedness. Scott notes that the sample was drawn from a Dun and Bradstreet database, which typically consists of "more mature and viable minority firms whose performance characteristics were largely unobserved in previous research."

Similar results were found by Bates and Furino, who report that MBEs are increasingly viable in a wide array of industries access to credit markets has been very beneficial to MBE development, and MBEs generally earned higher returns than their non-minority counterparts. Finally, Giunipero examined MBE performance from the perspective of the purchasing buyer/ manager. Buyers report that MBEs' performance is lower in all areas of comparison, especially in the areas of managerial and technical expertise. In addition to lower performance, buyers noted that finding qualified MBEs (with adequate capacity and competitive prices) is a substantial hurdle. Giunipero suggests a proactive approach to supplier development that involves technical, managerial, marketing, and financial assistance to help MBEs overcome their performance problems.

Third, insight into corporate purchasing perspectives of MBEs is critical to the future development of minority-owned business. Spratlen discussed the principal reasons for MBE purchasing programmes and presents a framework for an effective programme. Spratlen notes that MBE purchasing "links effective purchasing with company social responsibility" and is an underused and important source of competitive advantage.

Dollinger and Daily consider all three major themes but focus on buyer/ supplier relationships from the perspective of both the CPP and the MBE. Transaction cost economics provides the theoretical foundation for this extensive study. Important findings include that the costs of a "hostile" environment as well as the costs of opportunism are the principal impediments to establishing strong relationships. MBEs report that the complexity in doing business with large firms represents the greatest hurdle to strong relationships.

By contrast, CPPs emphasize the scarcity of qualified minority suppliers. Further, significant differences exist between MBEs and small business enterprises (SBEs), suggesting that MBEs face two types of challenges—size-related challenges and minority-related challenges. Cost-reducing activities found to be useful emphasize matching MBEs to CPPs and the provision of managerial assistance to help MBEs enhance their business performance. This study provides the foundation for the current research.

To better understand the buyer/supplier relationship between CPPs and MBEs, an empirical examination was undertaken in the fall of 1990 and the winter of 1991. A self-administered questionnaire was mailed to a random sample of 350 MBE owners/managers who were members of the National Minority Supplier Development Council. A similar questionnaire was sent to 1800 corporate purchasing managers (CPPs) of Fortune 500 organizations who have minority purchasing programmes.

An initial letter indicating the questionnaire would arrive in two to three weeks was mailed to each member of the sample population. A cover letter and questionnaire were then mailed. Usable responses were received from 135 MBEs (39 per cent response rate) and 620 CPPs (34 per cent response rate). These response rates compare very favorably with other studies of a similar nature.

The survey instrument consisted of three sections:

- A series of questions designed to help describe the study participants;
- Forty questions relating to the impediments facing MBEs and CPPs;
- Forty questions focusing on approaches to increase the success of MBE/CPP relationships.

The questions regarding both impediments and approaches use a seven-point scale (higher score = greater importance) to capture information from the respondents. This questionnaire was adapted from the instrument used by Dollinger and Daily.

Changes in the original survey were implemented following interviews with MBE owners/managers, corporate buyers/purchasing managers, and other purchasing experts. Some of the questions considered to be unnecessary were eliminated, and a set of approaches that MBEs can instigate to overcome the impediments to strong buyer/supplier relationships was added.

After modifying the survey, additional interviews were conducted with MBE owners/managers to determine the applicability of the modified questionnaire. Final modifications were made after a pilot test of the survey was conducted. This extensive survey development process was undertaken to assure the reliability of the study results.

A brief profile of the two respondent groups follows. The average age of the respondents from the corporate sample was 43 years. The vast majority of the respondents were Caucasian—86 per cent. Men outnumbered women by a two-to-one ratio. Corporate respondents averaged seven years experience in their current positions, and the vast majority were highly educated—the typical respondent possesses a college degree.

The "large" firms included in the corporate sample had annual sales of $7.6 billion and employed an average of 20,295 people. Approximately 93 per cent of the respondents classified their firms as manufacturers, with about 7 per cent service firms. These corporate firms are also quite profitable, with gross profit as a per cent of sales approaching 15 per cent. For these firms, purchases via minority purchasing programmes represent approximately 4.7 per cent of sales.

Finally, while the corporate respondents characterize themselves as successful (average score of 4.15 out of 5 with 5 = successful), they indicate that their MBE purchasing programmes are only satisfactory (average score of 3.16 out of 5 with 5 = successful).

The relatively low percentage of purchases via minority programmes (about the set-aside percentage established for government contracts) combined with the low rating for MBE purchasing programmes suggests a strong need to better understand the challenges and approaches to building better relationships between large firms and MBEs. The average age of the respondents from the minority-business sample was 44 years. The ratio of men to women was approximately 70 per cent to 30 per cent. MBE respondents averaged seven and a half years in their current positions. Like the corporate respondents, the MBE respondents were typically college graduates—in fact, a higher percentage of MBE respondents have obtained graduate degrees. By contrast to the corporate firms, over 90 per cent of the MBE firms classified themselves as service oriented.

On average, each MBE firm had annual sales of $3.5 million and employed 34 people. The MBE firms reported a higher level of profitability than their corporate counterparts, with the average MBE firm attaining a gross profit as a per cent of sales of almost 19 per cent. As expected, minority purchasing programmes are more important to MBEs since they do 29.5 per cent of their business through these programmes. Finally, MBE firms characterize themselves as somewhat successful (average score of 3.51 out of 5 with 5 = successful) while they suggest that MBE purchasing programmes at large firms are somewhat less than satisfactory (average score of 2.58 out of 5 with 5 = successful).

Not surprisingly, MBEs perceive minority purchasing programmes at large firms as less successful than do the corporations themselves. Again, this finding along with the low rating highlights the need for further study of these programmes. Impediments to Successful Relationships

Information regarding the respondents' perceptions of impediments to successful buyer/supplier relationships between MBEs and large corporations is contained. Two general observations quickly emerge from this data: CPPs and MBEs view the impediments quite differently, and MBEs perceive the impediments at higher levels than CPPs.

First, to highlight the fact that the two groups possess different perspectives regarding the challenges facing MBE development, the impediments are listed in decreasing order of the difference between the mean responses. The difference between the two mean scores is significant at the p =.01 level for 34 of the 40 impediments. This result is further emphasized by the ranking of impediments by CPP and MBE groupings.

These rankings are generally opposed—those impediments with high CPP rankings have low MBE rankings while those impediments with low CPP rankings have high MBE rankings. In fact, 27 of the 40 impediments have rankings that are separated by more than ten rank order positions.

This pervasive disagreement concerning the impediments is an important, though not entirely surprising, finding. To be successful, future policy efforts designed to assist MBE development must recognize these different viewpoints.

Second, based on the mean scores for each impediment, MBEs appear to perceive a higher level of difficulty in developing strong buyer/supplier relationships than their CPP counterparts. In fact, MBEs placed greater emphasis on the level of difficulty created by each impediment for 32 of 40 of the impediments. This finding most likely results from the fact that MBEs feel they have more at stake in developing relationships with large firms and therefore respond in a more assertive manner. Further, challenges to finding buyers tend to be internalized to a greater extent than challenges to finding suppliers. Special efforts should therefore be taken to help CPPs understand the nature and importance of successful buyer/supplier relationships for MBEs.

Additional insight is gained by examining the most prominent impediments as ranked by the CPPs and MBEs. Interestingly, while the two groups generally disagree on the type and magnitude of impediments that inhibit mutually beneficial relationships, they concur on the most prominent challenge—the undercapitalization of MBEs. Inadequate financing limits the ability of MBEs to sustain growth, establish leading edge operations, and develop highly visible market positions.

Inadequate financing is viewed as an underlying impediment that contributes to or exacerbates other impediments. Only two other impediments are common among the top ten listings for both groups: MBEs become disillusioned with corporate bureaucracy, and buyers use MBEs just to satisfy statistics.

Many MBEs (as well as their counterpart SBEs) are financially and managerially resource-poor such that understanding and complying with the "bureaucratic" hurdles inherent in doing business with large corporations is a particularly pervasive problem. Similarly, because many CPPs find MBE purchasing programmes to be cumbersome, the main efforts of CPPs are to meet established requirements rather than build long-term relationships.

Focusing specifically on the CPP perspective, the top ten impediment listing emphasizes two primary themes: the unavailability of qualified MBE suppliers and the perceived "hassles" involved in meeting MBE purchasing mandates. The overriding challenge from the CPP perspective appears to be to effectively match MBE capabilities to CPP requirements.

Five of the 10 most prominent impediments focus on the CPP's inability to find qualified MBE suppliers. CPPs perceive MBEs to be clustered in relatively few industries, to lack specialized skills, and to lack the flexibility to meet changing competitive requirements. CPPs also note that information regarding qualified MBEs is not readily available.

The fact that MBEs find it difficult to identify contracts to bid on and become disillusioned with corporate bureaucracy contributes to the perception that MBEs are unable to meet the needs of large firms. Unfortunately, the undercapitalization of MBEs limits their ability to directly affect this perception.

The second major theme (represented by the 9th, 10th, and 11th-ranked impediments) is that CPPs believe government programmes to develop MBEs are artificial and burdensome mandates that are sometimes abused by MBEs. MBEs view the prominent impediments quite differently, placing the greatest emphasis on a lack of effort by CPPs to build strong relationships with MBEs. Several issues are involved in the MBEs' assessment.

First, MBEs feel that institutional barriers involving "old-boy networks" make it difficult for MBEs to prove themselves as capable suppliers. Second, MBEs note that buyers are uninformed concerning minority owned firms. Finally, MBEs believe that large firms lack commitment to MBE purchasing programmes and use such programmes merely as a means of meeting government regulations and creating a favorable public image.

MBEs further feel that large corporations are inconsistent in implementing MBE programmes and only place small-volume and non-essential orders with MBEs.

From the MBE perspective, this lack of corporate commitment continues to exist in part because government fails to enforce regulations regarding MBE purchasing programmes. This generally negative perception regarding large corporations helps explain why MBEs become disillusioned when attempting to do business with large firms. Finally, MBEs believe that without greater access to capital, they will not be able to overcome the substantial barriers created by large corporations.

APPROACHES TO SUCCESSFUL RELATIONSHIPS

In contrast to the findings regarding impediments, a relatively high level of agreement exists between the two groups concerning the type of approaches that reduce barriers to strong relationships. In fact, based on the mean scores, CPPs and MBEs rank 34 of the 40 approaches within ten rank order positions of each other.

Despite this general concurrence regarding the approach rankings, the data show that the two groups place different levels of emphasis on the various approaches. The mean scores of 30 of the 40 approaches are significantly different at the $p = .01$ level (another five are significantly different at the $p = .05$ level). Given the MBE belief that they have more at stake in relationships with large firms, the fact that MBEs place greater emphasis on all but three of the approaches is not surprising.

As with the impediments, the CPPs and MBEs concur on the most important approach to success—MBEs should continually improve the product/service packages they offer. Such emphasis on improving the products/services offered by MBEs tends to support the implication that many MBEs are not competitive in today's rapidly changing business environment.

However, recognition of this issue among MBEs is an important step that indicates MBEs are serious about using their available resources to meet the needs of potential buyers. Information's role as a facilitator to reduce the transaction "distance" that separates CPPs and MBEs is highlighted by the four additional approaches common to the top listings for both groups.

Specifically, providing MBE vendor listings to all departments helps increase the visibility of MBEs. MBE attendance at trade fairs also increases MBE visibility and provides an opportunity to learn what other successful MBEs are doing. In addition, both groups rank the attendance by corporations at MBE trade fairs highly (CPPs rank = 5, MBEs rank = 12). As corporations identify and publicize long-term purchasing needs, MBEs are better able to identify opportunities and tailor their product/service mix. Finally, both groups feel that MBEs need to develop better information sources regarding sources of assistance.

A closer examination of the CPP top ten approach listing reveals four distinct issues, three of which rely heavily on information availability.

The information-related issues are:

- increasing MBE visibility,
- Increasing information concerning MBE opportunities,
- Assuring and monitoring MBE performance.

Approaches that increase MBE visibility and provide better information to MBEs regarding business opportunities. In addition to these approaches that reduce the transaction costs incurred by both sides, CPPs emphasize the need to verify MBE performance. Checking references, performing credit checks, and holding quality assurance meetings help large firms eliminate negative experiences with MBEs. The fourth major issue focuses on the actual capabilities that MBEs potentially bring to the buyer/supplier relationship. For CPPs to be truly interested in MBEs as suppliers over the long term, MBEs must offer the products/services required by large firms at competitive cost and quality levels.

If MBEs cannot meet the competitive needs of the large firm, then large firms will almost inevitably look at MBEs strictly in terms of meeting imposed (and burdensome) requirements. Unfortunately, CPPs placed relatively low levels of emphasis on using their firms' resources to help MBEs become more competitive. The MBE top 10 listing of approaches presents similar themes, including MBE visibility and competitiveness; however, a major emphasis is directed towards activities that large corporations should undertake to reduce the costs incurred by MBEs. For example, three of the top 12 approaches emphasize the need for large firms to identify their purchasing requirements and then publish those requirements so that MBEs can easily access the information.

Of particular importance is the MBEs' desire for large firms to make large volume and high value-added contracts available to MBEs. Similarly, MBEs stress the idea that corporate top management should be actively involved in MBE programmes to assure that the programmes are transformed from "minimal efforts to meet statistics" to strategic programmes. Regarding MBE visibility, the most highly ranked approach is for corporations to provide an

MBE listing to all departments (again, the emphasis is on what large firms should do). Interestingly, MBEs also noted that they need to be more persistent in the pursuit of contracts with large firms.

The final point of emphasis is on being aware of and acquiring outside sources of assistance. As MBEs develop multiple sources of finance and gain access to other resources (educational and technical), they are better able to position themselves as competitive suppliers.

Purchasing and Supply Chain Manager

The PSCM at the ALC has a direct link to the AFMC PSM Directorate. This person is the current Supply Chain Manager enhanced with "purchasing" responsibilities at the weapon system or major commodity. The PSCM coordinates with the SSM and weapons SPD, as well as the customer. He/she is an integrator and decision-maker across commodities and/or weapon systems. Categories of PSCMs may not always be the current categories of weapon systems and commodities. Just as the Air Force is a dynamic organization, this structure is dynamic and should change with the Air Force's needs.

STRATEGIC SUPPORT TEAM

This team provides strategic support to each sourcing team. Each member serves an internal ALC integrating function across the various sourcing teams and as an external integrator across the Air Force. Individuals belong to the PSCM organization, report to the PSCM leader, and are directly accountable for the sourcing team's performance.

This team's performance measurement is linked to meeting organizational sourcing objectives. Although the advisors are representatives of their function, the specific system complexity, uniqueness, and magnitude may warrant allocation of additional resources directly to the sourcing teams and additional resources of specific expertise may be subordinate to the appropriate strategic support team advisor.

PROCUREMENT ADVISOR

The Procurement Advisor will serve as an overarching procurement expert who is responsible for developing and continually improving the supply strategy and integration across all sourcing teams as well as liaison with Hq AFMC–level supply management activities. Because PSM requires that supplier relationships and contracts be designed at a higher, more strategic level, the procurement advisor serves as the PCO for all sourcing teams and will focus on the core, strategic, and analytic PCO activities, rather than the contract execution activities that can be accomplished by the sourcing teams. The procurement advisor must focus on and be involved with the strategic planning activities of PSM to include the requirements identification and generation activities, rather than execution and monitoring activities. This position may be best suited to serve as the PSCM deputy.

DEMAND PLANNING ADVISOR

The Demand Planning Advisor is a liaison and integrator both externally and internally across the sourcing teams. He/she is a customer liaison, focusing on supporting warfighter requirements, providing an aggregation of requirements by weapon system and commodity group. Collaboration and advanced planning and scheduling are key functions of this position. This position is an alternative option for the PSCM deputy. The commercial world may be slower than the Air Force in this realization of the value of early procurement involvement. "Though a proven best practice, involving procurement early in the product development cycle to ensure a quicker, smoother production rollout is often difficult because the role of procurement as value-adding partner represents a radical departure from the function's historically more limited activity as purchasing agent. In coming years, challenges, such as these (for example, the creation of centralized repositories of information and designs that can be shared across the organization and with external partners), must be overcome in order to make partnerships with suppliers as strong and innovative as possible".

TECHNICAL AND QUALITY ADVISORS

These advisors provide engineering, statistical process control, and other technical expertise to the sourcing leaders.

FINANCIAL/COST ADVISOR

This position is designated a GS-13 to enable both cost (including total ownership cost analysis, financial risk assessment, cost savings and cost benefit measurement) and budget competencies.

SOURCING LEADERS

These leaders are cross-functional, commodity-level managers involved in both purchasing and supply chain management activities. The sourcing leader is responsible for such core PSM commodity group–level activities as industry research, supplier selection, contract execution, and supplier relationship management at the commodity level or commodity subgroup. They are responsible for the leadership and integration of key functions such as procurement and logistics, as well as coordination with the weapon system level.

STRATEGIC MATERIALS MANAGER

This manager is responsible for logistics and production activities (*i.e.*, manufacturing inventory, requirements planning, production planning, and industrial packaging) previously known as item management, programme management, production management, and equipment specialist activities, except at a more aggregate level than individual items (*i.e.*, system, major assembly, or commodity group or subgroups). The manager will manage these items strategically, at a higher level than items or parts, requiring a single, higher-grade individual rather than numerous lower-grade specialists. He/she will be able to execute purchases using contractual vehicles designed by the PSCM team and established by the procurement advisor. The ability to establish this position is highly reliant upon the successful implementation of PSM enablers, including e-commerce (electronic transactions) and e-business (enterprise-wide) implementation. Realization of PSM tenets may require additional material management support.

The proposed changes to this point deal mainly with the need to elevate and integrate purchasing and supply strategy activities. The other key need is a function to manage a multitiered supplier network to leverage the Air Force's buying power with its suppliers.

THE AIR FORCE–WIDE HQ AFMC–LEVEL ORGANIZATION CONSTRUCT

In addition to managing purchasing and supply chains at the execution level, the supplier base must be managed at a strategic level to build long-standing performance-based relationships with suppliers and manage supplier production capacities over the life of Air Force systems. Supplier management is important not only for first-tier suppliers but also for second- and third-tier suppliers. This notion of having insight into suppliers' suppliers is a dramatic shift from current supply chain management practices. The proposed construct establishes a PSM directorate at Hq AFMC that capitalizes on the established SCM function. A reorganization at the Hq AFMC level involving the establishment of a Maintenance and PSCM Directorate.

Management of the supplier base is necessary to assure supply and build long-standing performance-based relationships with key suppliers. Weapon systems often share suppliers and many suppliers provide a range of goods and services. The proposed design establishes this supplier management activity at Hq AFMC and extends supplier management beyond first-tier suppliers. The new PSM Directorate would include a "supplier management" activity that would work at a level above the PSCMs for large cross-commodity suppliers and be organized around major suppliers or supplier groups of like capabilities (*e.g.*, electronic warfare (EW) equipment).

For example, there could be a Boeing Supplier Manager (SM), a Lockheed Martin SM, a Northrop Grumman SM, as well as a munitions SM, or a brakes, struts, wheels SM. The SM would be responsible for facilitating the strategic relationships between the Air Force and key suppliers and maintaining oversight of PSCMs and awareness of supplier lead times and production capacities for critical items. An additional function of the Hq-level PSM could be to maintain a database of inactive suppliers, with information on their lead-time requirements and surge capacities. These are key functions of a PSM organization; however, their value to the Air Force extends beyond PSM implementation and supports current initiatives aimed at more closely linking AFMC actions and production to war fighter requirements. One example of an initiative focused on tightening the link between AFMC and the war fighter is the combat support execution planning and control operational architecture study sponsored by AF/IL, which highlights the need for a virtual organization to manage supplier capacity to meet a range of operational requirements. In managing supplier capacities, a supplier manager, in this case the PSM, is constantly assessing active and non-active first-, second- and third-tier supplier capacities and developing agreements with them to respond within specified lead times, derived from known or projected operational requirements.

Given these needs, the PSM could be that element of a combat support execution planning and control operational architecture responsible for managing supply capacity and working with PSCMs and resource capacity managers in conducting capability assessments. With insight into multitiered supplier capacities and lead times, AFMC can provide better insight into the Air Force's long-range operational capability and make more enlightened tradeoff decisions. It is not all-inclusive but could serve as a starting point for establishing positions consistent with best practices.

ALC Level. The PSCM can be considered the execution level that will serve a resource capacity management function. Weapon systems/commodity groups are integrated, assessments are performed, and interaction with more global integration activities could occur from this point. Hq AFMC Level. Strategic supplier integration, relationships, and evaluations are managed at this level. Supply capacity is managed, working with weapon system and spares resource capacity managers in conducting capability assessments. Other roles include:

- Facilitate strategic relationship between the Air Force and key suppliers
- Oversee PSCMs, maintain awareness of supplier lead times and production capacities for critical items
- Aggregate demand planning and forecasting
- Perform supplier financial risk assessments
- Maintain database of inactive suppliers (lead time requirements and surge capacities, for example).

AIR FORCE–WIDE HQ AFMC–LEVEL ORGANIZATION CONSTRUCTS

To best complement the headquarters' existing strategic alignment, the core PSM responsibility is a direct reporting unit to Hq AFMC. PSM activities move from logistics, procurement, financial management, the ACE, and other necessary supporting resources to the new directorate. A PSM Directorate at this level maximizes crosscutting visibility and leadership, and allows integrated senior leadership focus. This structure will enable the organization to capitalize on AFMC's enterprise concept for operations objectives. A key purpose of the Air Force–wide, Hq AFMC–level organization is supplier management. Supplier/ Supply Base Managers ensure crosscutting activities, coordination, and integration across all PSCM teams. This is the ultimate integration point. A notional cross-reference between the PSCM and Supplier/Supply Base Managers.

The Supplier/Supply Base Manager's focus would be determined by major suppliers or groups of suppliers in a manner that best represents the allocation of resources, workload, and PSM benefit potential. Business units according to existing supply chain management leads. Once again, however, this is not a standard form fit approach; it is dynamic and should be aligned with organizational strategic objectives.

Two examples of relevant organizational structures are from major aeronautical corporations known for their best practices in PSM. Because the information was gathered by RAND team members through unattributed interviews, the company names are omitted.

A major worldwide aeronautical corporation has organized its supply chain management structure using a module centre strategy arranged by commodity types. In addition, this particular corporation has identified two commodity management business units. The first is core procurement, broken down into such categories as fabrication and composites and small machined parts, and the second is an externals and engines business unit, further broken down by such commodity types as electronics and electrical systems, forging/raw material, and large machined parts. This company stresses the effectiveness gained by linking the commodity management structure to the module centre strategy.

A major airline has aligned its supply chain management operations by engine maintenance sourcing, airframe sourcing, warranty recovery, indirect materials and services, and aircraft modifications. Using the engine maintenance unit as an example, six commodity managers have been handpicked and assigned to six commodity categories: Pratt and Whitney product line (spare parts), GE/ CFM spares product line, thrust reversers and engine accessories (spare parts and repairs, Pratt and Whitney outside repairs, and GE/CFM outside repairs). Each commodity manager has a different multidiscipline background such as financial, mechanic, repair technician, and materials and technology. Although there are no reporting lines between the commodity managers, they leverage their expertise and work together, as their individual discipline is not sufficient to fulfill all their responsibilities. This is a very lean organization of managers who accomplish their jobs by working with each other and with the rest of the organizational network. Other members of the organization are not matrixed or assigned to them but they help or support this team as needed. The airframe-sourcing unit, on the other hand, contains two commodity management categories.

The first is aircraft interiors and the second is component repairs. This unit also contains buyers for areas including airframe structures, aircraft interiors, aircraft systems component repairs, aircraft in-flight entertainment systems, and avionics. Furthermore, this unit has assigned analysts for finances, data analysis, and metrics.

Once again, the key point is that any approach should be derived according to the overall business strategy. Major worldwide corporations have successfully employed PSM and attribute their success to structuring the supply chain management business units according to organizational strategies. A prominent PSM pioneer, Dave Nelson, when he was the vice president of Worldwide Supply Management for John Deere, presented a briefing entitled "How the Winners Win, Mastering Supply Management Best Practices" at a Sourcing Interests Group conference. He stressed the importance of strategic intent. The supply chain strategy must be linked to the business objective and provide the framework to meet the overall business objective.

Furthermore, he described the need to move from decentralization to "centre-led" operations, not to be confused with "centralized" operations. His example portrayed a business model to strategically select and develop a global supply base from the top down. At the top of the inverted pyramid was enterprise-led common commodities and services. The smaller, midsection included enterprise/division teams—more highly engineered components, and the bottom section was division-led, product-specific components. This best practice supports the notion of an enterprise level of accountability for PSM as well as the establishment of centers of management for common commodities such as propulsion. A proposed team having responsibility for developing a core competency in PSM at the ALC level as well as at the AFMC Hq level. We also discussed establishing a PSM supporting role within Hq AFMC's ACE. This should help enable the ALC implementation teams to fully benefit from ACE initiatives, support, and resources while developing PSM competency through training and teaming among fellow purchasing and supply organizations as well as among the ALC-level implementation teams themselves. As a result, the establishment of an Hq AFMC PSM Directorate organization should be feasible.

The PSM focal point within the ACE can complete transformation by separating from the ACE and joining the Logistics (LG) supply and Contracting (PK) PSM organizations, along with other key functional representatives, to become the PSM Directorate.

The many functional resources that are key to PSM. Although PSM becomes a Directorate-level core function of Hq AFMC in this concept, it will rely heavily upon support from other organizations. Following a horizontal, truly integrated model, the functional home offices become coaches (teachers) or centers of excellence. The personnel should not simply be matrixed to the PSM organization (*i.e.*, personnel performance appraisals are written by their functional home office). They should become full members of the PSM organization (*i.e.*, personnel performance appraisals should be written by the appropriate PSM organization).

A strong case has been made in the business literature for coaches rather than managers. "In the long run, the quality of an organization's coaching is a key determinant of whether it succeeds or fails." "A single individual, no matter how talented or knowledgeable, can accomplish only so much. A teacher, however, multiplies the impact of his or her knowledge by sharing it with others." So, the "centre of excellence" is where the coaches of a particular skill or profession reside and teach, mentor, and develop the knowledge and skills base of the teams. The PSCM leaders are the process owners and teams do the process.

The centers of excellence are responsible for ensuring that skills are maintained and their success is measured by the success of the teams they support. This differs from the traditional functional home office perspective where the home office is also the process owner, has responsibility to do the work, and is measured by productivity and performance of the functional portion of the work. The resultant organization is ALC-led, has visibility to the Hq AFMC Commander, and is horizontally aligned with AFMC's enterprise managers.

The lines of interface and functional support that the AFMC PSM teams will provide to the ALC-level organization. The AFMC PSM team continues to work closely with the ALCs; but many vertical layers of management have been removed. Non-PSM-related AFMC and ALC interfaces remain intact.

RATIONALIZATION OF THE AIR FORCE–WIDE ALC-LEVEL ORGANIZATION

Our proposed Air Force–wide organizational construct supports many key PSM principles. It is centre-led at the Hq AFMC level where PSM is elevated to a recognized core competency. It enables enterprise-wide, strategic PSM application with a crosscutting weapon system or major commodity group perspective that is consistent with the Air Force's SCM function as well as Hq AFMC's Enterprise Management practices.

It is also consistent with PSM principles. Cross-functional integration of requirements, procurement, logistics, engineering, and finance is achieved by assigning personnel to the PSM teams, which ensures that team members share objectives. Moreover, the functional (AFMC and ALC home office) organizations are coaches, or centers of excellence, and are rated on the performance and results of the organizations they support. Our proposed organization also supports Air Force strategic objectives, such as capitalizing on significant strides the Air Force has undertaken. This structure is consistent with the Spares Campaign and Supply Chain Management structure, and is intended to change and be flexible with this strategy.

It has the potential to become a key resource capacity management component of the Air Force's combat support execution planning and control operational architecture. This structure also leverages SAF/AQ's Acquisition Excellence initiatives (*e.g.*, Roadblock Buster Lightning Bolts), as well as AFMC's Strategic Sourcing initiative. A horizontal organization enables an end-to-end view of purchasing and supply management and cross-functional integration. During the 1990s, when many companies were moving away from classic hierarchical organizations towards flatter ones, Business Week published an article entitled "The Horizontal Corporation" that summarized then-current best practices. Specifically, steps similar to our proposed approach were taken that include identifying strategic objectives and organizing around processes instead of functions, while preserving key expertise.

Although organizations differ by programme and centre, the F100 and its controls and accessories group serves as an example illustrating that PSM functions currently occur at approximately levels five, six, and seven. Also, there are separate stovepipes at each of these levels for such functions as procurement and engineering.

Many documented best practices serve as examples for a structure such as this. A case in point is Motorola's Space and Systems Technology Group (SSTG), one of four businesses within its communications enterprise. SSTG redesigned its supply management operation from a complicated, vertical, functionally divided, nine-level organizational hierarchy to only three levels. The original hierarchy greatly hindered the group's frontline employees' ability to voice suggestions or solve problems in real time. "Seven hundred workers performed various supply management tasks, but coherence and cross functional teamwork were virtually non-existent." SSTG began its redesign by defining its direction and value proposition, *i.e.*, by developing a vision and overall strategy. It established supply management as a core operating process. The result was a horizontal, cross-functional organization where self-directed, empowered, decisionmaking teams operate within an organization that is only three levels deep.

The director of operations and supply chain management reports directly to the SSTG general manager. A process owner team includes the vice president, the director of operations of supply chain management, and three commodity managers. Their commodity teams are arranged by such commodity/

technology types as electronic components and assembly, mechanical/electromechanical, and software and systems integration. These teams coordinate and employ the end-to-end supply management core process. Commodity teams work concurrently with purchasing, systems and software, and operations support teams; all reporting directly to the process owner team. A similar example is taken from a very well known IBM PSM success story. At the heart of this success story are the steps Gene Richter took in the early 1990s to move from a vertically integrated to a centralized organization with empowered commodity councils.

One consequence of a more horizontal organization is new opportunities for communication and knowledge-sharing. These opportunities not only multiply but also become key to the organization's success. The direct interface characteristics of the proposed Air Force–wide organization reflect the opportunities for and importance of knowledge-sharing.

5

Advances in Product Lifecycle Management

INTRODUCTION

Product lifecycle management, sometimes "product life cycle management", represents an all-encompassing vision for managing all data relating to the design, production, support and ultimate disposal of manufactured goods. PLM concepts were first introduced where safety and control have been extremely important, notably the aerospace, medical device, military and nuclear industries. These industries originated the discipline of configuration management, which evolved into electronic data management systems, which then further evolved to product data management. Over the last ten years, manufacturers of instrumentation, industrial machinery, consumer electronics, packaged goods and other complex engineered products have discovered the benefits of PLM solutions and are adopting efficient PLM software in increasing numbers.

PLM SOLUTIONS

PLM can be thought of as both:

- A repository for all information that affects a product, and
- *A communication process between product stakeholders*: Principally marketing, engineering, manufacturing and field service.

The PLM system is the first place where all product information from marketing and design comes together, and where it leaves in a form suitable for production and support. A few analysts use "PLM" as an umbrella term that includes engineering CAD. But product information creation tools include word processors; spreadsheet and graphics prigrammes; requirements analysis and market assessment tools; field trouble reports; and even e-mails or other correspondence. In our view, a PLM tool focuses exclusively on managing data that covers the breadth of a product's lifecycle, without regard to how that data is developed.

The essential elements of PLM:

- Manages design and process documents
- Constructs and controls bill of material records
- Offers an electronic file repository

- Includes built-in and custom part and document metadata
- Identifies materials content for environmental compliance
- Permits item-focused task assignments
- Enables workflow and process management for approving changes
- Controls multi-user secured access, including "electronic signature"
- Exports data for downstream ERP systems

LIMITATIONS

The PLC model is of some degree of usefulness to marketing managers, in that it is based on factual assumptions. Nevertheless, it is difficult for marketing management to gauge accurately where a product is on its PLC graph. A rise in sales per se is not necessarily evidence of growth. A fall in sales per se does not typify decline. Furthermore, some products do not experienced a decline. Coca Cola and Pepsi are examples of two products that have existed for many decades, but are still popular products all over the world. Both modes of cola have been in maturity for some years.

Another factor is that differing products would possess different PLC "shapes". A fad product would hold a steep sloped growth stage, a short maturity stage, and a steep sloped decline stage.

A product such as Coca Cola and Pepsi would experience growth, but also a constant level of sales over a number of decades. It can probably be said that a given product may hold a unique PLC shape, and the typical PLC model can only be used as a rough guide for marketing management. This is why its called the product life cycle.

PRODUCT LIFE CYCLE

A product's life cycle can be divided into several stages characterized by the revenue generated by the product. If a curve is drawn showing product revenue over time, it may take one of many different shapes, an example of which is shown below:

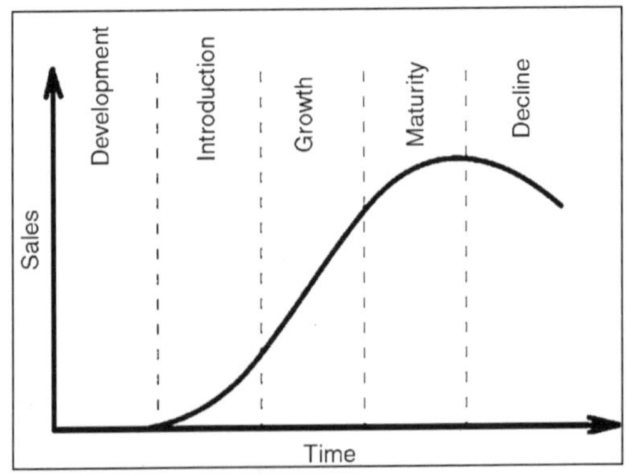

Fig. Product Life Cycle Curve

The life cycle concept may apply to a brand or to a category of product. Its duration may be as short as a few months for a fad item or a century or more for product categories such as the gasoline-powered automobile.

Product development is the incubation stage of the product life cycle. There are no sales and the firm prepares to introduce the product. As the product progresses through its life cycle, changes in the marketing mix usually are required in order to adjust to the evolving challenges and opportunities.

INTRODUCTION STAGE

When the product is introduced, sales will be low until customers become aware of the product and its benefits. Some firms may announce their product before it is introduced, but such announcements also alert competitors and remove the element of surprise. Advertising costs typically are high during this stage in order to rapidly increase customer awareness of the product and to target the early adopters. During the introductory stage the firm is likely to incur additional costs associated with the initial distribution of the product. These higher costs coupled with a low sales volume usually make the introduction stage a period of negative profits.

During the introduction stage, the primary goal is to establish a market and build primary demand for the product class.

The following are some of the marketing mix implications of the introduction stage:

- *Product*: One or few products, relatively undiffer-entiated
- *Price*: Generally high, assuming a skim pricing strategy for a high profit margin as the early adopters buy the product and the firm seeks to recoup development costs quickly. In some cases a penetration pricing strategy is used and introductory prices are set low to gain market share rapidly.
- *Distribution*: Distribution is selective and scattered as the firm commences implementation of the distribution plan.
- *Promotion*: Promotion is aimed at building brand awareness. Samples or trial incentives may be directed towards early adopters. The introductory promotion also is intended to convince potential resellers to carry the product.

GROWTH STAGE

The growth stage is a period of rapid revenue growth. Sales increase as more customers become aware of the product and its benefits and additional market segments are targeted. Once the product has been proven a success and customers begin asking for it, sales will increase further as more retailers become interested in carrying it. The marketing team may expand the distribution at this point. When competitors enter the market, often during the later part of the growth stage, there may be price competition and/or increased promotional costs in order to convince consumers that the firm's product is better than that of the competition. During the growth stage, the goal is to gain consumer preference and increase sales.

The marketing mix may be modified as follows:

- *Product*: New product features and packaging options; improvement of product quality.
- *Price*: Maintained at a high level if demand is high, or reduced to capture additional customers.
- *Distribution*: Distribution becomes more intensive. Trade discounts are minimal if resellers show a strong interest in the product.
- *Promotion*: Increased advertising to build brand preference.

MATURITY STAGE

The maturity stage is the most profitable. While sales continue to increase into this stage, they do so at a slower pace. Because brand awareness is strong, advertising expenditures will be reduced. Competition may result in decreased market share and/or prices. The competing products may be very similar at this point, increasing the difficulty of differentiating the product. The firm places effort into encouraging competitors' customers to switch, increasing usage per customer, and converting non-users into customers. Sales promotions may be offered to encourage retailers to give the product more shelf space over competing products.

During the maturity stage, the primary goal is to maintain market share and extend the product life cycle.

Marketing mix decisions may include:

- *Product*: Modifications are made and features are added in order to differentiate the product from competing products that may have been introduced.
- *Price*: Possible price reductions in response to competition while avoiding a price war.
- *Distribution*: New distribution channels and incentives to resellers in order to avoid losing shelf space.
- *Promotion*: Emphasis on differentiation and building of brand loyalty. Incentives to get competitors' customers to switch.

DECLINE STAGE

Eventually sales begin to decline as the market becomes saturated, the product becomes technologically obsolete, or customer tastes change. If the product has developed brand loyalty, the profitability may be maintained longer. Unit costs may increase with the declining production volumes and eventually no more profit can be made.

During the decline phase, the firm generally has three options:

- Maintain the product in hopes that competitors will exit. Reduce costs and find new uses for the product.
- Harvest it, reducing marketing support and coasting along until no more profit can be made.
- Discontinue the product when no more profit can be made or there is a successor product.

The marketing mix may be modified as follows:

- *Product*: The number of products in the product line may be reduced. Rejuvenate surviving products to make them look new again.
- *Price*: Prices may be lowered to liquidate inventory of discontinued products. Prices may be maintained for continued products serving a niche market.
- *Distribution*: Distribution becomes more selective. Channels that no longer are profitable are phased out.
- *Promotion*: Expenditures are lower and aimed at reinforcing the brand image for continued products.

LIMITATIONS

The term "life cycle" implies a well-defined life cycle as observed in living organisms, but products do not have such a predictable life and the specific life cycle curves followed by different products vary substantially. Consequently, the life cycle concept is not well-suited for the forecasting of product sales. Furthermore, critics have argued that the product life cycle may become self-fulfilling. For example, if sales peak and then decline, managers may conclude that the product is in the decline phase and therefore cut the advertising budget, thus precipitating a further decline.

Nonetheless, the product life cycle concept helps marketing managers to plan alternate marketing strategies to address the challenges that their products are likely to face. It also is useful for monitoring sales results over time and comparing them to those of products having a similar life cycle.

PRODUCTIVITY IMPROVEMENT

The aim of this section was first to identify the factors which managers find make the improvement of productivity difficult, second to attempt to establish which methods are used to improve productivity and their relative usefulness, and third the role of technology in improving productivity in services. Finally respondents were asked for their statements relating to the challenges for the future.

BARRIERS TO IMPROVING PRODUCTIVITY

Respondents were asked to rank their top five factors from a list of eleven factors which appear in the literature as factors which might impede improvement in productivity. The responses show the top three or four reasons as being lack of meaningful measures, organisation of work, frequent changes in demand, and the cost of gathering data, whose weighted averages were 1896, 16 per cent. 15 per cent and 12 per cent respectively. Lack of clear business targets at 12 per cent was the next factor. These results are perhaps not unforeseen but if they are representative for service organisations as a whole they give direction of the work which needs to be addressed to bring about improvements. The lack of meaningful measures restricts both the ability of managers to know the status of their operations with regard to productivity and thereby fails to identify the drivers for improvement.

The changes in the organisation of work presenting a barrier perhaps is associated with changes resulting from the ways in which people are required to work together and to take responsibility for their own work. It is interesting to note that frequent changes in methods was very low in the order suggesting that there may be problems in getting things right to start with. Consequently it may be inferred that respondents are not concerned with changes at the individual level but more fundamental structural changes in the ways of working. However even within this scenario one might have predicted that frequent changes of staff would have appeared further up the listing. Perhaps this is a result of the sample under investigation and it would require further investigation to establish if those sectors with high staff turnover such as hotel and restaurants would still reflect these findings. Anecdotal evidence suggests it would not be so.

The inclusion of frequent changes in demand as a major barrier to productivity improvement is not unexpected. Where demand changes frequently and if the changes are irregularly it makes the balancing of the capacity of the service operation with the demand that much more problematic, Cost of gathering data and the lack of clear business targets were identified also to be of importance as barriers. It would be interesting to know if there exists a link between these two factors and the lack of meaningful measures and whether the lack of meaningful business objectives make the establishment of meaningful productivity measures more difficult. Also does the difficult of finding meaningful measures increase the cost of gather data? It is perhaps interesting that the factors which might be classed as people factors appear low down in the rankings as barriers to productivity improvement. Lack of interest of senior management, poor supervisors, union resistance all fall in this category

METHODS OF IMPROVING PRODUCTIVITY

Respondents were asked about the techniques and methods used in their organisation to improve productivity and as an ancillary question asked to rank the three most useful. The question aimed to identify the extent to which traditional work study techniques are being used and the spread of newer approaches for improving quality and productivity and time productivity. The responses illustrate that not surprisingly many organisations use more than one technique and that all of the techniques are exmployed widely except those applying just-in-time approaches. Even though the numbers do not permit statistical analysis the use of skills training would seem to be the one approach which is favoured by a majority of those answering the question.

Other approaches not included in the listing included incentive payments and bonus schemes. The weighted average suggests that most respondents regard skills training as the most effective although the traditional techniques of work study are of significant importance. The other techniques which were offered as alternatives in many cases could be viewed as falling within the classifications listed.

However in addition the importance of communication and staff motivation was mentioned by a number of respondents and one indicated the link between understanding capacity planning and productivity improvement. Somcwhat surprisingly there was not a marked reference to the use of technology as route towards improving productivity even though it featured as the subject of the subsequent series of questions.

THE ROLE OF TECHNOLOGY IN IMPROVING PRODUCTIVITY

The series of questions relating to technology and technology improvement sort to gain an impression of the importance of technology for improving productivity and the type of technology which is most likely to give the desired improvement. Also respondents were asked to identify the aspects of technology which interfere with improving productivity.

An overwhelming number of respondents (80 per cent) indicated that productivity improvement is very important in their organisation. Aspects of information technology were thc cxamples given of the type of technology which most would be using to improve productivity.

Emphasis was placed on improved accuracy, availability, and speed of handling information. Electronic data interchange (EDI) was referred to by a number of respondents. In those sectors in which the operations involve handling of materials the introduction of mechanical handling, and sorting equipment, and the continued mechanisation of manual tasks were mentioned.

The problems presented by technology which might hinder the achievement of the—expected productivity gains fell within the categories of:

- Training of staff
- Costs of the technology (and by inference training)
- Compatibility of different systems
- Reliability of the technology, particularly software

The Changes in Approach and Challenges of Managing Productivity Improvement Respondents were asked their view of the changes in managing productivity and the main challenges facing those who have to improve productivity and the likely changes for the future. The issues identified were fairly common across the sectors. Many respondents raised the link between quality and productivity and the need to maintain or raise customer service while improving productivity. The influence of competition was seen a factor making this more difficult. The affect of quality programmes was raised in relation to reduction in errors, and the implementation of quality initiatives like total quality management programmes and the procedural discipline of standards like BS5750. The role of technology in improving productivity was again indicated confirming the answers to the previous questions.

The main challenges for the future can be summarised as:

- Increased business competition
- The rate of change managers have to cope with (by inference this is increasing).
- Gaining the commitment of staff and increasing their skills to carry out their tasks while at the same time adjusting cultural attitudes to attain levels of customer service.
- Containing costs (and by inference maintaining service levels) and utilising expensive resources to the full.
- Improving data collection and appropriateness of productivity measurements.
- Improving throughput efficiency.

CUSTOMER CARE AND TOTAL QUALITY MANAGEMENT PROGRAMMES

Respondents were asked to say if they had customer care programmes or total quality management programmes in operation in their organisation. It is clear that many more of the respondents have customer care programmes than total quality management.

This corresponds with other findings that service companies have tended to introduce customer care programmes first and then to follow with total quality. Productivity improvement would seem to be most inhibited by the organisation of work within the service delivery system and finding the most appropriate measures for productivity particularly when non-standard and complex tasks are being undertaken and in a climate of changing demand and where customer service levels must also be met at the same time. Traditional work study methods help but are not the full solution. Technology has a role to play but only in association with the part played by service personnel. The challenges for the future are to make the best use of systems as they are developed and to link them to needs of the organisation as a whole in meeting both productivity and customer service quality goals.

PRODUCT MIX COMBINATION OF PRODUCTS MANUFACTURE

Product mix is a combination of products manufactured or traded by the same business house to reinforce their presence in the market, increase market share and increase the turnover for more profitability. Normally the product mix is within the synergy of other products for a medium size organization. However large groups of Industries may have diversified products within core competency. *Larsen and Toubro Ltd, Godrej, Reliance in India are some of the examples.*

One of the realities of business is that most firms deal with multi-products.This helps a firm diffuse its risk across different product groups/Also it enables the firm to appeal to a much larger group of customers or to different needs of the same customer group.So when Videocon chose to diversify into other consumer durables like music systems,washing machines and refrigerators,it sought to satisfy the needs of the middle and upper middle income group of consumers.

Likewise, Bajaj Electricals.a household name in India, has almost ninety products in i8ts portfolio ranging from low value items like bulbs to high priced consumer durables like mixers and luminaires and lighting projects.The number of products carried by a firm at a given point of time is called its product mix. This product mix contains product lines and product items.In other words it's a composite of products offered for sale by a firm.

PRODUCT MIX DECISIONS

Often firms take decisions to change their product mix. These decisions are dictated by the factors and also by the changes occurring in the market place. Like the changing life-styles of Indian consumers led BPL-Sanyo to launch an entire range of white goods like refrigerators, washing machines, and microwave ovens.It also motivate the firm to launch other entertainment electronics.

Rahejas, a well-known builders firm in Bombay, took a major decision to convert one of its theatre buildings in the western suburbs of Bombay into a large garments and accessories store for men,women and children, perhaps the first of its kind in India to have almost all products required by these customer groups Competition from low priced washing powders forced Hindustan Levers to launch different brands of detergent powder at different price levels positioned at different market segments.

Customer preferences for herbs, mainly shikakai motivated Lever to launch black Sunșilk Shampoo,which has shikakai.Also,low purchasing power and cultural bias against shampoo market made Hindustan Lever consider smaller packaging mainly sachets, for single use.So, it is the changes or anticipated changes in the market place that motivates a firm to consider changes in its product mix.

PRODUCT-MIX MANAGEMENT AND RESPONSIBILITIES

It is extremely important for any organization to have a well-managed product mix. Most organizations break down managing the product mix, product line, and actual product into three different levels. Product-mix decisions are concerned with the combination of product lines offered by the company. Management of the companies' product mix is the responsibility of top management.

Some basic product-mix decisions include:

- Reviewing the mix of existing product lines;
- Adding new lines to and deleting existing lines from the product mix;
- Determining the relative emphasis on new versus existing product lines in the mix;
- Determining the appropriate emphasis on internal development versus external acquisition in the product mix;
- Gauging the effects of adding or deleting a product line in relationship to other lines in the product mix; and
- Forecasting the effects of future external change on the company's product mix.

Product-line decisions are concerned with the combination of individual products offered within a given line. The product-line manager supervises several product managers who are responsible for individual products in the line. Decisions about a product line are usually incorporated into a marketing plan at the divisional level. Such a plan specifies changes in the product lines and allocations to products in each line.

Generally, product-line managers have the following responsibilities:

- Considering expansion of a given product line;
- Considering candidates for deletion from the product line;
- Evaluating the effects of product additions and deletions on the profitability of other items in the line; and
- Allocating resources to individual products in the line on the basis of marketing strategies recommended by product managers.

Decisions at the first level of product management involve the marketing mix for an individual brand/product. These decisions are the responsibility of a brand manager. Decisions regarding the marketing mix for a brand are represented in the product's marketing plan. The plan for a new brand would specify price level, advertising expenditures for the coming year, coupons, trade discounts, distribution facilities, and a five-year statement of projected sales and earnings. The plan for an existing product would focus on any changes in the marketing strategy. Some of these changes might include the product's target market, advertising and promotional expenditures, product characteristics, price level, and recommended distribution strategy.

GENERAL MANAGEMENT WORKFLOW

Top management formulates corporate objectives that become the basis for planning the product line. Product-line managers formulate objectives for their line to guide brand managers in developing the marketing mix for individual brands. Brand strategies are then formulated and incorporated into the product-line plan, which is in turn incorporated into the corporate plan. The corporate plan details changes in the firm's product lines and specifies strategies for growth. Once plans have been formulated, financial allocations flow from top management to product line and then to brand management for implementation.

Implementation of the plan requires tracking performance and providing data from brand to product line to top management for evaluation and control. Evaluation of the current plan then becomes the first step in the next planning cycle, since it provides a basis for examining the company's current offerings and recommending modifications as a result of past performance.

PRODUCT-MIX ANALYSIS

Since top management is ultimately responsible for the product mix and the resulting profits or losses, they often analyse the company product mix. The first assessment involves the area of opportunity in a particular industry or market. Opportunity is generally defined in terms of current industry growth or potential attractiveness as an investment. The second criterion is the company's ability to exploit opportunity, which is based on its current or potential position in the industry.

The company's position can be measured in terms of market share if it is currently in the market, or in terms of its resources if it is considering entering the market. These two factors—opportunity and the company's ability to exploit it—provide four different options for a company to follow.

- High opportunity and ability to exploit it result in the firm's introducing new products or expanding markets for existing products to ensure future growth.
- Low opportunity but a strong current market position will generally result in the company's attempting to maintain its position to ensure current profitability.
- High opportunity but a lack of ability to exploit it results in either
  - Attempting to acquire the necessary resources or
  - Deciding not to further pursue opportunity in these markets.

- Low opportunity and a weak market position will result in either
  - Avoiding these markets or
  - Divesting existing products in them.

These options provide a basis for the firm to evaluate new and existing products in an attempt to achieve balance between current and future growth. This analysis may cause the product mix to change, depending on what management decides.

The most widely used approach to product portfolio analysis is the model developed by the Boston Consulting Group. The BCG analysis emphasizes two main criteria in evaluating the firm's product mix: the market growth rate and the product's relative market share.

BCG uses these two criteria because they are closely related to profitability, which is why top management often uses the BCG analysis. Proper analysis and conclusions may lead to significant changes to the company's product mix, product line, and product offerings.

The market growth rate represents the products' category position in the product life cycle. Products in the introductory and growth phases require more investment because of research and development and initial marketing costs for advertising, selling, and distribution.

This category is also regarded as a high-growth area. Relative market share represents the company's competitive strength. Market share is compared to that of the leading competitor.

Once the analysis has been done using the market growth rate and relative market share, products are placed into one of four categories:

1. *Stars*: Products with high growth and market share are know as stars. Because these products have high potential for profitability, they should be given top priority in financing, advertising, product positioning, and distribution. As a result, they need significant amounts of cash to finance rapid growth and frequently show an initial negative cash flow.
2. *Cash cows*: Products with a high relative market share but in a low growth position are cash cows. These are profitable products that generate more cash than is required to produce and market them. Excess cash should be used to finance high-opportunity areas. Strategies for cash cows should be designed to sustain current market share rather than to expand it. An expansion strategy would require additional investment, thus decreasing the existing positive cash flow.
3. *Problem children*: These products have low relative market share but are in a high-growth situation. They are called "problem children" because their eventual direction is not yet clear. The firm should invest heavily in those that sales forecasts indicate might have a reasonable chance to become stars. Otherwise divestment is the best

course, since problem children may become dogs and thereby candidates for deletion.

4. *Dogs*: Products in the category are clearly candidates for deletion. Such products have low market shares and unlike problem children, have no real prospect for growth. Eliminating a dog is not always necessary, since there are strategies for dogs that could make them profitable in the short term. These strategies involve "harvesting" these products by eliminating marketing support and selling the product only to intensely loyal consumers who will buy in the absence of advertising. However, over the long term companies will seek to eliminate dogs.

As can be seen from the description of the four BCG alternatives, products are evaluated as producers or users of cash. Products with a positive cash flow will finance high-opportunity products that need cash. The emphasis on cash flow stems from management's belief that it is better to finance new entries and to support existing products with internally produced funds than to increase debt or equity in the company. Based on this belief, companies will normally take money from cash cows and divert it to stars and to some problem children.

The hope is that the stars will turn into cash cows and the problem children will turn into stars. The dogs will continue to receive lower funding and eventually be dropped.

6

The Customer Perspective

CUSTOMER VALUE

As it is used in the business world, customer value is the amount of benefit that a customer will get from a service or product relative to its cost. Some businesspeople explain customer value as "realization" compared to "sacrifice." Realization is a formal term for what customers get out of their purchases. Sacrifice is what they pay for the product or service.

Businesses of all sizes use customer value as part of a greater analysis to determine how well they are supplying their customer base. Detailed research might include what customers generally do with the products they receive, or how they use services to increase the value of assets like real estate. Businesses also look at the prices of their products in order to price them competitively.

Businesses that identify the value of their wares to customers might go a step further and consider other similar ideas. In order to generate more thought about customer value, and to reach out to a customer base, a business might promote a customer value proposition. The customer value proposition is basically a promise of benefits from a vendor to customers.

We see examples of customer value propositions all the time in advertising. Companies pinpoint the benefits that they believe a customer will realise, and display them in advertising to attract more customers. The question is whether these propositions are made in good faith, or whether they may not be entirely true. When business leaders and others are talking about customer value, it is important that everyone at the table understands that customer value does not relate to the value of customers, but to the value that customers receive from the business. Those who are talking about how valuable customers are to a business might use terms like customer retention, or refer to the customer base as "valued customers," or VIPs. Since customer service is also a critical element for many businesses, it's possible that these two ideas might sometimes get confused.

Along with the basic idea of customer value, other terms help further define that value precisely. Relative performance identifies how the product or service gives customer value relative to what competitors offer. Access cost is something that business analysts add into the mix as an estimated cost of the effort involved in purchase. Value propositions often include these levels of detail to help leaders look at how well a business is serving its intended audience.

SATISFACTION

Customer satisfaction, a business term, is a measure of how products and services supplied by a company meet or surpass customer expectation. It is seen as a key performance indicator within business and is part of the four of a Balanced Scorecard. In a competitive marketplace where businesses compete for customers, customer satisfaction is seen as a key differentiator and increasingly has become a key element of business strategy. There is a substantial body of empirical literature that establishes the benefits of customer satisfaction for firms.

Measuring Customer Satisfaction

Organizations need to retain existing customers while targeting non-customers;. Measuring customer satisfaction provides an indication of how successful the organization is at providing products and/or services to the marketplace. Customer satisfaction is an abstract concept and the actual manifestation of the state of satisfaction will vary from person to person and product/service to product/service. The state of satisfaction depends on a number of both psychological and physical variables which correlate with satisfaction behaviours such as return and recommend rate. The level of satisfaction can also vary depending on other factors the customer, such as other products against which the customer can compare the organization's products.

Work done by Parasuraman, Zeithaml and Berry between 1985 and 1988 delivered SERVQUAL which provides the basis for the measurement of customer satisfaction with a service by using the gap between the customer's expectation of performance and their perceived experience of performance. This provides the researcher with a satisfaction "gap" which is semi-quantitative in nature. Cronin and Taylor extended the disconfirmation theory by combining the "gap" described by Parasuraman, Zeithaml and Berry as two different measures into a single measurement of performance relative to expectation.

The usual measures of customer satisfaction involve a survey with a set of statements using a Likert Technique or scale. The customer is asked to evaluate each statement in terms of their perception and expectation of performance of the service being measured.

Improving Customer Satisfaction

Published standards exist to help organizations develop their current levels of customer satisfaction. The International Customer Service Institute has released The International Customer Service Standard. TICSS enables organizations to focus their attention on delivering excellence in the management of customer service, whilst at the same time providing recognition of success through a 3rd Party registration plan. TICSS focuses an organization's attention on delivering increased customer satisfaction by helping the organization through a Service Quality Model.

TICSS Service Quality Model uses the 5 P's - Policy, Processes, People, Premises, Product/Services, as well as performance measurement. The implementation of a customer service standard should lead to higher levels of customer satisfaction, which in turn influences customer retention and customer loyalty.

SALES PROMOTION OF CONSUMER

Consumer sales promotions encompass a variety of short-term promotional techniques designed to induce customers to respond in some way. The most popular consumer sales promotions are directly associated with product purchasing. These promotions are intended to enhance the value of a product purchase by either reducing the overall cost of the product (*i.e.*, get same product but for less money) or by adding more benefit to the regular purchase price (*i.e.*, get more for the money).

While tying a promotion to an immediate purchase is a major use of consumer sales promotion, it is not the only one. As we noted above, promotion techniques can be used to achieve other objectives such as building brand loyalty or creating product awareness. Consequently, a marketer's promotional toolbox contains a large variety of consumer promotions.

The following 11 types of consumer sales promotions:

1. Coupons
2. Rebates
3. Promotional Pricing
4. Trade-In
5. Loyalty Programmes
6. Sampling and Free Trials
7. Free Product
8. Premiums
9. Contests and Sweepstakes
10. Demonstrations
11. Personal Appearances

Coupons

Most consumers are quite familiar with this form of sales promotion, which offers purchasers price savings or other incentives when the coupon is redeemed at the time of purchase. Coupons are short-term in nature since most (but not all) carry an expiration date after which the value may not be received. Also, coupons require consumer involvement in order for value to be realized. In most cases involvement consists of the consumer making an effort to obtain the coupon (*e.g.*, clip from newspaper) and then presenting it at the time of purchase.

Coupons are used widely by marketers across many retail industries and reach consumers in a number of different delivery formats including:

- *Free-Standing Inserts (FSI)*: Here coupon placement occurs loosely (*i.e.*, inserted) within media, such as newspapers and direct mail, and may or may not require the customer to cut away from other material in order to use.
- *Cross-Product:* These consist of coupons placed within or on other products. Often a marketer will use this method to promote one product by placing the coupon inside another major selling product. For example, a pharmaceutical company may imprint a coupon for a cough remedy on the box of a pain medication. Also, this delivery approach is used when two marketers have struck a cross promotion arrangement where each agrees to undertake certain marketing activity for the other.
- *Printout:* A delivery method that is common in many food stores is to present coupons to a customer at the conclusion of the purchasing process. These coupons, which are often printed on the spot, are intended to be used for a future purchase and not for the current purchase which triggered the printing.
- *Product Display:* Some coupons are nearly impossible for customers to miss as they are located in close proximity to the product. In some instances coupons may be contained within a coupon dispenser fastened to the shelf holding the product while in other cases coupons may be attached to a special display where customers can remove them (*e.g.*, tear off).
- *Internet:* Several specialized web sites, such as HotCoupons.com, and even some manufacturer's sites, allow customers to print out coupons. These coupons are often the same ones appearing in other media, such as newspapers or direct mail. In other cases, coupons may be sent via e-mail, though to be effective the customer's e-mail programme must be able to receive HTML e-mail (and not text only) in order to maintain required design elements (*e.g.*, bar code).
- *Electronic:* The Internet is also seeing the emergence of new non-printable coupons redeemable through web site purchases. These electronic coupons are redeemed when the customer enters a designated coupon code during the purchase process.

Rebates

Rebates, like coupons, offer value to purchasers typically by lowering the customer's final cost for acquiring the product. While rebates share some similarities with coupons, they differ in several keys aspects. First, rebates are generally handed or offered (*e.g.*, accessible on the Internet) to customers after a purchase is made and cannot be used to obtain immediate savings in the way coupons are used. (So called "instant rebates", where customers receive price reductions at the time of purchase, have elements of both coupons and rebates, but for our purposes we will classify these as coupons due to the timing of the reward to the customer.)

Second, rebates often request the purchaser to submit personal data in order to obtain the rebate. For instance, customer identification, including name, address and contact information, is generally required to obtain a rebate. Also, the marketer may ask those seeking a rebate to provide additional data such as indicating the reason for making the purchase.

Third, unlike coupons that always offer value when used in a purchase (assuming it is accepted by the retailer), receiving a rebate only guarantees value if the customer takes actions. Marketers know that not all customers will respond to a rebate. Some will misplace or forget to submit the rebate while others may submit after a required deadline.

Marketers factor in the non-redemption rate as they attempt to calculate the cost of the rebate promotion. Finally, rebates tend to be used as a value enhancement in higher priced products compared to coupons. For instance, rebates are a popular promotion for automobiles and computer software where large amounts of money may be returned to the customer.

Promotional Pricing

One of the most powerful sales promotion techniques is the short-term price reduction or, as known in some areas, "on sale" pricing. Lowering a product's selling price can have an immediate impact on demand, though marketers must exercise caution since the frequent use of this technique can lead customers to anticipate the reduction and, consequently, withhold purchase until the price reduction occurs again. Promotional pricing is also considered within the framework of the Price marketing mix component.

Trade-In

Trade-in promotions allow consumers to obtain lower prices by exchanging something the customer possess, such as an older product that the new purchase will replace. While the idea of gaining price breaks for trading in another product is most frequently seen with automobile sales, such promotions are used in other industries, such as computers and golf equipment, where the customer's exchanged product can be resold by the marketer in order to extract value.

Loyalty Programmes

Promotions that offer customers a reward, such as price discounts and free products, for frequent purchasing or other activity are called loyalty programmes. These promotions have been around for many years but grew rapidly in popularity when introduced in the airline industry as part of frequent-filer programmes.

Loyalty programmes are also found in numerous other industries, including grocery, pizza purchasing and online book purchases, where they may also be known as club card programmes since members often must use a verification card as evidence of enrollment in the programme.

Many loyalty programmes have become ingrained as part of the value offered by a marketer. That is, a retailer or marketing organization may offer loyalty programmes as general business practice. Under this condition loyalty programme does not qualify as a sales promotion since it does not fit the requirement of offering a short-term value (*i.e.*, it is always offered). However, even within a loyalty programme that is part of a general business practice, a sales promotion can be offered such as special short-term offer that lowers the number of points needed to acquire a free product.

Samples and Free Trials

Enticing members of a target market to try a product is often easy when the trial comes at little or no cost to the customer. The use of samples and free trials may be the oldest of all sales promotion techniques dating back to when society advanced from a culture of self-subsistence to a culture of trade.

Sampling and free trials give customers the opportunity to experience products, often in small quantities or for a short duration, without purchasing the product. Today, these methods are used in almost all industries and are especially useful for getting customers to try a product for the first time.

Free Product

Some promotional methods offer free products but with the condition that a purchase be made. The free product may be in the form of additional quantities of the same purchased product (*e.g.*, buy one, get one free) or specialty packages (*e.g.*, value pack) that offer more quantity for the same price as regular packaging.

Premiums

Another form of sales promotion involving free merchandise is premium or "give-away" items. Premiums differ from samples and free product in that these often do not consist of the actual product, though there is often some connection. For example, a cellphone manufacturer may offer access to free downloadable ringtones for those purchasing a cellphone.

Contests and Sweepstakes

Consumers are often attracted to promotions where the potential value obtained is very high. In these promotions only a few lucky consumers receive the value offered in the promotion. Two types of promotions that offer high value are contests and sweepstakes.

Contests are special promotions awarding value to winners based on skills they demonstrate compared to others. For instance, a baking company may offer free vacations to winners of a baking contest. Contest award winners are often determined by a panel of judges.

Sweepstakes or drawings are not skill based but rather based on luck. Winners are determined by random selection. In some cases the chances of winning may be higher for those who make a purchase if entry into the sweepstake occurs automatically when a purchase is made. But in most cases, anyone is free to enter without the requirement to make a purchase.

A sub-set of both contests and sweepstakes are games, which come in a variety of formats such as scratch-off cards and collection of game pieces. Unlike contests and sweepstakes, which may not require purchase, to participate in a game customers may be required to make a purchase. In the United States and other countries, where eligibility is based on purchase, games may be subjected to rigid legal controls and may actually fall under that category of lotteries, which are tightly controlled.

Demonstrations

Many products benefit from customers being shown how products are used through a demonstration. Whether the demonstration is experienced in-person or via video form, such as over the Internet, this promotional technique can produce highly effective results. Unfortunately, demonstrations are very expensive to produce. Costs involved in demonstrations include paying for the expense of the demonstrator, which can be high if the demonstrator is well-known (*e.g.*, nationally known chef), and also paying for the space where the demonstration is given.

Personal Appearances

An in-person appearance by someone of interest to the target market, such as an author, sports figure or celebrity, is another form of sales promotion capable of generating customer traffic to a physical location. However, as with demonstrations, personal appearance promotion can be expensive since the marketer normally must pay a fee for the person to appear.

TRADE SALES PROMOTIONS

A trade promotion aimed at retailers may encourage retailers to instruct their employees to promote a marketer's brand over competitors' offerings.

With thousands of products competing for limited shelf space, spending on trade promotion is nearly equal that spent on consumer promotions.

Many sales promotions aimed at building relationships with channel partners follow similar designs as those directed to consumers including promotional pricing, contests and free product. In addition to these, several other promotional approaches are specifically designed to appeal to trade partners. These approaches include:

- Point-of-Purchase Displays
- Advertising Support Programmes
- Short Term Allowances
- Sales Incentives or Push Money
- Promotional Products
- Trade Shows

Point-of-Purchase Displays

Point of purchase (POP) displays are specially designed materials intended for placement in retail stores. These displays allow products to be prominently presented, often in high traffic areas, and thereby increase the probability the product will standout. POP displays come in many styles, though the most popular are ones allowing a product to stand alone, such as in the middle of a store aisle or sit at the end of an aisle (*i.e.*, end-cap) where it will be exposed to heavy customer traffic.

For channel partners, POP displays can result in significant sales increases compared to sales levels in a normal shelf position. Also, many marketers will lower the per-unit cost of products in the POP display as an incentive for retailers to agree to include the display in their stores.

Advertising Support Programmes

In addition to offering promotional support in the form of physical displays, marketers can attract channel members' interest by offering financial assistance in the form of advertising money. These funds are often directed to retailers who then include the company's products in their advertising. In certain cases the marketer will offer to pay the entire cost of advertising, but more often, the marketer offers partial support known as co-op advertising funds.

Short Term Trade Allowances

This promotion offers channel partners price breaks for agreeing to stock the product. In most cases the allowance is not only given as encouragement to purchase the product but also as an inducement to promote the product in other ways such as by offering attractive shelf space or store location, highlighting the product in company-produced advertising or web site display, or by agreeing to have the retailer's sales personnel "talk-up" the product to customers. Allowances can be in the form price reductions (a.k.a. off-invoice promotion) and buy-back guarantees if the product does not sell in certain period of time.

Sales Incentives or Push Money

Since sales promotions are intended to stimulate activity that leads to meeting promotional objectives, it makes sense that these can also apply to those in a channel member's organization who also affect sales. Thus, a marketer may offer sales promotions to their reseller's sales force and customer service staff where they are used as incentives to help sell more of the marketer's product. Sometimes called push money, these promotions typically offer employees cash or prizes, such as trips, for those that meet sales requirements.

Promotional Products

Among the most widely used methods of sales promotions is the promotional product; products labeled with the brand or company name that serve as reminders of the actual product. For instance, companies often hand out free calendars, coffee cups and pens that contain the product logo.

Trade Shows

One final type of trade promotion is the industry trade show (a.k.a. exhibitions, conventions). Trade shows are organized events that bring both industry buyers and sellers together in one central location. Spending on trade shows is one of the highest of all sales promotions. In fact, the Promotion Marketing Association estimates that over (US) $20 billion is spent annually by marketers to participate in trade shows.

Marketers are attracted to trade shows since these offer the opportunity to reach a large number of potential buyers in one convenient setting. At these events most sellers attempt to capture the attention of buyers by setting up a display area to present their product offerings and meet with potential customers. These displays can range from a single table covering a small area to erecting specially built display booths that dominate the trade show floor.

SYSTEMS OF CUSTOMER MANAGEMENT

Companies need a method for viewing all customer and marketing-related information in an integrated way. Often marketing organizations maintain multiple databases for each business and marketing activity with data that is not easily integrated for strategic or operational purposes. A new generation of software that is Internet based gathers information from customer service, Web sites, direct mail operations, telemarketing, field sales, customer service, distributors, retailers and suppliers for the purpose of managing marketing, sales and customer service activities.

The major applications families are commonly referred to as sales force automation (SFA) and customer relationship management (CRM) systems.

Some CRM systems are fully integrated with SFA applications and some are standalone. The worldwide market for such systems is projected to grow five times faster than the overall software market, from $5 billion in 1999 to more than $22 billion in 2003.

Sales Force Automation

SFA is a customer management tool that is one of the fastest growing elements of the MkIS. SFA applications are often integrated with the CRM system. SFA involves the application of information technology to the sales function or, more appropriately, to the activities leading to a sale. These activities include acquiring sales leads, managing the sales opportunity, closing the sale and managing the customer relationship. The historic role of personal selling has been to move the product—to generate transactions.

As selling has become increasingly more professional, sales people emphasize building relationships with customers that will generate loyalty-based repeat transactions over time. Relationship building often necessitates that the sales person has consultative and advisory skills in addition to product knowledge and sales abilities. Team-based selling places emphasis on role specialization, collaboration and coordination. Customers have become more sophisticated as well.

Requirements for customised solutions, rapid response times and the need for concurrent and post-sale service have greatly increased the need for information technology in the sales process. The goals of SFA are to increase the effectiveness of the sales organization, improve its efficiency and to create superior value for the customer. Sales effectiveness focuses on getting the sale by improving lead generation, qualifying prospects, coordinating sales efforts, and tracking commitments.

Effectiveness is a function of improving the sales process. Sales efficiency is evaluated by measuring the return on sales efforts. SFA can improve sales efficiency by reducing sales cycle time, by managing workflow, and tracking the current status of critical activities related to the sale.

Proposal generation, opportunity management, fulfillment, and follow up are facilitated by SFA. Superior customer value is achieved when the customer expectations are exceeded. It is a primary determinant of customer satisfaction. SFA enables better understanding of customer expectations and management of the customer account.

The Sales Process

The typical field sales process consists of a series of steps that are designed to lead to a sale. The typical role of the MkIS is to support the sales process steps of lead generation, sales process management, and account management.

- *Lead generation*: Leads represent potential customers. The identification of a lead is the beginning of the sales cycle. After leads are identified, they must be qualified. This process involves gathering information about the lead and comparing the result against qualifying criteria. The lead generation process is becoming more automated with regard to obtaining more pre-qualifying information directly from the lead and augmenting it from commercial and other databases such as credit bureaus. The advent of Web-based technologies is driving this trend. Qualified leads are then distributed to the sales force.
- *Sales Process Management*: This process starts when the sales person receives the lead information. The primary information system need is for a convenient method to track the process and store data the data generated at each stage. There are a number of sub-steps to this stage of the process.
  - *Verification of the opportunity*: The sales person usually contacts the lead and attempts to verify the existence and nature of an opportunity including its size, timing, and appropriateness of the products and services of the selling company. Sales people will also desire to verify the lead's ability to purchase, identify the names of key decision-makers and influencers, and the level of budget authority. This information is entered into the sales database.
  - *The Sales Call*: If the lead is amenable and the opportunity justifies it, a sales call is scheduled. Information may be sent to the prospect and a custom presentation may be created. The SFA system is used to provide a single point of interface for the sales person to coordinate the activities leading up to the sales call. After the call, the SFA system is updated with customer requirements, new information and commitments made by the sales person.
  - *Opportunity Management*: If the sales person is successful, the next step is typically the receipt of a request for proposal (RFP) from the prospective customer. The RFP will generally state the customer's requirements and the date for the final submission. Follow-on visits may be necessary to clear up or identify new requirements. The prospect may want to visit the seller's manufacturing site. The final product of this stage is the creation of a proposal and price quote to be presented to the prospect. This document should build a sound economic case for the purchase. All these interactions, requirements, commitments, and

competitor information are tracked by the SFA system that provides the database, tools and templates to generate the proposal.

- *Closing the Sale*: The presentation of the proposal and the price quote is the start of the closing process. Even if the sales person has done a good job of presenting the business case, further negotiations may be necessary to close the sale. If all objections are met and the proposal is accepted the close is successful. If not, the sales team will need to debrief the sessions learned to determine why the proposal was not accepted. The outcomes are recorded in the SFA system.

- *Account Management*: The automation of the sales process may result in a standalone system that is not integrated with other management systems. However, SFA is increasingly being integrated with the overall CRM system. This is especially true of the account management function. Since the primary goal of the CRM system is to manage the customer relationship in order to generate repeat sales, a good sales person will want to keep track of the status of a new account and how well the customer is being served. This is especially true if the account is to become "referenceable" to other prospects. The account management function of the CRM system enables the sales person to track order entry, order processing, shipment, and installation. The sales person may need to ensure that post-sales service is delivered or monitor the results of and installation and track the customer's satisfaction. The ability to track outcomes and interact with the customer in order to reassess needs and create new opportunities is a major benefit that flows from effective account management.

Sales Force Automation Tools

SFA tools consist of software applications that enable the salesperson to better target sales opportunities and manage the sales cycle. The tools are increasingly available bundled as integrated suites that are Internet enabled, accessible through a browser and linked to the CRM system.

The software applications may be categorized as:

- *Document management tools*: These tools support all stages of the sales process. They include word processors, graphics programmes, spreadsheets, e-mail, expense reports, proposal generators, and "product configurators." A Web-accessible sales library or encyclopaedia of previously developed product information, brochures, product demonstrations, presentations, financial information, price lists, white documents, and public relations materials is a key resource for sales force productivity.

- *Personal management tools*: These tools focus on increasing the efficiency and effectiveness of the sales teams efforts. They typically include calendar and scheduling programmes, contact management systems, and call reporting capabilities.
- *Process management tools:* These tools are used to keep track of customer requirements and sales commitments. They include opportunity management systems, project management systems, account management systems, order-entry systems, telemarketing systems, team-selling systems.

Increasingly, with the rise of Web-based hosting and the application service provider (ASP) industry, SFA applications and databases are being hosted by third-party specialists and accessed remotely on the Internet. With the ASP model, client companies are essentially outsourcing all or part of there IS function. Remote hosting raises issues of security and scalability. The advantages of an ASP approach are its browser-based simplicity, rapid implementation, and lower cost of deployment. Most ASP applications use a subscription-based pricing model. Some vendors are proposing that renting the application or paying by the transaction may become the pricing model of the future.

Customer Relationship Management

The Internet has facilitated a fundamental shift in market power from sellers to buyers. Customers, newly endowed with the power of market information, have much different expectations than before. Customers can easily move their business to another vendor with the click of a mouse. They have access to the same cost data as their suppliers and they demand 24x7 customer service.

Customers now have almost unlimited ability for interactions with organizations through the Web in addition to the traditional phone and mail methods. Company web sites facilitate information search, shopping and customer support. E-mail communication can target specific offers on a one-to-one basis. Understanding and meeting demanding expectations has placed a renewed emphasis on managing customer relationships. The primary goal of CRM systems is to increase the return on marketing expenditures by enabling the understanding of the complete history of a firm's interactions with its customers.

CRM applications can deliver targeted solutions that promote customer loyalty as measured by increased response to promotions, purchase frequencies and volume, and minimizes the time between orders. CRM systems are able to target marketing communications to likely buyers, facilitate sales efforts and deliver customer service. CRM systems increase revenue, lower costs and optimize customer lifetime value.

Customer Relationship Management Design Principles

The CRM field is rapidly evolving into an integrated discipline that manages all of a company's touches with the customer.

Accordingly, several design principles have evolved as the foundation for CRM development:

- The CRM system should offer the customer multiple channels for communication such as the telephone, e-mail, fax, on-line or some combination. Each channel should lead to an interaction that satisfies customer expectations. Customers must be able to choose the method that best meets their needs on each occasion.
- Each CRM interaction should deliver value to the customer. The CRM system must be able to determine what value is required and deliver it quickly whether it is a product or service transaction or a customer service request.
- The CRM system integrates the customer throughout the firm's value chain. Customers should be able to reach into all necessary functions of the organization not just to the sales organization, or customer service, but to manufacturing and even the CEO. Better integration of the customer into the process can lead to higher levels of trust, loyalty and repeat purchases. The cost of acquiring a new customer often far exceeds that of retaining existing ones.
- Knowledge is captured during each CRM interaction. The CRM system should capture knowledge about the customer and the customer's relationship with the company over time. Sales and customer support histories should be analysed for indications of how well the vendor is doing in meeting customers' needs and how valuable the customer is to the marketer.

Customer Relationship Management Functions

CRM applications provide the customer-related information that is necessary to drive a firm's ebusiness activities. Better customer information enables more effective demand forecasting, product launches and marketing campaigns. CRM functions are sometimes referred to as the company's "front office."

CRM functionality includes:

- E-commerce support
- Sales force automation
- Telesales and call centre automation
- Direct mail and catalog sales
- E-mail and e-newsletter response
- Web sales and personalization
- Analysis of Web generated data

- Traditional customer support and service
- On-line support and customer service
- Mobile support through laptops, handheld devices.
- Training

Modern CRM systems are fully integrated with the "back office" elements of the enterprise resource planning (ERP) system such as accounting, manufacturing, project management, and human resources. This integration enables the sharing of customer information that can impact the operations of the enterprise and vice versa. Common customer definitions, price lists, employee definitions, service requests, call histories, order histories, contracts, service level agreements are accessible by all who need them. Correspondingly, marketing can access information on items such as new product development, product costs, order status, delivery dates and backorders.

CONSUMER MARKETING MANAGEMENT

The consumer market is composed of individuals who buy a specific good or service. Rarely does one product interest the entire population. This statement applies even to staples, such as sugar, flour, and salt. A small percentage of households do not eat these products, so even if a company did target the entire population, not everyone would be a potential consumer. The same statistical truth applies to cultural products. However, because of the extremely fragmented nature of the cultural sector, some distinctions are in order. For example, looking at this sector as a whole, it can be said that nearly 100 per cent of the population consumes one type of cultural product or another. Indeed, in its broadest sense, the cultural sector encompasses everything from the performing arts to heritage, compact disks, movies, book and magazine publishing, and radio and television, with each of these disciplines appropriating a more or less important share of global demand.

In Canada, for example, statistics1 show that 37.0 per cent of families attend a performing arts event at least once a year: movies 62.2 per cent, museums and art galleries 32.9 per cent. In the United States the figures for cultural consumption are: classical music 15.6 per cent, opera 4.7 per cent, musicals 24.5 per cent, plays 15.8 per cent, ballet 5.8 per cent, art museums 34.5 per cent, and historical parks 46.9 per cent.2 In Australia3 the figures are: musical theatre 19.3 per cent, classical music 7.7 per cent, festivals 21.9 per cent, concerts 23 per cent, and museums 27.8 per cent. Of course, within each of these sectors, consumers cluster just as to specific poles of interest.

This leads to sharper market segmentation. The consumer makes a discriminating choice among various cultural products to acquire or consume the type of product desired. The distribution of consumers just as to various market segments differs in both time and space. Markets undergo and reflect the influence of opinion leaders, trends, tastes, and societal characteristics.

Markets also vary from country to country just as to different social structures. Over the past 40 years, various surveys focusing on the sociodemographic profile of consumers of cultural products have been carried out in nearly every European country as well as in Canada, the United States, Australia, and Japan.4 It is fascinating to note that, regardless of whether the surveys were conducted in the 1970s, 1980s, or 1990s, they all obtained the same attendance rates and the same sociodemographic profiles.

Differences in the measuring tools used can sometimes make it difficult to compare countries; nonetheless, these studies have consistently and systematically revealed strong polarization of audiences between high art and popular culture across all countries over the past four decades. They show, for example, that cultural products catering to high art attract educated consumers, whereas those catering to popular culture draw on all segments of the population, in accordance with the relative weight of each.

The proportion of university graduates making up Canadian audiences, for example, ranges between 50 per cent and 70 per cent for high art, compared with 10 per cent to 25 per cent for popular culture. By way of comparison, the overall percentage of university graduates in Canada is 25 per cent. Similar results have been found in other countries, most notably in France5 but also in Russia, where university graduates make up 50 per cent of performing arts audiences but only 7 per cent of the general population. Other sociodemographic variables are also linked to attendance, including average income and type of occupation. It should be pointed out once again that this profile is based on averages. Less-educated individuals with lower income may be great consumers of culture, as is the case for students and those specialized or working in the cultural milieu.

Indeed, it is well known that, as a rule many people active in the arts are highly educated yet so ill paid that they struggle to stay above the poverty line. On the other hand, there are people with both very high salaries and very high educational levels who are not interested in the arts and gladly keep their distance. Four factors are known to influence an individual's penchant for complex cultural products: family values that encourage or discourage high art; the educational milieu and the value it places on high art; the fact of having attended performances or visited museums as a child; and amateur art practice.

A more detailed analysis of the typical cultural consumer's traits reveals other nuances based on the different disciplines. For example, dance audiences are relatively younger and even more female in composition than those of the other performing arts; similarly, more women than men read novels, although a larger proportion of men read daily newspapers. In the film sector, there are two very different segments of avid cinema-goers; one of these segments is dominated by a young clientele, while the other is made up of educated people.

The majority of consumers in the film sector belong to one or the other of these two segments.

CONSUMER BOYCOTTS AND CERTIFICATION SCHEMES

Consumer markets also offer opportunities to punish and/or reward corporate behaviour. Product boycotts and product certification schemes represent contrasting mechanisms used by civil society groups, occasionally with governmental involvement or support, to influence MNE activities. Organized consumer boycotts usually target individual companies, either because the specific firm's actions are deemed particularly offensive or the company plays a prominent and influential role within an industry whose common practices generate opposition.

Boycott mechanisms do not work equally well in all situations. Boycotts enjoy greatest success when directed against recognizable consumer goods whose market position relies on brand-name image and reputation and where substitute products of satisfactory quality and price are readily available. In addition, the issue motivating the boycott must be conveyed in an easily understandable fashion that will evoke broad sympathy in the general consuming public. By contrast, companies that engage in minimal advertising and produce intermediate products for sale to other businesses are less vulnerable to a consumer boycott mechanism.

The use of consumer boycotts to protest MNE actions developed from the same general time period and set of issues that produced the capital market mechanisms. Anti-apartheid campaigns included product boycotts, including the adoption by many US state and city governments of selective procurement regulations that restricted purchases from companies maintaining investments in South Africa. The loss of large sales contracts to state and municipal agencies may have provided more measurable effective leverage against MNEs than stock divestment actions by activist pension funds. Another high-profile campaign urged a boycott of Nestlé's numerous consumer products to protest the corporation's methods of promoting its infant formula in developing counties.

Similar to shareholder activism, the potential effects of consumer boycotts often surpass the actual financial loss in terms of immediate sales. In order to reach the broad consuming public, boycott organizers generally seek maximum publicity and may organize demonstrations, marches or even engage in acts of civil disobedience to draw media attention to their cause. The short-term demand on management response time and potential for longer-term damage to a company's reputation can add significantly to overall boycott costs. Opponents often assert that boycott campaigns unfairly single out one or a small number of companies to protest actions undertaken by many enterprises, including MNEs in countries where comparable consumer actions seldom occur. Sometimes boycott targets show only minimal or distant causal connections to wrong actions. Similar to secondary rather than primary boycotts, the targeted firm or product may simply be used as a means to exert leverage on a different offending actor.

For example, in 1990 a civil society group called Neighbour to Neighbour helped organize a boycott action against Folger's coffee, sold by Procter and Gamble. In this case, the boycott campaign stemmed from opposition to human rights violations by right-wing death squads in El Salvador, allegedly connected with that country's government. Although less than 2 per cent of the beans in Folger's coffee reportedly came from El Salvador, those purchases represented an important share of the country's coffee exports which in turn provided significant revenue to the government.

To help publicize their cause, the boycotting groups sponsored a dramatic television advertisement attacking Folger's and showing blood running from an overturned coffee cup. The advertisement was characterized by a P&G spokesperson as "inaccurate, grossly misleading and offensive." The company responded with its own type of boycott action, suspending advertising on some television stations that aired the anti-Folger's commercial. US government officials offered clear statements supporting P&G's coffee bean purchases, calling the actions "in the best interest of the peace process and the people of El Salvador." The case illustrates how boycotts, even when motivated by laudable objectives, may become ethically problematic as causal and capability connections grow more distant between a targeted product or company and the offending actor and actions. Another case of a successful boycott describes a campaign organized by the Rainforest Action Network (RAN) against Scott Paper, aimed at stopping Scott's plans to use a rain forest concession on the Indonesian island of Irian Jaya to develop a eucalyptus plantation and sawmill to supply pulp for its various paper products.

An observer reports that, despite corporate efforts to work with local representatives to limit the project's environmental and social impact, "RAN convinced environmental groups from all over the world to boycott Scott products if the company did not withdraw from Irian Jaya. The campaign focused on a single thing: Scott's name, the company's most valuable, and most vulnerable, asset." The company announced its withdrawal from the project just before the boycott began, prompting RAN to take out newspaper advertisements "declaring victory" and "hailing the power of consumer boycotts."

Without necessarily disputing the impact of the boycott mechanism, some critics subsequently questioned the substance of the victory as a state-owned forestry company replaced Scott in the project and, not subject to similar consumer pressures, reportedly engaged in broad deforestation actions. This case points up the challenge of projecting a boycott's effects which may depend on when outcomes are measured and whether or not potential impacts on other boycott actions are considered. Product certification schemes also depend on consumer choice to provide leverage for influencing corporate behaviour. Contrasted with boycott mechanisms, certification schemes focus less on penalizing bad corporate conduct to induce change and more on rewarding good corporate operations by giving their products a market advantage over uncertified competitors. To be credible, groups using this mechanism must demonstrate that consumers are sufficiently aware and concerned about an issue to affect their purchasing decisions. In addition, consumers need enough knowledge and understanding about the certification process to recognize and favour certified products. These requirements place a premium on media coverage and the development of alliances and support networks among sympathetic civil society groups, particularly in major consumer market economies.

No clear consensus exists regarding either the breadth or the depth of probable consumer response to product certification schemes. Certainly participation will vary depending on the nature of the issue, the location of the consumer market and the effectiveness of a particular campaign. Other important variables include the cost, quality and convenience differential in choosing certified over uncertified products.

Some polling data suggests that a core of committed individuals will act on certification criteria while a larger portion of the general public is open to considering corporate actions and reputation in their purchasing decisions. For example, a Mori survey in Great Britain defined 15 per cent of the population as corporate responsibility activists, reporting that ethical considerations led 17 per cent of adults to boycott a product and 14 per cent to purchase a company's product during 2003. The survey also reported that 38 per cent of the public stated corporate social responsibility was very important in making their purchases. The head of Mori's CSR research speculated that more individuals from this broader group might follow through with concrete actions if provided with more effective information.

The proliferation of product certification schemes touches many of the issues. A broad government-backed mechanism emerged to certify that international trade would be free of "conflict diamonds" associated with human rights violations in Africa. Exports of soccer balls and rugs from South Asia feature certification processes to assure the goods were not produced using child labour. "Green" labels tout the environment-friendly record of many products, from recycled paper or plastic products to energy-saving devices to "dolphin-safe" tuna. Remarkable variety exists in the types of issues addressed and certification measures employed. The constellation of certifying and supporting organizations can also mix public agencies, business organizations and civil society groups. Fair Trade initiatives represent a particular application of product certification schemes, usually but not exclusively applied to products based on agricultural commodities. The basic concept seeks to establish a dependable, long-term relationship with commodity growers in developing countries, offering them a higher price for their products by eliminating middlemen traders.

Many schemes also provide an additional premium to growers for using environmentally friendly methods and/or for community social development projects. The general approach reportedly stems from efforts begun in 1986 by the Max Havelaar Foundation in the Netherlands to respond to desires for development projects that emphasize trade rather than aid. Starting with coffee and expanding to honey, bananas, tea and orange juice, the Foundation supported Fair Trade products sold primarily in Europe.

During the 1990s fourteen other Fair Trade organizations were established, reaching over $200 million in sales by the end of the decade, still largely concentrated in European markets. Some approaches expect consumers to pay a somewhat higher price for certified Fair Trade products while other efforts try to remain price-competitive, using cost savings in the distribution chain to redistribute profits towards developing country growers. An important extension of the Fair Trade mechanism to the US market occurred in 2000 when Starbucks announced the introduction of a blend of Fair Trade coffee certified by the non-profit TransFair organization that encourages farmer co-operatives in developing countries to sell direct to coffee roasters or retailers. The breakthrough with Starbucks came after some of its coffee houses were vandalized during anti-globalization protests at a World Trade Organization meeting hosted in the company's hometown of Seattle, Washington. This initiative complemented Starbucks' broader social responsibility programmes and helped expand Fair Trade coverage in the United States beyond craft shops and a few grocery stores. Subsequent discussions between Starbucks and Oxfam also led to cooperation on a project to aid coffee growers in poverty-stricken areas of Ethiopia. The Rainforest Alliance, which promotes another certification scheme covering several products, has forged agreements with major coffee MNEs that could broaden the Fair Trade mechanism beyond the market for specialty coffees that represents only about 2 per cent of supply.

DECISIONS OF CONSUMER PURCHASE MANAGEMENT

Consumers are faced with purchase decisions nearly every day. But not all decisions are treated the same. Some decisions are more complex than others and thus require more effort by the consumer. Other decisions are fairly routine and require little effort. In general, consumers face four types of purchase decisions:

- *Minor New Purchase*: These purchases represent something new to a consumer but in the customer's mind is not a very important purchase in terms of need, money or other reason (*e.g.*, status within a group).
- *Minor Re-Purchase*: These are the most routine of all purchases and

often the consumer returns to purchase the same product without giving much thought to other product options (*i.e.*, consumer is brand loyalty).

- *Major New Purchase*: These purchases are the most difficult of all purchases because the product being purchased is important to the consumer but the consumer has little or no previous experience making these decisions. The consumer's lack of confidence in making this type of decision often (but not always) requires the consumer to engage in an extensive decision-making process..
- *Major Re-Purchase*: These purchase decisions are also important to the consumer but the consumer feels confident in making these decisions since they have previous experience purchasing the product.

For marketers it is important to understand how consumers treat the purchase decisions they face. If a company is targeting customers who feel a purchase decision is difficult (*i.e.*, Major New Purchase), their marketing strategy may vary greatly from a company targeting customers who view the purchase decision as routine. In fact, the same company may face both situations at the same time; for some the product is new, while other customers see the purchase as routine. The implication of buying behaviour for marketers is that different buying situations require different marketing efforts.

WHY CONSUMERS BUY

Customers make purchases in order to satisfy needs. Some of these needs are basic and must be filled by everyone on the planet (*e.g.*, food, shelter) while others are not required for basic survival and vary depending on the person. It probably makes more sense to classify needs that are not a necessity as wants or desires. In fact, in many countries where the standard of living is very high, a large portion of the population's income is spent on wants and desires rather than on basic needs. In this tutorial when we mention the consumer we are referring to the actual buyer, the person spending the money. But is should also be pointed out that the one who does the buying is not necessarily the user of what is bought and that others may be involved in the buying decision in addition to the actual buyer. While the purchasing process in the consumer market is not as complex as the business market, having multiple people involved in a purchase decision is not unusual. For example, in planning for a family vacation the mother may make the hotel reservations but others in the family may have input on the hotel choice. Similarly, a father may purchase snacks at the grocery store but his young child may be the one who selected it from the store shelf.

So understanding consumer purchase behaviour involves not only understanding how decisions are made but also understanding the dynamics that influence purchases.

WHAT INFLUENCES PURCHASING

As we discussed the decision-making process for consumers is anything but straight forward. There are many factors that can affect this process as a person works through the purchase decision. The number of potential influences on consumer behaviour is limitless. However, marketers are well served to understand the KEY influences. By doing so they may be in a position to tailor their marketing efforts to take advantage of these influences in a way that will satisfy the consumer and the marketer (remember this is a key part of the definition of marketing).

For the purposes of this tutorial we will break these influences down into three main categories: Internal, External and Marketing. However, those interested in learning more about customer buying activity may want to consult one or more consumer behaviour books where they will find additional methods for explaining consumer buying behaviour. For the most part the influences are not mutually exclusive. Instead, they are all interconnected and, as we will see, work together to form who we are and how we behave. For each of the influences that are discussed we will provide a basic description and also suggest its implication to marketers. Bear in mind we only provide a few marketing implications for each influence; clearly there are many more.

INTERNAL INFLUENCES

We start our examination of the influences on consumer purchase decisions by first looking inside ourselves to see which are the most important internal factors that affect how we make choices.

Perceptual Filter

Perception is how we see ourselves and the world we live in. However, what ends up being stored inside us doesn't always get there in a direct manner. Often our mental makeup results from information that has been consciously or subconsciously filtered as we experience it, a process we refer to as a perceptual filter. To us this is our reality, though it does not mean it is an accurate reflection on what is real. Thus, perception is the way we filter stimuli (*e.g.*, someone talking to us, reading a newspaper story) and then make sense out of it.

Perception has several steps:

- *Exposure*: Sensing a stimuli (*e.g.* seeing an ad)
- *Attention*: An effort to recognize the nature of a stimuli (*e.g.* recognizing it is an ad)
- *Awareness*: Assigning meaning to a stimuli (*e.g.*, humorous ad for particular product)
- *Retention*: Adding the meaning to one's internal makeup (*i.e.*, product has fun ads)

How these steps are eventually carried out depends on a person's approach to learning. By learning we mean how someone changes what they know, which in turn may affect how they act. There are many theories of learning, a discussion of which is beyond the scope of this tutorial, however, suffice to say that people are likely to learn in different ways.

For instance, one person may be able to focus very strongly on a certain advertisement and be able to retain the information after being exposed only one time while another person may need to be exposed to the same advertisement many times before he/she even recognizes what it is.

Consumers are also more likely to retain information if a person has a strong interest in the stimuli. If a person is in need of new car they are more likely to pay attention to a new advertisement for a car while someone who does not need a car may need to see the advertisement many times before they recognize the brand of automobile.

Marketing Implications

Marketers spend large sums of money in an attempt to get customers to have a positive impression of their products. But clearly the existence of a perceptual filter suggests that getting to this stage is not easy. Exposing consumers to a product can be very challenging considering the amount of competing product messages (ads) that are also trying to accomplish the same objective (*i.e.*, advertising clutter). So marketers must be creative and use various means to deliver their message. Once the message reaches consumer it must be interesting enough to capture their attention (*e.g.*, talk about the product's benefits). But attending to the message is not enough. For marketers the most critical step is the one that occurs with awareness. Here marketers must continually monitor and respond if their message becomes distorted in ways that will negatively shape its meaning. This can often happen due in part to competitive activity (*e.g.*, comparison advertisements). Finally, getting the consumer to give positive meaning to the message they have retained requires the marketer make sure that consumers accurately interpret the facts about the product.

Knowledge

Knowledge is the sum of all information known by a person. It is the facts of the world as he/she knows it and the depth of knowledge is a function of the breadth of worldly experiences and the strength of an individual's long-term memory. Obviously what exists as knowledge to an individual depends on how an individual's perceptual filter makes sense of the information it is exposed to.

Marketing Implications

Marketers may conduct research that will gauge consumers' level of knowledge regarding their product. As we will see below, it is likely that other factors influencing consumer behaviour are in large part shaped by what is known about a product. Thus, developing methods (*e.g.*, incentives) to encourage consumers to accept more information (or correct information) may affect other influencing factors.

Attitude

In simple terms attitude refers to what a person feels or believes about something. Additionally, attitude may be reflected in how an individual acts based on his or her beliefs. Once formed, attitudes can be very difficult to change. Thus, if a consumer has a negative attitude towards a particular issue it will take considerable effort to change what they believe to be true.

Marketing Implications

Marketers facing consumers who have a negative attitude towards their product must work to identify the key issues shaping a consumer's attitude then adjust marketing decisions (*e.g.*, advertising) in an effort to change the attitude. For companies competing against strong rivals to whom loyal consumers exhibit a positive attitude, an important strategy is to work to see why consumers feel positive towards the competitor and then try to meet or beat the competitor on these issues. Alternatively, a company can try to locate customers who feel negatively towards the competitor and then increase awareness among this group.

Personality

An individual's personality relates to perceived personal characteristics that are consistently exhibited, especially when one acts in the presence of others. In most, but not all, cases the behaviours one projects in a situation is similar to the behaviours a person exhibits in another situation. In this way personality is the sum of sensory experiences others get from experiencing a person (*i.e.*, how one talks, reacts). While one's personality is often interpreted by those we interact with, the person has their own vision of their personality, called Self Concept, which may or may not be the same has how others view us.

Marketing Implications

For marketers it is important to know that consumers make purchase decisions to support their self concept. Using research techniques to identify how customers view themselves may give marketers insight into products and promotion options that are not readily apparent. For example, when examining consumers a marketer may initially build marketing strategy around more obvious clues to consumption behaviour, such as consumer's demographic indicators (*e.g.*, age, occupation, income). However, in-depth research may yield information that shows consumers are purchasing products to fulfill self-concept objectives that have little to do with the demographic category they fall into (*e.g.*, senior citizen may be making purchases that make them feel younger). Appealing to the consumer's self concept needs could expand the market to which the product is targeted.

Lifestyle

This influencing factor relates to the way we live through the activities we engage in and interests we express. In simple terms it is what we value out of life. Lifestyle is often determined by how we spend our time and money.

Marketing Implications

Products and services are purchased to support consumers' lifestyles. Marketers have worked hard researching how consumers in their target markets live their lives since this information is key to developing products, suggesting promotional strategies and even determining how best to distribute products. The fact that lifestyle is so directly tied to marketing activity will be further examined as we discuss developing target market strategies.

Roles

Roles represent the position we feel we hold or others feel we should hold when dealing in a group environment. These positions carry certain responsibilities yet it is important to understand that some of these responsibilities may, in fact, be perceived and not spelled out or even accepted by others. In support of their roles, consumers will make product choices that may vary depending on which role they are assuming.

As illustration, a person who is responsible for selecting snack food for an office party his boss will attend may choose higher quality products than he would choose when selecting snacks for his family.

Marketing Implications

Advertisers often show how the benefits of their products aid consumers as they perform certain roles. Typically the underlying message of this promotional approach is to suggest that using the advertiser's product will help raise one's status in the eyes of others while using a competitor's product may have a negative effect on status.

Motivation

Motivation relates to our desire to achieve a certain outcome. Many internal factors we have already discussed can affect a customer's desire to achieve a certain outcome but there are others. For instance, when it comes to making purchase decisions customers' motivation could be affected by such issues as financial position (*e.g.*, *Can I afford the purchase?*), time constraints (*e.g.*, *Do I need to make the purchase quickly?*), overall value (*e.g.*, *Am I getting my money's worth?*), and perceived risk (*e.g.*, *What happens if I make a bad decision?*).

Marketing Implications

Motivation is also closely tied to the concept of Involvement, which relates to how much effort the consumer will exert in making a decision. Highly motivated consumers will want to get mentally and physically involved in the purchase process. Not all products have a high percentage of highly involved customers (*e.g.*, milk) but marketers who market products and services that may lead to high level of consumer involvement should prepare options that will be attractive to this group. For instance, marketers should make it easy for consumers to learn about their product (*e.g.*, information on web site, free video preview) and, for some products, allow customers to experience the product (*e.g.*, free trial) before committing to the purchase.

EXTERNAL INFLUENCES

Consumer purchasing decisions are often affected by factors that are outside of their control but have direct or indirect impact on how we live and what we consume.

Culture

Culture represents the behaviour, beliefs and, in many cases, the way we act learned by interacting or observing other members of society. In this way much of what we do is shared behaviour, passed along from one member of society to another.

Yet culture is a broad concept that, while of interest to marketers, is not nearly as important as understanding what occurs within smaller groups or Sub-Cultures to which we may also belong. Sub-cultures also have shared values but this occurs within smaller groups. For instance, sub-cultures exist where groups share similar values in terms of ethnicity, religious beliefs, geographic location, special interests and many others.

Marketing Implications

As part of their efforts to convince customers to purchase their products, marketers often use cultural representations, especially in promotional appeals. The objective is to connect to consumers using cultural references that are easily understood and often embraced by the consumer. By doing so the marketer hopes the consumer feels more comfortable with or can relate better to the product since it corresponds with their cultural values. Additionally, smart marketers use strong research efforts in an attempt to identify differences in how sub-culture behaves. These efforts help pave the way for spotting trends within a sub-culture, which the marketer can capitalize on through new marketing tactics (*e.g.*, new products, new sales channels, added value, etc.).

Other Group Membership

In addition to cultural influences, consumers belong to many other groups with which they share certain characteristics and which may influence purchase decisions. Often these groups contain Opinion Leaders or others who have major influence on what the customer purchases. Some of the basic groups we may belong to include:

- *Social Class*: Represents the social standing one has within a society based on such factors as income level, education, occupation
- *Family*: One's family situation can have a strong effect on how purchase decisions are made
- *Reference groups*: Most consumers simultaneously belong to many other groups with which they associate or, in some cases, feel the need to disassociate

Marketing Implications

Identifying and understanding the groups consumers belong to is a key strategy for marketers. Doing so helps identify target markets, develop new products, and create appealing marketing promotions to which consumers can relate. In particular, marketers seek to locate group leaders and others to whom members of the group look for advice or direction. These opinion leaders, if well respected by the group, can be used to gain insight into group behaviour and if these opinion leaders accept promotional opportunities could act as effective spokespeople for the marketer's products.

Purchase Situation

A purchase decision can be strongly affected by the situation in which people find themselves. In general, a situation is the circumstances a person faces when making a purchase decision, such as the nature of their physical environment, their emotional state, or time constraints. Not all situations are controllable, in which case a consumer may not follow their normal process for making a purchase decision. For instance, if a person needs a product quickly and a store does not carry the brand they normally purchase, the customer may choose a competitor's product.

Marketing Implications

Marketers can take advantage of decisions made in uncontrollable situations in at least two ways. First, marketers can use promotional methods to reinforce a specific selection of products when the consumer is confronted with a particular situation. For example, automotive services can be purchased that promise to service vehicles if the user runs into problems anywhere and at anytime. Second, marketers can use marketing methods that attempt to convince consumers that a situation is less likely to occur if the marketer's product is used. This can also be seen with auto products, where marketers explain that using their product will prevent unexpected damage to their vehicles.

CONSUMER BUYING BEHAVIOUR

Consumer Buying Behaviour the decision processes and acts of final household consumers associated with evaluating, buying, consuming, and discarding products for personal consumption. Consider the purchase an automobile. You generally will not consider different options until some event triggers a need, such as a problem needing potentially expensive repair. Once this need has put you "on the market", you begin to ask your friends for recommendations regarding dealerships and car models. After visiting several dealerships, you test drive several models and finally decide on a particular model. After picking up your new car, you have doubts on the way home, wondering if you can afford the monthly payments, but then begin to wonder if instead you should have purchased a more expensive but potentially more reliable model. Over the next five years, the car has several unexpected breakdowns that lead you to want to purchase a different brand, but you have been very happy with the services of the local dealership and decide to again purchase your next car there.

In this particular case, the following *generic model of consumer decision making* appears to hold:

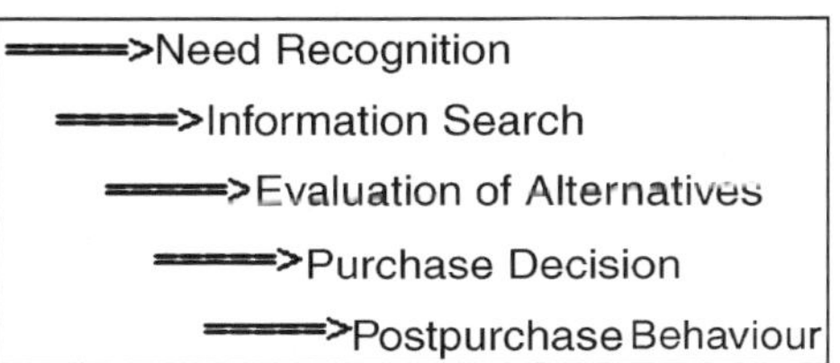

Now consider the purchase of a quart of orange juice. You purchase this product when you do your grocery shopping once per week. You have a favourite brand of orange juice and usually do your grocery shopping at the same store. When you buy orange juice, you always go to the same place in the store to pick it up, and never notice what other brands are on the shelf or what are the prices of other brands. How is it that the generic model above works differently in this second scenario? Why does it work differently? Why would we generally need the ministrations of a sales person in the sale of a car, but we generally do not need the help of a salesperson in the purchase of orange juice? How can the marketer of orange juice get a consumer like you to exert more effort into information search or to consider alternative products? How is it that the marketer of your brand got you to ignore alternative competing brands? What is the involvement of salespeople in *sales promotions* that might be associated with products such as orange juice? Consumer behaviour researchers are not so interested in studying the validity of the above generic model, but are more interested in various factors that influence how such a model might work.

GROUP INFLUENCES ON CONSUMER BEHAVIOUR

- *Culture*: Culture the set of basic values, beliefs, norms, and associated behaviours that are learned by a member of society Note that culture is something that is *learned* and that it has a relatively long lasting effect on the behaviours of an individual. As an example of cultural influences, consider how the salesperson in an appliance store in the U.S., must react to different couples who are considering the purchase of a refrigerator. In some subcultures, the husband will play a dominant role in the purchase decision; in others, the wife will play a more dominant role.
- *Social Class*: Social Class a group of individuals with similar social rank, based on such factors as *occupation*, *education*, and *wealth*
- *Reference Groups*: Reference groups, often temporary, that affect a person's values, attitude, or behaviours
- *Family*: Family a group of people related by blood, marraige, or other socially approved relationship

INTERNAL INFLUENCES ON CONSUMER BEHAVIOUR

Personality

Personality a person's distinguishing psychological characteristics that lead to relatively consistent and lasting responses to stimuli in the environment We are each unique as individuals, and we each respond differently as consumers. For example, some people are "optimisers" who will keep shopping until they are certain that they have found the best price for a particular item, while other people are "satisficers" who will stop shopping when they believe that they have found something that is "good enough." If you are a salesperson in a retail shoe store, how might you work differently with these two personalities?

Lifestyle and Psychographics

- Lifestyle is a pattern of living expressed through a person's activities, interests, and opinions
- Psychographics is a technique for measuring personality and lifestyles to developing lifestyle classifications

Motivation: Multiple Motives

Consumers usually have multiple motives for particular behaviours. *These can be a combination of:*

- Manifest known to the person and freely admitted
- Latent unknown to the person or the person is very reluctant to admit

Note: different motives can lead to the same behaviour; observing behaviour is not sufficient to determine motives.

Involvement

Involvement has to do with an individual's

- *Intensity of interest* in a product and the
- *Importance* of the product for that person

The purchase of a car is much more risky than the purchase of a quart of orange juice, and therefore presents a higher involvement situation. This modifies the way that the generic model works. As involvement increases, consumers have greater motivation to comprehend and elaborate on information salient to the purchase. A life insurance agent, for example, would typically be more interested in contacting a young couple who just had a baby than an eighteen year old college student—even though the new parents might be struggling to make ends meet while the student is living more comfortably. Although the annual investment into a policy is much lower if started at a younger age, most young college students are not open to thinking about long term estate planning. A young couple with a new child, however, is much more open to thinking about issues associated with planning for the child's future education, saving to buy a house, or even saving to take an extended vacation upon retirement.

TYPES OF CONSUMER PROBLEM-SOLVING PROCESSES

Routenised

- Used when buying frequently purchased, low cost items

- Used when little search/decision effort is needed
- *E.G.,* buying a quart of orange juice once per week

Limited Problem Solving

- Used when products are occasionally purchased
- Used when information is needed about an unfamiliar product in a familiar product category

Extended Problem Solving

- Used when product is unfamiliar, expensive, or infrequently purchased
- *E.G.,* buying a new car once every five years

POST-PURCHASE CONSUMER BEHAVIOUR

Satisfaction

After the sale, the buyer will likely feel either satisfied or dissatisfied. If the buyer beleives that s/he received more in the exchange than what was paid, s/he might feel satisfied. If s/he believes that s/he received less in the exchange than what was paid, then s/he might feel dissatisfied. Dissatisfied buyers are not likely to return as customers and are not likely to send friends, relatives, and acquaintences. They are also more likely to be unhappy or even abusive when the product requires post-sale servicing, as when an automobile needs warranty maintenance.

The idea can be modeled as Homans' basic exchange equation:

- Profit = Rewards - Costs

Unfortunately, even a buyer who "got a good deal" with respect to price and other terms of the sale might feel dissatisfied under the perception that the salesperson made out even better. This idea is called equity theory, where we are concerned with:

Outcomes of A Input of A
Vs.
Outcomes of B Inputs of B

Consider, for example, that you have purchased a used car for $14,000 after finding that the and quote;blue book" value is listed at $16,000. You are probably delighted with the purchase until you accidentally meet the prior owner who had received a trade-in of $10,000 on the car just a few days before. That the dealer appears to have received substantially greater benefit than you could lead to extreme dissatisfaction, even though you received good value for the money spent. An issue related to this is attribution theory. Attribution theory, people tend to assign cause to the behaviour of others. Mary's life insurance agent advises her to purchase a whole life policy, while her accountant advises her, "buy term insurance and invest the difference.". The reason, explains the accountant, "is that insurance agents receive substantially higher commission payments on sales of whole life policies." If Mary believes that the insurance agent is recommending a product merely because he receives a higher commission, she will likely be displeased with the relationship and will not take his recommendation. If the agent is able to show Mary that the recommended product is the best solution for her situation, then she will likely attribute his recommendation to having her best interests in mind and will not be concerned about how it is that he is compensated for his services.

Cognitive Dissonance

Cognitive dissonance has to do with the doubt that a person has about the wisdom of a recent purchase. It is very common for people to experience some anxiety after the purchase of a product that is very expensive or that will require a long term commitment. Jane and Fred, for example, signed a one year lease on an apartment, committing themselves to payments of $1500 per month. A week later, they are wondering if they should have instead leased a smaller $900 apartment in a more rough part of town; they are not sure if they really can afford this much of a monthly obligation. Dick and Sally, on the other hand, ultimately rented the $900 apartment, and now are wondering if the savings in rent will be offset by noisy and sometimes unsafe conditions in this neighbourhood.

Perhaps neither couple would be experiencing this anxiety if their landlords had given them just the smallest of assurances that they had made a good decision. After a close on products that are expensive or that require a long term commitment, the salesperson should provide the prospect with some reasons to be happy with the decision. Allow the car buyer to reinforce her own positive feelings by calling her a week after the purchase to ask how things are going. Call the new life insurance policy holder after two months to see if there are any questions; a lack of questions can only help the buyer to convince himself that he did the right thing.

BUYING DECISION PROCESS

Whenever folks make a buying decision, that decision represents the culmination of a process. It may take place almost instantaneously or stretch out over a long period of time – but it's a process, not an event. No matter how long the process takes, the buying decision always begins when folks become aware of a need. Once they have identified that need, they begin to search for and explore possible avenues for meeting it. While gathering information, they refine and evaluate all the buying criteria that will affect the decision to purchase and narrow the field of choice to the "best few" alternatives. Once they reach a decision and choose, they take action by making a purchase. The final step in the process involves a reevaluation of the decision and its results.

To summarise, the steps of the buying decision process are:

- Identify
- Search
- Evaluate
- Decide
- Purchase
- Reevaluate

THE NATURE OF THE BUY

The way folks make buying decisions depends on the complexity of the problem they are trying to solve and the complexity of each step in the decision process. This will affect how you manage the sale. If their needs and the decision-making process are simple, all you need to do is make your visitors aware of you, build confidence, differentiate yourself, demonstrate value and guide them through a very simple shopping and buying process. This is why lower-end, branded products sell so well. Think of buying a book from Amazon.com. If the needs and the decision-making process are highly complex, then you need to make people aware of you, build relationships, educate them show sensitivity to the different decision-makers, influencers and groups, and resolve conflicting needs, so you can custom-tailor your solutions and make the buying process as painless and positive as possible. Think of purchasing a multi-million dollar piece of equipment that needs five departments to sign off to close the deal. It also helps if you understand and incorporate how folks think about buying what you offer.

Are they going to compare similar models in different brands? Are they looking for the range offered by one manufacturer? Do they think of the purchase in terms of a hierarchy of benefits, with some more important than others? Is the best way to showcase your product or service to compare it with someone else's stuff?

PROPENSITY TO BUY

You get four types of traffic, and each group is primed with a different level of motivation and preparedness – the classic "propensity to buy." First, you've got the to-die-for perfect visitors; they are the ones who know exactly what they want and come to you looking for features, brands, and model numbers. Then you've got the visitors who sort of know what they want. These are folks who have identified a strongly felt need, but they're still in the process of narrowing down their search criteria. Then there are the window shoppers, folks who aren't sure they want anything, but might buy if they saw something that interested them. They have no strongly felt need in mind, but one could be suggested to them. The fourth group aren't really prospects.

They're lost or there by mistake. Be happy when they go away. You don't know where your visitors are in the process when they land on your site, so you've got to plan for each possibility. You've got to help the folks who know exactly what they want get to it quickly; make them jump through too many hoops and they're gone. You've got to help the ones still mulling it over by offering pertinent information where and when they are most likely to need it, as well as persuading them you're the logical business choice. You've got to be most engaging and appealing for the window shopper, and you've got to let the lost soul quickly figure out he doesn't belong there. It also helps to consider that not all your visitors are prepared or even inclined to make a decision when they first visit your site – sometimes a successful conversion is the result of multiple visits. So you'd like to give folks a reason to come back.

BUYING IS AN EMOTIONAL DECISION

It really is the piece that pulls it all together. Folks rationalise the decision to buy based on facts, but they make the decision to buy based on feelings. The single biggest motivator in buying is emotional response. And that takes place on two levels. In part, it's the emotional response that comes when folks imagine themselves enjoying the benefits of what you offer. Put them in the driver's seat, and they are that much closer to being able to see themselves making the decision to buy. Am I saying "Ditch the features?" Absolutely not. You should make your features available and present them as corollaries to benefits.

After all, some of your visitors, particularly analytic types who will pointedly look for this stuff, feel more comfortable emotionally with facts and specifications. And that brings me to the other aspect of emotional response. Folks buy when they feel comfortable, when they feel they can trust you, when the process feels natural and reassuring, and when they come to believe that buying will make them feel good. Ignore this, and most of your visitors will bail out. Tap into it, and watch your conversion rate climb. Because, at then end of the day, it's not facts that convince customers to go with your company. It's emotion.

PACKAGE BUYING WITH SELLING

The persuasive architecture of your entire site must recognise every step of the buying decision process. Each step feeds and leads to the others. Although the process ultimately is linear, there can be feedback loops within the process as folks reevaluate information. So, it's not unusual to address multiple steps on a single page. To successfully get your visitors to take action you must be able to see the world from their "buying" point of view. So learn how to address and package the buying process within your selling process. It will make a world of difference!

STAGES OF THE CONSUMER BUYING PROCESS

Six Stages to the Consumer Buying Decision Process. Actual purchasing is only one stage of the process. Not all decision processes lead to a purchase. All consumer decisions do not always include all 6 stages, determined by the degree of complexity...discussed next.

The 6 stages are:

1. *Problem Recognition*: Difference between the desired state and the actual condition. Deficit in assortment of products. Hunger—Food. Hunger stimulates your need to eat.
2. Can be stimulated by the marketer through product information—did not know you were deficient? *I.E.*, see a commercial for a new pair of shoes, stimulates your recognition that you need a new pair of shoes.
3. *Information search*:
   - Internal search, memory.
   - External search if you need more information. Friends and relatives. Marketer dominated sources; comparison shopping; public sources etc.

     A successful information search leaves a buyer with possible alternatives, the evoked set. Hungry, want to go out and eat, evoked set is:
   - Chinese food
   - Indian food
   - Burger king
   - Klondike kates etc
4. *Evaluation of Alternatives*: Need to establish criteria for evaluation, features the buyer wants or does not want. Rank/weight alternatives or resume search. May decide that you want to eat something spicy, indian gets highest rank etc.
5. If not satisfied with your choice then return to the search phase. Can you think of another restaurant? Look in the yellow pages etc. Information from different sources may be treated differently. Marketers try to influence by "framing" alternatives.
6. *Purchase decision*: Choose buying alternative, includes product, package, store, method of purchase etc.
7. *Purchase*: May differ from decision, time lapse between 4 and 5, product availability.
8. *Post-Purchase Evaluation*: Outcome: Satisfaction or Dissatisfaction.

Cognitive Dissonance, have you made the right decision. This can be reduced by warranties, after sales communication etc. After eating an indian meal, may think that really you wanted a chinese meal instead.

TYPES OF CONSUMER BUYING BEHAVIOUR

Types of consumer buying behaviour are determined by:

- Level of Involvement in purchase decision. Importance and intensity of interest in a product in a particular situation.
- Buyers level of involvement determines why he/she is motivated to seek information about a certain products and brands but virtually ignores others.

High involvement purchases—Honda Motorbike, high priced goods, products visible to others, and the higher the risk the higher the involvement.

Types of risk:

- Personal risk
- Social risk
- Economic risk

The four type of consumer buying behaviour are:

1. *Routine Response/Programmed Behaviour*: Buying low involvement frequently purchased low cost items; need very little search and decision effort; purchased almost automatically. Examples include soft drinks, snack foods, milk etc.
2. *Limited Decision Making*: Buying product occasionally. When you need to obtain information about unfamiliar brand in a familiar product category, perhaps. Requires a moderate amount of time for information gathering. Examples include Clothes—know product class but not the brand.
3. Extensive Decision Making/Complex high involvement, unfamiliar, expensive and/or infrequently bought products. High degree of economic/ performance/psychological risk. Examples include cars, homes, computers, education. Spend alot of time seeking information and deciding. Information from the companies MM; friends and relatives, store personnel etc. Go through all six stages of the buying process.
4. Impulse buying, no conscious planning.

The purchase of the same product does not always elicit the same Buying Behaviour. Product can shift from one category to the next.

For example:

- Going out for dinner for one person may be extensive decision making but limited decision making for someone else. The reason for the dinner, whether it is an anniversary celebration, or a meal with a couple of friends will also determine the extent of the decision making.

FINANCING THE CONSUMER

To facilitate the process of consumption, some goods are sold to the ultimate consumer on credit, or loans of cash are made to him. The subject was analyzed as one determinant of consumer behaviour. At this point, consumer finance is treated as a marketing activity, with attention given both to its business and social implications.

NATURE OF CONSUMER CREDIT

The credit granted to ultimate consumers for the purpose of facilitating the process of consumption is known as consumer credit. Theoretically, it is the power which an individual uses in obtaining goods and services, or in borrowing money, for consumption purposes, on the promise to repay an equivalent at an agreed future time. Broadly conceived, consumer credit includes all credit extensions for personal use, whether granted by manufacturers that sell directly to consumers, by retailers, professional men, servicc businesses, or by the various types of financial institutions. Reasons for and Basic Types of Consumer Credit From the standpoint of creditors, the principal reason for credit is profit. To the retailer, credit spells increased sales volume and remunerative business; to the money lender, it means a worth-while return on his investment. To the ultimate consumer, however, the matter is not so simple.

In general, however, the consumer is prompted to use credit by one or more of three sets of motives: *convenience, a desire for immediate improvement in his standard of living,* and *necessity.* Each of these motives constitutes, in the main, the fundamental explanation for a different type of consumer credit: *the charge account, installment sale credit, and consumer cash credit, respectively.*

Importance and Composition of Consumer Credit

The importance of consumer credit may be judged in several ways. First, it may be pointed out that about one-third of all retail store sales is made on a credit basis, with about two-thirds of such credit sales being made on a charge account basis and about one-third on some type of installment credit arrangement. The importance of credit sales varies considerably among different lines of trade, being of greatest significance to large establishments, with a wide range of merchandise classifications, serving a relatively permanent clientele.

For example, department stores, which account for only 6.7 per cent of retail store sales, hold 19 per cent of the total consumer indebtedness arising out of the use of charge accounts in all retail stores, including credit card plans. Another indication of the importance of consumer credit is the volume of credit outstanding at a particular time. Such data, which are published regularly in very comprehensive fashion, measure the amount due creditors as of a particular date rather than the volume of credit granted during a particular period. Nevertheless, trends in such data at least reflect increasing or decreasing use of various means of financing consumption through credit.

In 1960, for example, consumers owed $54 billion in connection with previous uses of all forms of short-term and intermediateerm installment credit. This was the equivalent of 15 per cent of total disposable personal income during that year. On an annual basis, consumer credit outstanding (debt) has tended to increase gradually but consistently, from 9.2 per cent in 1950 to 15 per cent of disposable personal income in 1960. Greater use of consumer credit, as so measured, is explained by a variety of factors, including:

- Growing acceptance of credit as an institution of modern society, as opposed to a puritanical aversion to indebtedness;
- Increasing levels of per family income which has enhanced the demand for types of goods commonly sold on a credit basis and caused a larger proportion of the population to qualify as acceptable credit risks;
- A wider variety of credit or financing arrangements, available from a growing number of marketing and financial institutions, especially designed to meet the particular needs of families in different income groups and financial circumstances.

Of total consumer indebtedness in 1960, 78 per cent arose out of the use of one form or another of installment credit and 22 per cent reflected non-installment credit. Installment debt was, however, only 11.7 per cent, or less than one-eighth, of total annual disposable personal income. It appears, therefore, that the total population could safely carry considerably larger amounts of installment financial obligations, without impairing its ability to repay on a reasonable basis, provided such debt is of high quality by virtue of being wisely extended in the vast number of individual cases that comprise the aggregate.

The composition of consumer credit, in terms of debt outstanding. These data do not correspond with the magnitude of consumer expenditures made on a credit basis since expenditures which involve long-term financing tend to be overstated in terms of marketing significance and those which are short-term obligations tend to be understated. However, provide a frame of reference for appraising the composition of consumer credit by major parts or uses and by various sources of credit (holders), and do serve as a background for discussion of types of credit and kinds of financial institutions.

Charge Accounts

Consumers utilize charge accounts chiefly because it is convenient for them to obtain goods on that basis. Orders can be placed by telephone, better service can be obtained from stores, several members of a family may buy on an account, home budgeting may be facilitated, and family budgeting may be controlled through monthly payments. Merchants who operate on a charge account basis do so for several reasons. It is claimed that charge accounts serve to build regular customers who tend to concentrate their purchases and to buy more merchandise. Credit customers are believed to be less resistant to sales and advertising appeals and are more likely to buy on considerations of quality and style rather than price.

Stores extending charge account credit also have a more uniform distribution of sales than do cash stores which experience pronounced peaks in business on and following paydays and lulls in activity between such times.

In spite of the advantages explained above, many stores do not choose to make charge accounts available to their customers. If the basic appeal of an establishment is price, all services, including credit, are usually minimized. Charge accounts are not usually used in the sale of goods of low unit value, as in the case of variety store items, for which customers are accustomed to paying cash. Furthermore, merchants with limited financial resources are often forced to operate on a cash basis because charge accounts involve financing consumer purchases for periods of 50 or 60 days on the average.

Retail store charge accounts have tended to be a relatively stable or declining component of total consumer credit out standings, but service credit, which is closely akin to charge accounts, has increased significantly in the post-World War II era. Service credit consists principally of amounts owed to doctors, hospitals, and public utility companies. Its steady growth reflects wider acceptance of credit financing of medical and household operation expenses, but is also partly attributable to the increased relative significance of service expenditures in the typical family budget.

Most charge accounts involve a relationship between an individual retail store and an individual consumer; however, some group arrangements are of interest. In some cities, numerous independent retailers and service establishments sell on credit through bank charge account plans. Usually a number of stores are affiliated with a given bank; the bank makes credit investigations and approves the accounts; customers may make charge purchases in any of the participating stores; the retailer receives cash for the sale, minus a service charge, at the daily presentation of the sales checks to the bank; and the bank bills the customer monthly for all purchases he made in all participating stores.

Major oil companies have promoted the use of credit cards or credit check books which are accepted by any of the independent dealers associated with the company and by the dealers of other affiliated companies. National credit card plans, such as Carte Blanche of Hilton Hotels Corporation and the American Express Company Credit Card, are similar in many respects but are used to a greater extent for handling business travel and entertainment expense than for financing ultimate consumption. Such group arrangements have made it possible for many individual firms to offer charge account services when they would otherwise have found it impossible or uneconomical to do so.

Installment Sale Credit

Installment sale credit differs from charge account credit in one major way. Instead of paying the full amount of the bill at the end of a given period of time, the purchaser, when using installment credit, agrees to pay his obligation in fixed portions or installments at stated intervals. Other common, although not universal, distinctions are that a down payment is often made on installment transactions and that a finance charge is levied on the unpaid balance.

Although it is an old business practice, the installment method did not evoke much attention until about the middle of the 1920's when its use was greatly extended together with the expansion of the automobile market. During the 1930's the method became more common as it was extended to numerous types of durable goods and even to "soft" goods which have been later sold extensively on deferred multiple payment plans. Installment sale credit accounts for about one-third of total credit sales of retail establishments in non-war years.

During war years and periods of national emergency marked by scarcities of durable goods, the total volume of installment sale credit has been as little as one-fourth of total credit sales and as low as less than 5 per cent of the total sales of retail establishments. More than one-half of the *installment sale* credit *extended* annually represents automobile financing. Other lines of business in which installment sale credit is of great significance are furniture stores, household appliance stores, jewelry stores, automobile tire and accessory stores, and department stores.

Installment selling has also been applied to the marketing of various kinds of services. Airlines, for example, have made it possible for consumers to take expensive vacation trips which are financed over a number of months. Similarly, many doctors, dentists, and hospitals have made arrangements with financing institutions so that people with limited incomes may finance major medical expenses on definite installment arrangements.

Sales Finance Companies and Installment Sale Credit

Finance companies are of two types: *consumer* or *personal finance companies* engaged chiefly in making cash loans and which are discussed at a later point, and *sales finance companies* engaged principally in financing the sale of products.

Sales finance companies, in turn, may be divided into two principal classes: manufactured-owned companies, such as General Motors Acceptance Corporation, and independent financial institutions, as illustrated by Commercial Credit Corporation. Regardless of ownership, both types of companies do the bulk of their business in connection with automotive sales, but both types also are heavily engaged in financing sales of appliances, electronic products, furniture, and other durable goods. The nature of their operations may be illustrated with respect to automobile financing.

When an automobile is sold on the installment plan (and the same applies to other articles financed by sales finance companies), a promissory note covering the transaction is made out by the purchaser.

The note, secured by a chattel mortgage on the car, or by a conditional sales contract, is indorsed by the dealer, with or without recourse, as the case may be, and is then discounted by the finance company. Prior to acceptance of the risk by the finance company, a credit investigation is made in order to determine the purchaser's willingness and ability to meet the installments when due. An agreement must be reached on the amount of down payment and the number of, and the amount of time between, installment payments.

On automobiles, the usual down payment required has, from time to time, varied from about 10 per cent to 15 per cent to onethird of the purchase price; the time interval between payments is generally one month; and the number of payments has varied from about 12 to 36. In some cases, however, automobiles are sold on terms involving no down payment and with terms of 48 months.

In determining the amount to be paid under the installment sales contract a regular service charge is added to the unpaid balance. This charge, which is all too often confused and compared with pure interest rates, must cover interest on the money lent, credit and collection expense of the lending agency, a reasonable allowance for bad debt losses, allowance for expenses involved in repossession, reconditioning, and sale of cars of delinquents, and certain types of insurance as specified.

This charge is quoted in terms of a *nominal* rate, *i.e.*, the amount of service charge expressed as a percentage of the total unpaid amount on a per annum basis, that is, on the total initial unpaid balance. The *actual* effective rate of charge is generally about twice the nominal rate because the debtor is constantly decreasing the outstanding balance by monthly payments made throughout the period.

Installment Credit Handled by Retailers

Installment credit is generally used in many types of retail stores that operate without assistance from sales finance companies. Department stores, mail order companies, furniture stores, and home appliance stores are some of the major types of establishments that maintain their own installment credit departments, make credit investigations, and handle collections, which are accepted at accounts receivables offices in the store or are made by consumers by mail. Many of these stores finance their receivables through commercial banks or other financial institutions. Some large-scale retailers have subsidiary corporations which have been established to handle their time-sales financing activities and which operate in the same manner as sales finance companies. Durable goods items of high unit value are usually sold on straight installment contracts which customarily involve a down payment and payments of a specified amount for a definite number of weeks or months.

Since about the middle 1940's, various types of "budget," "revolving" or "optional" credit plans have been adopted extensively by department stores, mail order companies, and apparel retailers, to facilitate the sale of soft goods on installments. According to a common arrangement, the consumer contracts to pay a certain amount each month and thus is granted a credit limit which is a multiple of the monthly payment. In a 12-month revolving account, if the customer contracts to pay $20 per month the credit limit is set at $240. The consumer can make purchases of any kind of goods sold by the store, so long as the credit limit is not exceeded. Each month a carrying charge is added to the outstanding balance as of the end of the month.

The "optional" or multiple-purpose account used by many retailers serves either as a regular charge account or as a deferred payment account. If the customer wishes to pay the total amount of the monthly billing, he may do so, and there is no service charge. On the other hand, if the billing is large (*e.g.*, owing to seasonal purchases such as at school opening time, Christmas, or Easter) payments may be spread over several or many months, with a service charge added to the outstanding balance, as in the case of revolving credit. The various forms of revolving credit are classified, for statistical purposes, along with regular installment credit. Their popularity in the 1950's and early 1960's has resulted in the shifting of some debt balances from the category of charge account to installment.

Arguments for Installment Credit

The real nature of installment credit can be but little understood merely from a knowledge that it involves periodic payments. Installment credit is not merely a technique; rather it is a pervasive influence and an explanation of its nature must be sought in the effects it has upon all whom it touches. These effects are reputedly both beneficial and detrimental. The advantages of installment credit may be considered from the standpoint of the business establishments that use it as a selling technique and from the view of the consumer and society in general.

To merchants selling on the installment plan, it is not a matter of conjecture that the plan tends to increase sales volume. It does increase the total demand for goods of the type that may be sold on this plan, and it brings people into stores at frequent intervals to make payments. Each such call is an opportunity to make additional sales, with payments for one purchase leading to still additional purchases and greater familiarity with the credit-granting establishment.

From the standpoint of society, the installment plan is desirable, first, because it *enables people to obtain, without delay, many commodities of high unit value and much usefulness,* without the necessity of waiting long periods before they are acquired, or of doing without them altogether. The buyer is thus enabled to use the article while paying for it; as a result he can enjoy life more fully than would otherwise be possible.

A second social advantage, and one contrary to much popular opinion, is that installment buying *tends to encourage thrift.* It is an enforced form of saving, *provided* that the terms of payment are such that the consumer's equity in the purchased article is increased at a rate greater than the rate at which the article is used up or consumed. Many people will economize in order to be able to meet installments when they come due, even though they may be unable, or lack the discipline, to economize merely for the sake of accumulating money for future use. Third, *because installment credit has widened the market for the type of consumer goods sold in this manner, it has contributed to lower prices on such goods.*

Most of the industries manufacturing durable goods of high unit value operate on a decreasing cost basis; consequently, as their output is increased, the unit cost is materially reduced. The advantage of lower prices resulting from market expansions attributable to consumer credit inures to the benefit, therefore, of cash and credit customers alike. There can be no doubt, furthermore, that installment credit *has contributed to a substantially higher standard of living for large segments of the consuming public.*

This argument is a natural corollary of the two just stated, in that it results both from the savings feature of the plan and the broadening of the market through price reductions of many types of goods. Standards of living are judged in large measure by the number and kinds of durable goods and costly articles in the possession of consumers, as well as by the consumption of items yielding cultural and aesthetic satisfaction.

Much of the income that is now used for purchasing automobiles, television, radios, dishwashers, washing machines, garbage disposals, vacuum cleaners, floor coverings, furniture, and refrigerators would be expended upon highly perishable satisfactions in the absence of installment credit. Furthermore, in the absence of economies of scale enjoyed by industries manufacturing such goods, unit prices would necessarily be much higher and at such a level that it would be impossible for the masses to purchase items of this kind.

Objections to Installment Credit

Installment credit is sufficiently well established as a business practice that it is only upon rare occasions that objections to it arise from within the business community. Some strong arguments have been set forth against it, however, by those who view the subject from a consumer or social standpoint.

Most such objections are either made by those who have no understanding of this type of credit, or objections are directed to abuses rather than to sound applications of it. Among the most common criticisms is that it causes people to live beyond their means by the consumption of luxuries to which they are not entitled on the basis of current income. Tastes and desires of different individuals vary so much, however, as to make any attempt to dictate that one commodity be purchased instead of another, or that it be bought on a certain basis, the height of absurdity.

A second and somewhat related objection is that installment credit has led consumers to mortgage their future incomes, both through the consumption of luxuries and overconsumption in general, to the extent that the slightest interruption in normal earnings would effect a very serious and straitened condition in their ability to meet obligations. Such criticisms are apparently based upon two assumptions:

- That a person's income is static
- That installment purchases are made on top of what would be normally bought in the absence of such purchases. In numerous individual cases the person who bought an expensive article on the installment plan may justly expect an increase in his present earnings during the life of the contract. Again, he may so reapportion and redirect his purchases that less of other types of goods will be bought, or he may have been saving to the extent that this distribution of his income can be modified without impairing his security. Furthermore, many buyers on the installment plan have resources other than their immediate income, which can be converted into cash if desired or necessary in order to meet obligations.

One of the most serious objections to installment credit is its costliness. In operating on a charge account basis, there is but one collection to be made for purchases during the credit period and, ordinarily, only one chance that payment will be delayed or not made at all. From the standpoint of the store or finance company, there are repetitive chances that the installment purchaser will become delinquent. Elaborate collection machinery must be established to insure that payments are kept forthcoming and that the purchaser remains satisfied with the goods and the service of the selling establishment. In addition to collection expenses, carrying charges must also include, as previously indicated, interest on the funds used, bookkeeping and clerical costs, credit investigation expense, reserves for bad debt losses, and allowances for the cost of repossession and resale of articles.

An objection voiced by many is that charges are exorbitant, that is, even greater than warranted by actual costs of carrying installment accounts. This criticism arises in part from misunderstanding and in part because certain less reputable vendors have taken advantage of the ignorance of some consumers.

All too often the carrying charge on installment purchases is inappropriately related to the economic concept of interest which involves merely a price paid for the use of money.

Learning that the actual rate of installment charge per annum on a given transaction is, for example, 12 or 18 per cent per annum, a consumer may unrealistically compare this rate with a rate of interest, say 3 or 4 per cent, that his funds will yield if deposited in a savings account. The conclusion may be drawn that the charge is exorbitant, without cognizance of the fact that interest is only a fraction of the total charge which must cover all of the various costs detailed in the preceding paragraph. In other cases, the charge of exorbitance results from the practice of certain vendors who do not quote any percentage rate of installment charge, but emphasize in the sales presentation merely the amount of the down payment and the amount of the periodic payments. Apparently there are many consumers who are unable or too indifferent to figure the cost of purchasing on the installment plan at the time purchases are made if the amount of the monthly or weekly payment is something they feel they can reasonably afford. Consequently, certain stores have been able to make very high charges on installment transactions and under such circumstances that the amount of the charge is not actually known by many customers. Fortunately, this is a practice that has never been common among more reputable dealers. A fifth important criticism of installment credit is concerned solely with *abuses,* as for example, when carrying charges are not disclosed or are misrepresented.

Many vendors and finance companies have quoted only nominal rather than actual rates of charge per annum and, even so, have failed to indicate whether the rate applied to the unpaid balance after the deduction of the down payment or to the full purchase price of the article. With respect to this criticism, it is significant that steps have been taken in the direction of regulation relating to the use of clear forms of installment contracts which reveal just what the customer gets and how much he is paying for the product and how much for the financing of it.

Cash Credit as a Supplement to Installment Sale Credit

Consumer cash credit may be distinguished from installment sale credit in that consumers obtain cash funds, rather than merchandise, in exchange for a promised future repayment. A large proportion of such credit has its origin in human want and misery and is explained by the urgent need for immediate funds in order to cope with emergency situations. To an important extent, however, cash credit is a supplement to installment sale credit; and in this respect it is of great significance as a factor in the marketing of goods. There are numerous instances in which a consumer has a choice as to the type of credit he might use.

For example, in buying a major electrical appliance, he might make the purchase on the installment plan, arranging for payments with the store from which the purchase is made. On the other hand, he might obtain a cash loan from a lending agency, pay cash to the store selling the merchandise, and repay the loan to the lending agency in periodic installments. In some instances, the latter procedure may be used to circumvent the down payment that is required by the store selling on the installment plan. There are no statistics that reveal the extent to which cash credit directly supplements installment sale credit and to what extent it is used for emergency purposes arising out of unforeseen events or from past financial mismanagement. That cash credit is of considerable significance in facilitating the sale of goods is, however, generally recognized, both by marketing authorities and by those engaged in the cash-lending business.The principal sources of consumer cash credit are as follows:

- Consumer or personal finance companies: These are lending agencies licensed under state laws to engage in the business of lending money to consumers. Typical examples are Household Finance Company, Personal Finance Company, and City Loan Company.
- Banks: Most commercial and industrial banks have consumer loan departments. In general, they make loans of larger amounts at lower rates of installment payment charges than is the case with personal finance companies, owing to their tendency to confine lending activities to high-grade credit risks.
- Credit Unions: Cooperative organizations formed for the purpose of encouraging thrift among members and making loans to them at relatively low rates are known as credit unions. Such organizations are chartered under, and regulated by, state or federal law. Members are ordinarily otherwise affiliated in some way, as employees of a particular company or members of the same church, labour union, or lodge. Since much of the work of the credit union is done by members without compensation, because its facilities are often subsidized by employers or other associated institutions, and because of certain tax advantages owing to status as cooperatives, loans are made at lower rates than are available from financial institutions. Credit is, however, available only to members.

Control of Consumer Credit

As consumer credit has grown in stature in the course of this century, it has led to ever-broadening concepts of its social and economic significance. Consumer credit, particularly of the installment sale or installment cash type, has been, accordingly, the subject of increasing control and regulation by state and federal government. This control is of two types, quality and quantity control.

Quality Control

Regulations pertaining to the quality of consumer credit are designed to prevent usurious, deceptive, unfair, or monopolistic practices by credit-granting agencies.

At the beginning of this century, many consumers in need of cash funds were forced to look to illegal lenders or "loan sharks" as a source for loans, and had to pay exorbitant rates. The reason for this was that the usury laws of most states limited interest rates to 6 per cent per annum or, in the presence of a special contract, to 8 per cent. Such rates were inadequate to attract agencies to make consumer loans in small amounts at inevitable high costs. After making a thorough study, the Russell Sage Foundation, a philanthropic organization working for the improvement of social conditions, drafted a model bill for submission to state legislatures in 1916. This Uniform Small Loan Law, has subsequently been enacted, in some cases with modifications, in 44 states.

The main provisions of the law permit specially authorized rates on loans up to $300. A charge of 3 ½ per cent per month on unpaid balances of $100 or less and 2 ½ per cent per month on the remainder up to the $300 limit is recommended. The law provides that no special fees may be collected on the loans, nor may any charges be made other than the rates applying on the unpaid balance. Companies operating under the law are licensed and bonded and are subject to state inspection.

State laws concerning the control of installment sale credit were first enacted in the 1930's but have since been passed in more than 30 states containing more than three-fourths of the population. Some of these laws pertain solely to automobile financing whereas others cover all kinds and types of installment sale credit. Practically all of them are intended to combat excessive finance charges and non-price abuses by requiring installment sellers to provide written contracts that give a dollar itemization of the following: commodity price, down payment, finance charge, and insurance and/or other charges, if any. In a few states, such laws have specific provisions establishing maximum allowable finance charges.

The broadening interest in the quality of available installment sale credit is also evident from a code of fair trade practices covering certain aspects of automobile sale financing. Rules promulgated by the Federal Trade Commission Trade Commission in 1951 prohibited a variety of abusive or deceptive practices which had become somewhat common among less scrupulous automotive dealers. These rules apply, of course, only to dealers engaged in interstate commerce and subject to the jurisdiction of the FTC.

From time to time there has been considerable sentiment in favour of a federal law which would prescribe standard conditions of disclosure of credit terms in all cash and sale installment credit transactions. One proposal bill, the improperly designated "Truth in Lending Act," was the subject of much publicity in 1961. If enacted, it would require that the installment charge in every transaction be stated in terms of simple "interest" per annum. Owing to the wide variety of installment plans in use, it would be practically impossible to comply with the terms of such a law in each particular retail transaction. Moreover, referring to such a charge as "interest" is fallacious when due consideration is given to the other, and quantitatively more significant, types of clerical and operating costs which must be recovered in installment finance charges. Such a law would, furthermore, greatly extend federal control of local and retail business activity and duplicate to a substantial extent the provisions of numerous and increasing state laws on the same subject but which, significantly, require disclosure of finance charges only in amounts or in some other simple fashion.

7

Distribution Management

Distribution involves getting the product from the manufacturer to the ultimate consumer. Distribution is often a much underestimated factor in marketing. Many marketers fall for the trap that if you make a better product, consumers will buy it. The problem is that retailers may not be willing to devote shelf-space to new products. Retailers would often rather use that shelf-space for existing products have that proven records of selling.

SALES AND DISTRIBUTION MANAGEMENT

Sales refers to the exchange of goods or services for an amount of money or its equivalent in kind. Selling helps an organization achieve its business goals. Thus, managing sales in an organization is a critical activity. A sales manager needs to ensure that the salespeople are motivated to perform the selling function in a way that will help the organization attain its goals. The sales team continuously monitors the changes taking place in the external environment regarding competitors, customers, government and other regulatory agencies, advances in technology, and industry trends.

This provides the sales personnel with vital information regarding trends in organizational sales, product development, and budgets. By offering the management vital inputs pertaining to such information, the sales team helps the management to develop plans regarding sales, production, and design. Over the years, substantial changes have taken place in the selling environment, leading to changes in the sales function.

The trends that have shaped the sales function include shorter product life cycles, longer and more complex sales cycles, reduced customer loyalty, intense competition among manufacturing firms, rising customer expectations, increasing buyer expertise, electronic revolution in communications, and the entry of women into the sales force. In addition to having a strong sales function, companies should also have efficient distribution channels to make the products available to the end consumer. Management of distribution channels involves efficient channel design, conflict management and implementation of sophisticated channel information systems which will enhance the process of making the products available to the end consumer in a timely manner. Sales and Distribution Management provides an overview of the sales and distribution function. It discusses various aspects of the sales function ranging from various sales organization structures to the role of the sales manager in improving sales by hiring, training, motivating and leading the sales force. The second half of the book deals with the distribution function and discusses logistics and channel management.

SALES ORGANIZATION

Owing to intense global competition, slow growth in markets and different customer expectations, sales organizations have to reengineer their organization structures and streamline their processes. An inefficient organization structure can frustrate top managers as it may result in strategic plans going astray due to absence of clearly defined responsibilities and reporting relationships. Developing customer-centric organizations, building strong relationships within and outside the organization, modifying the traditional top-down hierarchical structure and introducing cross-functional teams are some steps companies are taking to improve their efficiency and profitability. The organizational structure should fulfill the purpose for which it has been designed.

The role of a sales organization is to achieve company objectives, streamline reporting relationships, facilitate effective coordination and control and develop an efficient sales force structure to ensure effective selling strategy. Designing the sales organization plays a crucial role in a company's overall success. One must consider the influence of external and internal factors while designing a sales organization. External factors include the markets targeted and the technology prevailing in the target market. Internal factors influencing the design of a sales organization include the company objectives, the size of the sales force, core competence of the company, compensation system, reporting relationships, etc. Based on the span of control, authority, hierarchical levels and departmentalization, four basic organization structures are possible. These are formal and informal structure, centralized and decentralized structure, vertical and horizontal structure and line and staff organization structure. To efficiently serve the ever-changing needs of customers in the best possible manner, a company can have a product-based, geographic-based, customer-based or a combination-based sales force structure.

The type of customers, the market size and its potential, the type of industry in which the company is operating, level of sales desired, size of the sales force and the width and depth of the product mix are some factors that influence the decision on the type of sales force structure to be adopted. Sales culture plays an important role in the success of a sales organization. Sales culture is a collective impression of the values, attitudes and personality of top management in an organization. It pervades down to the lower levels of hierarchy over time. Sales culture has a significant influence on sales force activities and attitudes. The various components that make up sales culture include symbols, language, ceremonies, rites and rituals, role models, tales and stories, and values and beliefs. The strength and direction or fit of the sales culture also play a crucial role in developing a sound sales organization.

SALES FUNCTIONS AND POLICIES

A sales person's professional life is characterized by various highs and lows. At times he may clinch a deal and close a sale, at other times he may have to face the customer's rejection. Thus, the life of a salesperson is certainly not an easy one. What differentiates a successful company from a not-so-successful one is its sales force. The sales force of a company comprises the sales managers and the sales personnel. Both have distinct roles to play and responsibilities to fulfill towards the achievement of the sales objectives of the organization. The sales manager who occupies a middle-level position in an organization satisfies the demands and expectations of not only those him and those whom he is supervising, the sales persons, but also various other groups of people.

These include people who belong to the organization as well those who are external to it. The sales manager has several functions to perform, which fall in the sphere of sales as well as marketing management. Likewise, a sales manager also plays a variety of roles - planner, recruiter, leader, controller, market analyst, sales forecaster, budget manager, and communicator. In addition to playing a variety of roles in sales management, a sales manager also has a set of responsibilities to fulfill. These include the responsibility of hiring, training, coaching, motivating, setting targets for sales people and tracking the results, providing leads and sales support, organizing the sales effort, conducting sales meetings, and allocate scarce resources.

The salesperson's job is also a demanding one. He has to play the role of a persuader, a service provider, an information-gatherer and reporter, an advocate, a traveler, a coordinator and scheduler, a problem-definer, a customer-ego builder, a display arranger for the wholesaler or the retailer, a merchandiser as well as an ombudsman. Like a sales manager, a salesperson too has his own set of responsibilities to fulfill. Further, the operations and functioning of a sales organization is governed by certain policies. The sales-related policies that have an impact on the sales achieved by an organization fall into three categories, namely, policies related to the product, policies related to the distribution aspects, and policies related to the pricing of the product.

The product related policies determine the products and product lines the company should be involved in, and whether to add or drop a particular product or product line. The product-related policies also help specify the company's stand regarding product design and quality, after-sales service, product recall, warranties and repair. The distribution-related policies in a sales organization deal with how the distribution of a product affects its sales. These policies also highlight the relationship between various factors such as product quality, its positioning, the marketer's reputation, marketing efforts, product promotion and sales, and the need for coordination among these various factors. The policies that relate to pricing of the product discuss the relationship between product or service pricing and its impact on sales.

INTERNATIONAL SALES MANAGEMENT

Globalization has opened up markets and provided hitherto untapped opportunities to companies across the world. With increasing competition, changing customer needs and stagnation of demand in domestic markets, many companies have started looking at international opportunities. International sales management plays an important role in implementing the marketing policies and selling programmes of the company in the foreign market at the ground level.

The international sales manager plays the crucial role of planning and organizing this effort and ensuring that the desired results are obtained. A thorough understanding of the overall operations of the organization in the global context, an open approach to multi-cultural differences and the ability to implement both the basic and advanced levels of sales management functions is necessary for the sales manager to succeed. Companies enter foreign markets in search of opportunities. The chances of diversifying the market base, attaining low costs of labour and manufacturing, economies of scale, first-mover advantage and faster growth rate of the economy in comparison to the home market, are some of attractions that woo companies to enter these markets.

An awareness of the pitfalls that accompany entry into foreign markets is also necessary to fully reap the benefits. These pitfalls may be in the form of economic, socio-cultural and legal factors. The decision to enter and operate in international markets is a strategic one. An awareness of various strategic issues is necessary to ensure success in foreign markets. The strategic issues to be considered pertain to the marketing mix, sources of information and mode of entry into the foreign market. The timing, scale and mode of entry are also crucial to the success of a company. The modes of entry include long-distance selling, direct or indirect exporting, franchising, licensing agreements, strategic alliances, turnkey contracts, greenfield investments, joint-ventures and wholly-owned subsidiaries. Variations in economic, socio-cultural and political conditions in different countries makes selling in international markets a challenging task. It requires a great deal of sensitivity to local customer needs, expectations, business approach and personal philosophy. Companies can adopt different structures while operating in foreign markets.

These include use of long-distance selling, piggybacking with local distributors, using intermediaries or operating independently by establishing a direct sales force. Finally, due to differences in culture and traditions and associated problems, most organizations employ local people to sell their products. An awareness of the recruitment, selection, training and compensation procedures for the sales force appropriate for the host country is necessary to successfully operate in different regions of the world.

SALES PLANNING

Most organizations find themselves operating in highly competitive markets with varying customer needs and expectations. This has made them redefine the importance of meticulous planning to be successful in the globalized environment. An understanding of the sales planning process is essential to effectively manage the sales management function. It provides a framework and direction to all actions involved in sales management.

It also helps sales personnel understand where the organization is headed, how it will reach the desired position and what activities must be undertaken to fulfill the organization's mission. Sales planning is very important to an organization because it helps in better implementation of plans, provides a sense of direction, improves coordination and control and reduces uncertainty and risk. The sales manager's role has gradually shifted over the years to that of a planner and administrator. As a planner, the sales manager has to forecast, develop objectives, design the sales organization, formulate policies, procedures and standards and prepare sales budgets. As an administrator, the sales manager has to supervise, coordinate, delegate and motivate the sales force. Managers must also ensure that ethical standards are followed by the sales force during selling. The planning process involves - setting objectives, determining operations to meet these objectives, organizing action, implementing the sales plan, measuring results against standards, re-evaluating, and control of the sales force performance. Most plans fail due to a host of reasons.

The primary reason is the habit of sales managers to duplicate the successful plans of other organizations without trying to understand the specific requirements of their organization. Lack of awareness of important aspects, absence of proper planning, absence of sales force participation and lack of effective communication of planning elements also lead to failure of sales plans. The accuracy of the sales plan is dependent on the time- frame. Plans are generally accurate for shorter time spans than for longer periods. The rate of profits, size of the organization, involvement of top management, communication and sales force participation affect the accuracy of the sales plan.

SALES BUDGETS

A budget is a plan expressed usually in monetary terms. It is a process of allocating a portion of an organization's resources for its various activities for a specified period of time. It helps in planning and coordination of the organization's activities. Sales budgets are developed for the smooth functioning of the sales function. Developing sales budgets serve two purposes - as a mechanism of control and an instrument of planning. There are several benefits an organization derives from budgeting. They are—improved planning, better communication and coordination, perf-ormance evaluation, psychological benefits and avoiding uncontrolled expenditure. In practice, sales managers prepare three types of budgets - sales budgets, selling expense budget and administrative budget. A sales budget gives a plan showing the expected sales for a specified period in the future. Selling expense budgets details the schedule of expenses that may be incurred by the sales department to achieve planned sales. Administrative budget specifies the budgetary allocations for general administrative expenses that would be incurred by the sales department.

The different methods for budgeting include the affordability method, percentage-of-sales method, competitive parity method, objective-and-task method and return-oriented method. The success or effectiveness of each of these depends on the involvement and support received from the top management and the flexibility built into the budgets. To develop an efficient sales budget a manager has to follow certain steps like review and analysis of the situation, identifying specific market opportunities and problems, sales forecasting, communicating sales goals and objectives, preliminary allocation of resources, preparing the budget and getting approval for it.

A meticulously developed sales budget provides many benefits to an organization. But, like any other management concept, budgeting has its share of limitations. They include inability to project the course of future events, inability to gain acceptance by all people in the organization, consumption of significant amount of managerial time and avoidance of expenditures that will bear fruit only in the long run. Once adequate care is taken to overcome the limitations of budgeting, it will performance as a tool to enhance the profitability of the organization.

ESTIMATING MARKET POTENTIAL AND FORECASTING SALES

Estimating the potential of a market is very important for a company planning to enter a new market. This is a process where an organization estimates the attractiveness of the market for selling its products or services. Before venturing into a market and investing huge sums of money, it is very important to asses it in order to avoid irrecoverable losses. Besides studying the broad market factors such as the size of the population, GDP and the spending capacity of the market, firms should also analyse market specific factors such as customers'tastes and preferences, the cultural factors prevailing, their willingness to buy the products and so on. Data regarding customer and market specific factors can be obtained through primary and secondary sources.

Estimating the future sales of the company in a given market is called sales forecasting. Over the years, the importance of sales forecasting has been on the rise across the world. Apart from the mathematical models developed earlier, many new software tools have emerged for forecasting sales in a better fashion. Forecasting can be classified into qualitative forecasting and quantitative forecasting. The methods used in qualitative forecasting are user expectations, sales force composite, jury of executive opinion, Delphi technique and market test. The methods used in quantitative forecasting are time series analysis, moving averages, exponential smoothing, regression and correlation analysis, and multiple regression models. Selecting the appropriate forecasting method is of great importance for a firm.

The method of sales forecasting is selected on the basis of factors such as accuracy, available time, costs, pattern of data, experience of the company and requirements of the software. For effective forecasting, certain criteria in terms of accuracy, plausibility, durability, flexibility, availability of statistical indexes, organizational participation and demand patterns, should be met. Sales forecasting faces several difficulties such as lack of adequate sales history, lack of time, money and qualified personnel. The changing customer attitudes, and changing fashions and fads also performance as hurdles to effective forecasting.

SALES QUOTAS

Sales quotas are a way of life for the sales force. All activities of the sales force revolve around the fulfillment of sales quotas. Sales quotas are targets assigned to sales personnel. They signify the performance expected from them by the organization. Sales quotas help in directing, evaluating and controlling the sales force. They form an indispensable tool for sales managers to carry out sales management activities. Sales quotas are prepared on the basis of sales forecasts and budgets. Sales quotas serve various purposes in organizations. They provide targets for sales personnel to achieve, performance as standards to measure sales force performance and help motivate the sales force. Compensation plans are invariably linked to quotas. The commission and bonuses given to sales persons are based on their meeting quotas set for them.

The four categories of sales quotas widely used are — sales volume quotas, expense quotas, activity quotas and profit quotas. A sales quota should be fair, challenging yet attainable, rewarding, easy to understand, flexible and must satisfy management objectives. It must also help in the coordination of sales force activities. Setting motivating and easy to understand quotas is essential to obtain the cooperation of the sales force. Various methods are used to set sales quotas, among which, quotas based on sales forecasts and market potential are the most common. Skilful administration by sales managers is required for effective implementation of quotas.

Convincing salespeople about the fairness and accuracy of quotas helps the sales management to successfully implement quotas. Sales quotas have certain limitations such as being time consuming, difficulty in comprehending if complicated statistical calculations have been used and focusing on attaining sales volumes at the cost of ignoring important non-selling activities. Quotas may reduce risk-taking among sales personnel and may influence them to adopt unethical selling practices. With changes in the competitive environment and variations in customer expectations, many companies have started developing compensation plans that are increasingly based on non-traditional aspects, thereby reducing dependency on quotas.

SALES AND COST ANALYSIS

Control is one of the most critical functions performed by a sales manager as it measures the performance of the system and helps the manager take corrective action if the performance of the system is not in agreement with the formulated plans. The present day dynamic marketplace has forced sales managers to shift their focus in sales control from sales volume alone and to lay equal emphasis on costs incurred in implementing the sales effort.Group.

The objective of sales control is to ensure that the company's sales efforts are in tune with its sales plan by taking necessary measures in case of deviations. The sales control function measures the performance of the sales force and identifies the problems and opportunities that the firm is exposed to. The process of sales control involves setting goals, comparing actuals with the targets, and taking up corrective action if necessary. The sales efforts of a company can be studied through a sales analysis that involves gathering, classifying, comparing, and studying the sales data of the company. A typical sales analysis involves deciding on the purpose of evaluation, comparing the sales figures with some standards and processing the data to generate reports. A sales analysis can be most informative when the sales data is broken down hierarchically.

An analysis of volume of sales by categories is very helpful in identifying the root causes of the problems in the sales activities of the firm. Though a sales analysis helps identify the problems associated with the sales activities of the firm, it is also bound by a few limitations like dependency on accounting records, inability to reflect the profitability of sales, etc.

Sales analysis involves analyzing the sales volume or the total sales of the company. It includes the total sales of the company by territory, customer, and product category.

A sales audit is periodically taken up by the sales management to examine the entire selling operations of the firm. The audit involves an audit of the sales organization, the sales environment, planning systems, and sales management functions. While a sales analysis measures the sales volume achieved, the marketing cost analysis looks into the costs and expenses incurred to achieve the sales volume and their justification. A cost analysis involves spreading the natural costs, allocating them to functional units, studying the profitability of the units, and implementing appropriate action depending on the findings of the analysis.

Just as a sales audit examines the entire sales operations of a firm, a marketing audit evaluates and enhances the effectiveness of a firm's marketing operations by studying its marketing strategies, policies, and practices. Sales managers use profitability analysis to relate the sales revenues to marketing costs. This helps sales managers to take necessary measures to ensure higher profitability of the firm's sales transactions. A number of principles such as the iceberg principle, the 80/20 principle and cross-classifications guide sales managers in conducting effective sales and cost analysis. These principles reveal the behaviour of sales data and the actual reasons underlying them. They forewarn sales managers of impending dangers and help them to take measures to counter them.

HIRING AND TRAINING SALES PERSONNEL

Hiring is a personnel function that consists of various stages such as the recruitment of candidates with the right qualifications, selection of those who match the organizational requirements, and placing them in a suitable position in the organization. The quality of a company's sales force plays a crucial role in determining the ability of the company to compete and survive in the competitive business environment. While super salesmen can increase a company's revenue significantly, poor performers can hinder the company's growth and drive it towards losses. The greatest challenge faced by all companies is to be able to hire the best talent and to be able to utilize that talent to achieve organizational objectives. Recruiting the wrong person costs a great deal to a company in terms of recruitment cost, cost of placing advertisements, cost of screening potential candidates and interviewing them, assessing, placing and training them after selection.

In addition to these costs, the company also has to bear the cost of paying them a salary at least till the time they are asked to leave the organization. Reimbursement for the sales expenses incurred by such sales persons is yet another cost which has to be borne by the company. A greater area of concern is the opportunity cost that is involved in hiring an unsuitable candidate for a position and missing out on the profits that could have been generated by the company by hiring a competent person instead.

An ineffective salesman can cause great damage to the company's reputation due to his poor product knowledge, failure to serve the customer properly and poor selling techniques which only tend to alienate the customers.

Companies seek specific characteristics in a potential salesperson. These characteristics are clubbed together into two categories - mental aptitude dimensions, and personality dimensions. The mental aptitude dimensions of salespersons include mental alertness, business terms and memory recall aptitude, communication skills, numerical ability and mechanical interest. The personality dimensions, on the other hand, include honesty or character strength, sociability, cynicism, high energy levels, dominance, competitiveness, emotional maturity, work habits, and work motivation. Salespersons are hired on the basis of the satisfactory fulfillment of a company's requirements. The selection process for hiring a salesman involves a number of stages.

These include sourcing the candidates, screening the candidates, conducting the selection test, holding personal interviews, checking letters of recommendations, conducting reference checks, physical examination, and making the employment offer. Once a suitable candidate has been hired for the position of a salesman, the candidate needs to be properly trained to increase his effectiveness and productivity in selling. Sales training is of four types - initial sales training, refresher or follow-up training, training offered by the manufacturer to the sales force of its distributor and training offered by the manufacturer to its customers. Sales training offers several benefits, both to the sales persons as well as to the organization. These benefits range from decrease in sales force turnover, enhanced morale of the sales force, to improved company image and customer relations. Sales training programmes consist of three components: designing the training programme, implementing the training programme and evaluating the training programme. The designing of training programmes should be done keeping in view the organizational objectives. However, a company's efforts must not just end with designing a training programme to achieve its objectives. The company must also take measures to implement the training programme effectively so that it helps the company achieve its objcctives.

The impleme-ntation of the training programme takes into consideration issues such as - Selecting the right trainer, timing of training, place of training, etc. Looking at the large amount of expenditure that companies incur to train their sales force, evaluation of training programmes becomes essential to justify this expenditure and to objectively examine whether the training programmes have been successful in accomplishing their objectives. Kirkpatrick's four-stage model of sales force training evaluation is the most widely used method of evaluating training programmes and evaluates the training programme on four levels, namely, reactions, knowledge acquisition, behaviour change/ transfer of learning, and organizational outcomes.

TIME AND TERRITORY MANAGEMENT

Effective time management will significantly help a salesperson improve his performance. There has been a fundamental shift in organizations' approach to time management with the advent of better technological options. Advancements in technology have simultaneously led to a significant increase in time pressure on the salesperson. However, technological advancements have also provided several techniques to help salespersons manage their time efficiently.

Efficient time management leads to better customer coverage, helps in reducing selling costs, improving customer service and helps in accurate evaluation of salespeople. A sales territory comprises a number of present and potential customers, located within a given geographical area and assigned to a salesperson, branch, or intermediary. Sales territories should be designed efficiently so that the potential of salespersons can be exploited to the maximum. Sales territories are designed using the three methods – buildup method, breakdown method and incremental method.

The buildup method consists of designing sales territories by assessing the attractiveness of current and prospective customers. In this method, current and prospective customers are identified and their sales requirements analysed individually. Subsequently the salespersons are assigned territories on the basis of the sales volumes and the number of calls they are supposed to make to these accounts. The breakdown method is the reverse of the buildup method and in this, the market potential for the product is identified and then the market share that the company is targeting assessed. Based on this, sales are forecast.

This is followed by determining the average number of sales that each salesperson is required to make and the territories are then accordingly allocated to individual salespersons. In the incremental method, additional territories are created as long as the revenues generated from them exceed the cost of serving them. Once the designing of territories is completed, salespersons are allocated to individual territories according to their capabilities. Routing and scheduling are two widely accepted techniques for territory management. Routing refers to the process of deciding the pattern of movement of a salesperson in his territory for making sales calls in a way that minimizes the total distance traveled, the travel expense and the travel time. Scheduling involves allocation of time to the various activities that a salesperson is involved in during a day, week and a month.

COMPENSATING SALES PERSONNEL

There is no single sales compensation plan that is suitable for all organizations. Every organization has to design its own compensation plan that will enable it to fulfill sales objectives and to attract and retain sales personnel. A truly successful sales compensation plan must help achieve overall organizational goals and not just sales goals. The objectives of a compensation plan should be clearly stated, so that it becomes easier to determine whether the organization is able to achieve them. The compensation plan must fulfill the primary objective of balancing the needs of the sales personnel, and provide them income and security. It should also be effective in all business conditions – good or bad. It should be fair, flexible, easy to administer, fulfill the needs of sales personnel and lead to the achievement of organizational objectives. Organizations compensate sales forces in many ways. The compensation plan may be a straight salary type, a commission-based type or a combination of salary, commissions and incentives. While deciding on the type, it is necessary to consider the differences in territory characteristics, sales activities and objectives of sales personnel. Sales contests are widely used as a source of compensation, especially when an organization wants to emphasize certain activities with the primary aim of increasing profits.

A sales manager must plan a sales contest well in advance and avoid indiscriminate usage. Otherwise, sales contests will lose their efficacy. Compensation plans have an impact on recruitment, training, evaluation and control functions too. While designing a compensation plan, its objectives must be stated. Next, the level of payment should be established. Different industries have different levels of payments. The last step in designing the plan is deciding on the method of payment for the sales force. It may be in the form of a straight salary, commission or bonus or a combination. Drawing account, special cash and non-cash incentives and fringe benefits are also used as a form of payment to the sales force.

The effectiveness and success of a compensation plan depend on its execution. The plan should be tested in a territory before it is implemented throughout the organization. To ensure success, periodic monitoring is also essential. Sales force expenses make up a large portion of total organizational expenditure. To ensure profitability, a sales manager should control sales force expenses in the form of expense quotas. An expense plan must be easy to administer, beneficial to the organization and sales personnel and must be communicated clearly to the sales force.

In most organizations, selling expenses are be reimbursed either completely, partially or in the form of an excess commission that sales personnel must use for meeting selling expenses. Fringe benefits have become a common method of compensation in most organizations. This is also called indirect compensation. Fringe benefits may be in the form of retirement benefits, insurance schemes, employee stock options, medical benefits and paid holidays. With changes in the global environment, organizations have started formulating tailor-made sales compensation plans for individual sales personnel. Ultimately, the success or failure of a compensation plan is dependent on its ability to motivate sales personnel to fulfill organizational objectives and to retain the best talent in the organization.

LEADING THE SALES FORCE

Motivation is the process that produces goal-directed behaviour in an individual. It helps to initiate desired behaviour in an individual and direct it towards the attainment of organizational goals. Motivation consists of three elements - need, drive and goal. Satisfaction of the need in the individual cuts off the drive in him to work towards satisfaction of the need. The effectiveness of the sales force plays a crucial role in the success and growth of an organization. In order to attain the goals of the organization, it is essential that the sales force is highly motivated.

Motivation in the sales function refers to the amount of effort a salesperson is willing to expend in the selling job. While some salespersons are self-motivated, there are others who need to be motivated to perform. Sales managers can motivate their team by following any of the theories of motivation, namely, Maslow's hierarchy of needs theory, Herzberg's two-factor theory, goal-setting theory, expectancy theory, and job design theories. Maslow's hierarchy of needs theory classifies the needs of an individual into five categories - physiological, safety or security, social, self-esteem and self-actualization needs. Physiological needs are the lowest order needs while self-actualization needs are the highest order needs. Further, as lower order needs get satisfied, an individual strives to satisfy higher order needs. Herzberg's two-factor theory states that the job environment of an individual is characterized by two types of factors - hygiene factors and motivational factors.

The goal-setting theory presumes that people have specific needs and aspirations to fulfill for which they set certain goals for themselves. They then go about achieving these goals by taking purposeful action. Further, setting higher goals produces higher output. The expectancy theory states that an individual is motivated by the perceived consequences of his or her actions. This theory, motivation is a function of expectation, valence and instrumentality. Job design theories assume that all individuals have the same needs, and that ensuring certain job characteristics can satisfy these needs. A salesperson's motivation plays a crucial role in influencing his performance and thereby his productivity.

Salespersons having a high level of motivation tend to perform well in the selling job and have high productivity. On the other hand, salespersons who lack motivation tend to be poor performers and fail to achieve their sales targets. Such salespersons hence tend to have low productivity. Sales managers can take various measures to motivate the sales force and boost its productivity. These measures can be in the form of sales quotas, sales contests, well- designed compensation plans and reward systems, etc. Further, the personality traits of the salesperson play a vital role in influencing his motivation. Salespersons can be divided into four types - competitor, achiever, ego-driven, and service-oriented. Sales managers are increasingly concerned about the need to motivate salespersons as they move through various stages in their career. The primary concern of sales managers is to motivate salespersons in the various stages of their career to direct them towards greater selling efforts and enhanced sales performance. A salesperson's career passes through four stages - exploration, establishment, maintenance and disengagement.

EVALUATING SALES FORCE PERFORMANCE

One of the most important responsibilities of sales managers is to evaluate the performance of the sales personnel. The performance appraisal period can become one of those times that a salesperson dreads, unless the appraisal is effectively conducted. Ineffective performance appraisal tends to become a time-consuming and unpleasant activity for the sales manager as well as the sales personnel.

The factors affecting sales peoples' performance are many. Some of these are beyond the control of the individual, while some can be modified. Aspects like motivation, skill-set, job satisfaction, role perception, personal factors like age, sex, height, etc; the ego drive, and empathy towards the customers are inherent in the individual salesperson. Environmental and organizational factors, along with the different functions of sales management come under external factors. It is difficult for the sales manager to predict the influence of the external factors on the performance of the sales force. To measure performance, it is necessary for the sales manager to put in place a performance evaluation procedure.

A proper evaluation process ensures that the organization is well managed. It also provides the sales personnel with information on their performance and gives recommendations for further improvement. Performance evaluation can also help in improving the relationships between the sales force and superiors by minimizing suspicion and improving interaction. The performance evaluation process generally involves five steps. The first step is to determine the factors that affect the performance of the sales force. The next step involves the selection of criteria that will be used to evaluate the performance. Step three involves establishing performance standards that can be used as a basis to compare the performance of the sales force. Step four involves monitoring actual performance.

The last step is to review and provide feedback to the sales personnel. The purpose of conducting performance evaluation is to crosscheck whether the sales force activities are in alignment with organizational objectives. It also helps monitor the sales force activities and provide remedial action, if required. Performance evaluation also helps to prepare a future action plan for the sales personnel and fulfill the organizational objectives. It exerts an influence on the mode of compensation, fixing of sales quotas, and decisions on the transfer or removal of the salesperson from the organization. In most organizations, it is the immediate superior or the sales manager who conducts the performance appraisal. Sometimes a team of people including the personnel manager and the department head, along with the sales manager, appraise the sales personnel. The timing of appraisal also varies for different organizations. It depends on the complexity of the sales plan, the costs involved, and the current objectives of the organization.

Periodic performance appraisal is necessary to identify any discrepancies in the overall sales plan and correct them. The sales manager or the concerned person involved in appraising the sales force can take the help of quantitative or qualitative criteria. These are also termed the behaviour and outcome components. Qualitative criteria include sales skills, territory management skills, personality traits, etc. The quantitative factors include the sales volume, average calls per day, sales orders, etc. Quantitative criteria are those aspects that measure the sales performance in terms of the end results whereas qualitative criteria involve all those activities that the sale person does to achieve the end results.

The sales manager must ensure that the performance standards are set to compare and evaluate the actual performance of the sales force. The standards vary from industry to industry and are different for different job profiles. Performance standards come under quantitative standards, qualitative standards, time-based standards, or cost-based standards. All the sales force activities can be segregated into one of these four categories and compared with the base standard. Many methods of performance evaluation have been developed over the years. Yet, there is no single method that can be considered ideal for all organizations. Some of the commonly used methods are essays, rating scales, rankings, management by objectives and behaviourally-anchored rating scales. Several modern methods like critical incident appraisal, work-standards method, family of measures, etc., have been developed to suit variations and other requirements. Finally, regular monitoring and review of the sales force activities is also necessary to ensure that the organizational activities are aligned to the sales plan.

MARKETING LOGISTICS

Companies today are finding it extremely difficult to maintain their competitive advantage over others purely on the basis of innovative strategies pertaining to the product, price, place, or promotion. Since competitors can easily imitate each of these competitive advantages, the emphasis on building a sustainable competitive advantage has made companies focus their attention on logistics, which provides such a means for companies to successfully differentiate themselves from competing firms.

Logistics is a complex process by which companies transport products, parts, and materials from the place where they are manufactured to the place where they are required. There are several reasons for the overriding importance being given to logistics by businesses across the world. These reasons include wider availability of alternatives to maintain cost and service standards, need for location of retail outlets closer to the market, the growing complexity of product lines, the increasing shortage of raw materials, and the perceived need for an effective system of computerized inventory control.

Logistics is a complex process and involves several functions such as procurement or purchasing, inward transport, receiving, warehousing, stock control, order picking, materials handling, outward transport, physical distribution management, recycling, and returns and waste disposal functions. Effective logistics management requires that the actual status of goods and services be communicated in real-time to the various groups of people involved in the logistics process. This helps logistics service providers to improve their service by keeping a closer watch on inventory and taking the steps necessary to avoid losing customers. Communication using satellite technology and sophisticated devices makes it possible for the various players involved in the logistics chain of processes to remain in constant communication with one another and with the end customer. Technology is playing a key role in communication as well as in other processes in the logistics function and helping logistics firms to attain a competitive advantage. The various types of technology being implemented in logistics activities include Electronic Data Interchange, artificial intelligence, expert systems, communication technology in the form of satellite and wireless communication, and bar coding and scanning. It is necessary to streamline the logistics process to maintain the efficiency of the logistics network.

In addition to integrating information technology and advanced logistical approaches into their business operations, businesses are beginning to realise the need to focus on their logistics strategy in order to efficiently maintain their supply chain capabilities. A logistics strategy examines logistical operations and activities and provides logistical firms with a sense of unity, direction, and purpose. It helps firms involved in the business to attain a competitive advantage over others by allowing them to promptly respond to the opportunities and threats in the business environment.

In their efforts at logistical management, firms face several challenges, which may be local or global in their scope. While the need for integration of logistics activities and lack of qualified personnel are the primary challenges faced in logistics management at the local level, the global challenges include challenges arising due to greater distance, modes of transport, documentation, coordination of intermediaries, cultural and political differences, globalization, need for flexibility and speed, need to integrate supply chain activities, and challenges due to emphasis of companies on green logistics.

MARKETING CHANNELS

A marketing channel acts as a differentiating factor and provides businesses with a competitive advantage. Marketing channels comprise several individuals and interdependent organizations that facilitate the process of making a product or service available to end users. Marketing channels have evolved over time, from being production-oriented to customer- centric.. The evolution of marketing channels has primarily been a response to changes taking place in businesses due to the environment. Channel members play a dominant role in moving products across the marketing channel. They facilitate the search process of buyers and sellers.

They also perform the role of sorting, making transactions routine and contractual efficiency. In addition, marketing channels perform several functions. These involves all activities that facilitate the flow of products from the manufacturer to the end user. As the product moves through different stages, different members in the distribution channel perform the functions of exchange, logistics and other supporting functions. Designing an appropriate marketing channel is crucial to the success of a business. The channel design has to be meticulously planned taking into consideration the channel functions and other strategic business objectives. The most important elements in channel design are channel structure, channel intensity and the type of intermediaries at each level. Marketing channels ensure the smooth flow of products between channel members. In the process, a marketing channel witnesses eight basic types of flows. These are flow of possession, ownership, promotion, negotiation, financial, risk, ordering and payment. Each flow is associated with certain costs. Therefore, it is necessary that marketing channels be designed to eliminate redundancy of flows.

CHANNEL INTEGRATION

Companies the world over produce millions of dollars worth of goods for consumers. These goods reach the end-consumer through a maze of distribution systems. Over the last few decades, companies have realised that effective distribution systems can be a source of competitive advantage. Companies can develop their own distribution channels or delegate the functions to different channel members through channel integration. Channel integration involves streamlining the different channel activities and information flow in a manner that leads to mutual benefits to all the partners concerned. The advantages of channel integration are manifold. It reduces transaction costs, improves inventory management, reduces business opportunism, acts as a barrier to new entrants, bridges the time, space, and variety gaps between production and consumption and reduces the business opportunities lost due to stock-outs and delayed delivery. To gain the advantages of integration, companies have adopted vertical marketing systems.

VMSs have emerged as the dominant mode of distribution over the traditional systems. In a VMS, one of the channel members may own the others, influence the others due to better bargaining power, or develop a contractual arrangement with the different channel members. The three types of VMS's are administered, contractual, and corporate. An administered VMS is similar to a conventional distribution system except that there are greater inter-organizational relationships and sharing of an overall objective. Contractual VMS consists of independent firms operating at different channel levels and forming a system on a contractual basis. Contracts direct the channel members to cooperate with each other for mutual benefits. Franchising is one of the best known forms of this system. The other popular forms of contractual system are the retailer-sponsored cooperative organizations (RCOs) and the wholesaler sponsored voluntary organization (WVOs). In a corporate VMS, one of the channel members exerts complete control over the rest of the channel partners and everyone follows the objectives and procedures as dictated by this dominant channel member.

The benefits of VMSs include improved profitability, better control on the product quality, increased efficiency in inventory management, increased ability to respond to changing market needs, better economic control, improved marketing know-how, decrease in costs leading to better competitive advantage, stability in operations, and reduction in risks arising from competitor actions. Another principal benefit that prompts many companies to vertically integrate is differentiation. A new concept that has emerged is value-added partnerships. In this form of integration, small firms come together and form a system. Here, each participating channel member performs a single channel function at a particular channel level. A horizontal marketing system is another approach that has gained widespread support. It is an arrangement within a distribution channel in which two or more firms at the same channel level work towards a common goal. In this system, the participating organizations usually operate in different segments and are unrelated.

The advantage of this type of arrangement is that the firms pool together resources and skills the others do not have, with the objective of exploiting the available market opportunity. Most companies operate through a strategic alliance or a joint venture. Hybrid channel systems develop when organizations begin to use a number of channels to sell their products. These channels include a direct sale force, direct mail, telemarketing, catalog selling, and retail selling. The advantages of using hybrid channels include better product promotion, reduction in transaction costs, increase in market and customer coverage, and the benefit of developing a customised approach to selling and distribution of products.

Designing hybrid systems involves identifying the tasks required to fulfill the desired objectives and then segregating the selling tasks and assigning them to the respective channels. Designing hybrid systems involves determining the channel characteristics, identifying the channel mix properties and selecting the number of channels that will bring about the desired outcomes. To effectively manage the hybrid channel system, the manager must be able to identify the source of any conflict, assess its magnitude, observe the reaction of customers and channel members, and analyse the time needed to solve the conflict. Modern information systems have enabled organizations to effectively manage the hybrid channels and avoid overlap of activities and draining of resources.

CHANNEL MANAGEMENT

Managing channels is one of the most important dimensions of businesses across the world for improving their value in the market. Customers are constantly on the look out for convenience and service, when purchasing goods. Effective channel management helps companies decrease costs and reach potential customers profitably. Effective channel management involves proper recruitment of channel members. Recruiting channel members should be a continuous process. In the recruitment process, screening involves elimination of applicants who do not match the criteria set for the position. After effective screening, the company has to make the final selection based on some criteria.

These criteria can be divided into sales factors, product factors, experience factors, administrative factors and risk factors. After selecting channel members, they have to be constantly evaluated and based on their performance, the company will either retain existing channel members or try to forge relationships with new channel members. Channel members can be evaluated by using parameters like sales quota attainment, average inventory levels, proper management of inventory, channel members'cooperation in promotional and training programmes, etc. The distribution requirements of a company will keep changing according to changes in the product life cycle. Modifying channels accordingly is essential for the success of the organization. However, care should be taken in dealing with channel members for proper channel management. Conflict management among channel members is another important activity for the management of the organization.

MANAGING CHANNEL CONFLICTS

All channels are based on the premise that anyone joining the channel and performing channel functions stands to benefit. Channel conflicts arise in channel systems when one or more channel members start perceiving the behaviour and actions of another channel member as an impediment to goal attainment. There are many sources of channel conflicts. They can originate from competing roles, clash of domains and differing perceptions of reality. Marketing channel strategies and channel structures are also important sources of conflict. Channel conflicts can be of different types. They can be primarily divided into pre-contractual and post-contractual conflicts and conflicts based on channel levels. Based on the timing of conflicts, they are divided into conflicts that arise before channel members enter into agreements and those that arise after channel members enter into agreements. Channel level conflicts may be vertical, horizontal or multi-level. To ensure effective coordination and channel functioning, different conflict management techniques can be used. They are primarily segregated into structural and behavioural conflict resolution strategies. Some commonly used strategies include negotiation, persuasion, problem solving, co-optation, arbitration and mediation.

Channel members can also resolve conflicts by exchange of personnel between channels and by association with different trade organizations. Channel power is also frequently used as a conflict management tool. Power sources are usually effective when wielded by channel leaders. Channel leaders can use referent, expert, legitimate, coercive and reward power to minimize channel conflicts. Creative and effective channel leadership result in channel members moving towards shared goals. If this ideal situation is achieved, distribution channels will be in a better position to satisfy the demands of target customers and maximize profits of individual channel members.

CHANNELS OF DISTRIBUTION MANAGEMENT

Still another method of judging the magnitude and complexity of the marketing task is by giving consideration to the multiplicity of channels through which products move from origin to destination.

CHANNEL OF DISTRIBUTION DEFINED

The course taken in the transfer of title to a product constitutes its channel of distribution. The title may be transferred directly, as when the product is bought or sold outright, or indirectly, as when the transaction is negotiated through a functional middleman such as an agent or broker who does not himself actually take title to it. It is the *route taken by the title to a product in its passage from its first owner*, the agricultural producer or manufacturer as the case may be, *to the last owner*, the ultimate consumer or the business user. The links in the channel or chain of distribution of necessity include both such owners inasmuch as they always participate to some extent in the marketing process.

Vertical Aspects

Normally, the channel of distribution is viewed vertically, that is, from the standpoint of the various *types* of links of which it is composed. It is concerned with the number of levels through which the title to goods is passed in the flow from source to final destination. For example, a manufacturer may sell direct to consumers, or he may utilize different types of middlemen who perform a variety of functions at different stages in the flow of title transfer. The most common vertical variations in channels for consumer and industrial goods, respectively.

The simplest channel is obviously that where manufac-turers sell direct to consumers. This is sometimes accomplished by those who make a wide line of related merchandise, the sales of which can support the operation of company-owned retail establishments. Stores operated by some manufacturers of paint or of men's clothing are illustrative. The direct channel is also used by manufacturers of articles that have qualities sufficiently distinctive to make possible mail-order sales.A third method of direct sale is through house-to-house salesmen.

A number of situations account for the manufacturer-retailer-consumer channel. Many manufacturers of men's and women's clothing sell direct to retailers, because the retailers handling such goods ordinarily purchase in fairly large quantities. This may be true because the stores are large. Vertical aspects of channels of distribution, illustrating channels commonly used by manufacturers of consumer and industrial goods, respectively.

The channel is also used by some manufacturers of perishable commodities. The meat packing industry is illustrative; here, sale to retailers through company-owned branches is common because of the financial strength of large producers and because of the special storage and handling requirements of the commodity. A less direct channel is to use agents or brokers to contact the retail trade. Such a channel is usually favored by small or specialized manufacturers who cannot afford to maintain their own sales organizations. Sales may be made more economically through agents or brokers because their costs of distribution are spread over the product lines of several manufacturers. This channel is generally used in contacting large retailing organizations, such as chain stores, department stores, and larger specialty stores.

The manufacturer-wholesaler-retailer-consumer channel is most common in the distribution of convenience goods to independent retail stores. Most manufacturers of tobacco, hardware, drugs, groceries, and other convenience goods have only a few products in their line of merchandise and cannot economically contact the thousands of retail stores needed for adequate distribution. Consequently, they call upon wholesalers who stock merchandise and cultivate the entire retail market, even in the remotest regions. Then there are numerous companies whose potential sales volume is so small or whose business is of such a seasonal nature that they cannot develop a sales organization to contact even wholesalers. This accounts in large measure for the use of agents and brokers who serve as substitutes for a manufacturer's own selling organization. In the canned fruit and vegetable industry, for example, many small manufacturers market through food brokers, who render a comparable service to other grocery product companies, including many flour millers and beet sugar refining companies.

In marketing business or industrial goods, direct manufacturer-user relationships are more common. Industrial installations usually involve sales of high unit value and require factory-trained sales engineers for effective sale and service. Semimanufactured goods, such as sheet steel and parts, like motors for washing machines, are usually sold in large individual contracts. Consequently, many manufacturers of such items are able to sell direct.

Producers of standardized equipment and tools of the type used in numerous factories often find it more economical to distribute through industrial wholesalers. Operating in a manner similar to the consumer goods wholesaler, but selling to industrial users rather than to retail stores, these organizations are to be found in all principal cities and are known by such terms as *industrial distributors, mill supply houses, equipment distributors*, and so on. Short-line manufacturers of industrial goods often use agents and brokers for the same reason that these functional middlemen are used in consumer goods marketing.

Marketing Establishments of Integrated Firms

An important vertical phase of channels—namely, the position of marketing establishments that are owned and operated by integrated companies. Examples are manufac-turer-owned retail stores, manufacturer-owned wholesale branches, warehouses, or petroleum bulk tank distributing stations, and retailer-owned wholesale warehouses.

According to a strict interpretation of the definition of the term *channel of distribution*, one may question the inclusion of such establishments in a discussion of channels. Actually, there is no *legal* transfer of title between factory and manufacturer-owned sales branch or retail store, nor is there any between the chain store warehouse and retail units in the same organization. Since, however, the census is taken on the basis of establishments and the information must be published for individual industries and lines of trade and by states and local areas, it is necessary that each reporting *unit* of a multiple-unit organization report as though it were operated as an independent establishment.

That procedure is followed by the Bureau of the Census, even when goods are transferred from one plant of a manufacturing company to another for further processing; and while they are designated as *interplant transfers*, they are viewed as in the nature of sales or shipments. Furthermore, manufacturers' wholesale branches and chain store wareho-uses operate similar to independent wholesale establishments of the same character, and manufacturers' own retail stores operate similar to independent or chain retail stores of the same type and character. *Functionally*, therefore, such establishments operating on the same level are fairly identical irrespective of differences in ownership. Failure to consider them as links in the chain of distribution would lead to confusion when comparing one channel with another or in comparing costs of distributing through alternative channels. From a practical standpoint, therefore, transfers of goods to different kinds of establishments within an integrated company must be considered in the nature of sales.

Horizontal Aspects

Many manufacturers also have important alternatives to consider with regard to the *horizontal* aspects of different levels in the channel. On any given level (wholesale or retail) there are many different kinds of establishments when classified by line of goods handled or by method of operation.

Although the situation varies considerably from one line of goods to another, the character of the problem may be illustrated with an example. Prepared baby foods were originally marketed as specialty goods and were sold chiefly through drugstores, because they were purchased by mothers upon the advice of pediatricians or general medical practi-tioners who prescribed feeding programmes for babies. When the first mass producer of such goods began to sell them through the grocery trade, a different channel was used even though it may have comprised the same types of links. More recently, this was illustrated by the change made by another manufacturer of such items who primarily produced drug merchandise and hence found it natural to sell also the few baby food items through such line of business.

This manufacturer originally distributed these products through wholesale drug firms who, in turn, sold them to the retail drug trade. As such products became more widespread in use, they were purchased by the housewife as convenience goods and mostly in retail grocery outlets. Because wholesale druggists did not have contact with retail grocery outlets, many wholesale grocers purchased the products from wholesale druggists and in this unnatural manner the items eventually found their way to the retail grocer.

The marketing pattern changed to such an extent that about 85 per cent of total consumer purchases of these baby foods was being made from grocery stores. When this was recognized by the manufacturer, a decision was made to simplify the channel of distribution by making the product directly available to wholesale grocery organizations. This change was fraught with real significance. National distribution was formerly accomplished by direct dealings at the most with only about 300 wholesale drug firms. Wholesale grocers, however, are much more numerous. It would be essential to contact at least about 3,000 such firms to provide dense nation-wide coverage among retail grocery outlets.

This called for basic marketing changes. Since it was not feasible for the manufacturer to expand his own sales organization to the extent necessary to handle such a large number of channel contacts, food brokers were employed to sell from the manufacturer to wholesale grocery organizations.

Thus, a decision to modify the channel horizontally on the wholesale level, by shifting from drug wholesalers to grocery whole-salers, was a channel problem of very great importance. Even in the absence of the introduction of brokers, the shift from drug to grocery wholesale outlets was of sufficient significance to constitute a change in the channel of distribution. Horizontal modifications of channels have become increasingly important. In former decades, it was rather common to find that there was a single natural channel for many kinds of commodities. Especially since the middle 1940's, however, there has been considerable diversification of merchandise lines by many kinds of stores. Many drug items, toilet goods, and housewares are now sold in food stores, especially of the supermarket type.

The modern large drugstore sells many items of general merchandise not formerly part of drugstore retailing. Many automobile accessory stores have become rather complete hard-line stores, handling all kinds of household appliances, hardware, lawn and garden supplies, and housewares. Such changes, sometimes popularly described as "scrambled merchandis-ing," have increased the complexity of horizontal aspects of many manufacturers' distribution efforts.

Other Channel Variations

There are additional reasons which complicate the channel question. Many manufacturers find it necessary or desirable to use more than one kind of channel (in the vertical or horizontal sense) for the same product. The vertical aspect is particularly true of commodities which have a double market. Automotive tires are an important example. That portion of the industry's output which is sold for original equipment on new cars is distributed direct from tire factories to automobile manufacturers. Tires for replacement equipment on cars on the road are sold principally through manufacturers' branches to retailers, or through regular wholesalers to retailers.

Some manufacturers have different products that require separate distribution channels. Illustrative is the meat packing industry. In addition to meat sales to retail stores, the industry is confronted with the problems of selling numerous types of by-products to different classes of customers, each of which poses a special channel-selection problem. Finally, some manufacturers find it feasible to use different channels in different parts of the country. Many manufacturers of factory machinery and store equipment sell direct to industrial consumers in regions where customers are highly concentrated but rely on manufacturers' agents for effecting sales in those areas where potential customers are widely scattered.

The foregoing discussion has been concerned with the distribution of manufactured goods. Channels for agricultural commodities involve a greater multiplicity of types of middlemen. Distribution of such goods is more complicated because they come from large numbers of small producers. In local growers' markets, various types of assembling middlemen are found. These include independent cash buyers of farm products, trucker-buyers, and the assembling agencies of cooperative marketing associations. Then there are also unique types of concentrating agencies in the major city wholesale markets. Of particular importance are the fruit and vegetable auctions found in a number of our leading cities.

Selection of Channels

It must not be assumed that every manufacturer has a wide range of alternatives to consider in selecting channels. Many middlemen, particularly wholesalers and retailers who handle a wide range of merchandise items, regard themselves as purchasing agents for a group of customers rather than as distributing organizations for manufacturers. At any given time, they are likely to be stocking what they consider to be the maximum feasible number of items in a particular classification. Thus, a manufacturer often finds it difficult to obtain distribution among new outlets. The point is that the channel of distribution may be determined as much by the middleman, acting as a buyer, as it is by the manufacturer, acting as a seller.

Another factor which limits freedom in selection consists of changes in consumer buying habits. The trend towards consumer buying of baby food items in food stores forced a drug firm to market its baby food items through such outlets, even though from a standpoint of operating convenience and utilization of an existing sales organization, it would have preferred to continue distribution through the drug trade. No manufacturer of a highly competitive product can maintain his historic share of market by confining his distribution to types of outlets which are of decreasing relative importance for a class of products. In the last analysis, the relative importance of different channels for consumer and industrial goods items is determined by the buying decisions of ultimate consumers and business purchasers, respectively.

Moreover, in some cases a variety of types of middlemen is not available. In certain lines, such as high-fashion apparel, wholesalers are of such limited significance that they do not constitute a practical alternative. In other cases, such as elaborate industrial machinery, the requirements of each potential customer are so unique that a direct manufacturer-to-user channel is dictated by unalterable circumstances.

Nevertheless, many manufacturing sellers have considerable freedom in channel selection. Whether to sell direct or to utilize the services of one or a number of types of middlemen is often a perplexing question of marketing strategy. The manufacturer may also be faced with determin-ing whether one channel will suffice, or whether two or more different channels are required because of differences in the products made or markets served. Finally, he may have to decide upon the kinds of business or lines of trade through which his goods should move, which will, in turn, determine not only the types of links to be used but the number of links. Cases abound where such decisions have been reached in a haphazard manner. To approach this problem scientifically, it is essential to know how various products are distributed and what factors govern the choice of given channels.

Policies of different vendors in the choice of trade channels vary widely. The authors have deemed it best to analyse and discuss such policies in connection with the treatment of each important marketing institution. This approach tends to make the presentation of marketing institutions more complete and rounded, it emphasizes the strategic role of customers in the determination of channels which is in line with modern concepts of marketing orientation, and it gives the study of trade channels a more realistic setting.

DISTRIBUTION INTERESTS: RETAILERS VS. MANUFACTURERS

Manufacturers of different kinds of products have different interests with respect to the availability of their products. For convenience products such as soft drinks, it is essential that your product be available *widely.* Chances are that if a store does not have a consumer's preferred brand of soft drinks, the consumer will settle for another brand rather than taking the trouble to go to another store. Occasionally, however, manufacturers will prefer *selective* distribution since they prefer to have their products available only in upscale stores.

Parallel distribution structures refer to the fact that products may reach consumers in different ways. Most products flow through the traditional manufacturer--> retailer —> consumer channel.

Certain large chains may, however, demand to buy directly from the manufacturer since they believe they can provide the distribution services at a lower cost themselves. In turn, of course, they want lower prices, which may anger the traditional retailers who feel that this represents unfair competition. Firms may also choose to utilize factory outlet stores. To allay concerns held by conventional stores, however, these factory outlet stores are usually located in areas where they are not easily accessible.

We must consider what is realistically available to each firm. A small manufacturer of potato chips would like to be available in grocery stores nationally, but this may not be realistic. We need to consider, then, both who will be willing to carry our products and whom we would actually like to carry them. In general, for convenience products, intense distribution is desirable, but only brands that have a certain amount of power—*e.g.*, an established brand name—can hope to gain national intense distribution. Note that for convenience goods, intense distribution is less likely to harm the brand image—it is not a problem, for example, for Haagen Dazs to be available in a convenience store along with bargain brands—it is expected that people will not travel much for these products, so they should be available anywhere the consumer demands them.

However, in the category of shopping goods, having Rolex watches sold in discount stores would be undesirable—here, consumers do travel, and goods are evaluated by customers to some extent based on the surrounding merchandise.

In general, a brand can expect lesser distribution in its early stages—fewer retailers are motivated to carry it. Similarly, when a product category is new, it will be available in fewer stores—*e.g.*, in the early days, computer disks were available only in specialty stores, but now they can be found in supermarkets and convenience stores as well. Certain products that are not well established may have to get their start on "infomercials," only slowly getting entry into other types out outlets.

Different parties involved in the marketing of products tend to have different, and often conflicting, interests:

- Full service retailers tend dislike intensive distribution.
- Low service channel members can "free ride" on full service sellers.
- Manufacturers may be tempted towards intensive distribution—appropriate only for some; may be profitable in the short run.
- Market balance suggests a need for diversity in product categories where intensive distribution is appropriate.
- Service requirements differ by product category.

Diversion occurs when merchandise intended for one market is bought up by a distributor that then ships it to a different market. Sometimes, a manufacturer will run a promotion in one region but not in another, and speculators will then buy extra quantity in the promoted area and ship it another area. The speculator will then sell it to local retailers or distributors for a price slightly lower than what is being charged through the regular channel but at a price that still allows a nice profit.

Certain products sell for different prices in different countries. As we discussed in the unit of international marketing, a gray market occurs when a product is bought in one country and exported to another where the price is generally higher. Both Louis Vuitton suitcases and golf clubs were imported to Japan, depressing prices there.

Recent retail trends: Over the past decade, there has been considerable growth in both extremes of the continuum from low price, low service to high price, high service retailers. There has been considerably growth both in the Wal-Mart *and* Nordstrom-type retailers than there has been in between.

For some time, during difficult economic times in the mid 2000s, discount stores like Wal-Mart actually tended to *increase* sales as consumers seemed to switch their purchases of the same products from higher priced to lower priced stores rather than reducing the quantity and quality bought in the product categories. It appears that consumers have done most of the switching that can be reasonably done this way already. More recently, Wal-Mart has felt more of an effect of weak economic times. Observations have been made that more and more customers seem to be running out of money at the end of the month.During the last two decades, there has been strong growth in the "category killer" chains which specialize in a moderate assortment of goods. Chains like Comp USA, Best Buy, Staples, Circuit City, Office Depot, and Home Depot—which were rare before the 1990s—have expanded rapidly and have captured a very large share of the market in their respective areas of emphasis.

These chains operate from two sources of strength:

- Although their total purchase volumes are usually smaller than those of the giants such as Wal-Mart and Target, these purchases are focused in more limited areas. Thus, the purchases of each "giant" account for a large proportion of the sales of many firms. Best Buy, for example, accounts for a large percentage of the sales of firms that make DVD players, TV sets, video games, and, to a lesser extent, computers and printers.
- The mega store chains will often negotiate very large contracts early in the purchasing cycle. Manufacturers are often willing to offer especially low prices to a buyer who will commit to taking large quantities well ahead of the time that these products are actually needed. This guarantees the manufacturers a certain volume—albeit at small margins—freeing the firm to commit to production and produce large quantities without having to worry about selling a large portion the production. Such deals often account for the very low sale prices that can be offered on select models in various product categories.

8

Retailing Management

INTRODUCTION

Retail consists of the sale of goods or merchandise from a fixed location, such as a department store, boutique or kiosk, or by mail, in small or individual lots for direct consumption by the purchaser. Retailing may include subordinated services, such as delivery. Purchasers may be individuals or businesses. In commerce, a "retailer" buys goods or products in large quantities from manufacturers or importers, either directly or through a wholesaler, and then sells smaller quantities to the end-user. Retail establishments are often called shops or stores. Retailers are at the end of the supply chain. Manufacturing marketers see the process of retailing as a necessary part of their overall distribution strategy. The term "retailer" is also applied where a service provider services the needs of a large number of individuals, such as a public utility, like electric power.

Shops may be on residential streets, shopping streets with few or no houses or in a shopping mall. Shopping streets may be for pedestrians only. Sometimes a shopping street has a partial or full roof to protect customers from precipitation. Online retailing, a type of electronic commerce used for business-to-consumer (B2C) transactions and mail order, are forms of non-shop retailing.

Shopping generally refers to the act of buying products. Sometimes this is done to obtain necessities such as food and clothing; sometimes it is done as a recreational activity. Recreational shopping often involves window shopping (just looking, not buying) and browsing and does not always result in a purchase.

Retail is India's largest industry. It accounts for over 10 per cent of the India's GDP and around eight per cent of the employment. Retail sector is one of India's fastest growing sectors with a 5 per cent compounded annual growth rate. India's huge middle class base and its untapped retail industry are key attractions for global retail giants planning to enter newer markets. Driven by changing lifestyles, strong income growth and favourable demographic patterns, Indian retail is expected to grow 25 per cent annually. It is expected that retail in India could be worth US$ 175-200 billion by 2016. The organized retail industry in India had not evolved till the early 1990s. Until then, the industry was dominated by the un-organized sector. It was a sellers market, with a limited number of brands, and little choice available to customers. Lack of trained manpower, tax laws and government regulations all discouraged the growth of organized retailing in India during that period. Lack of consumer awareness and restrictions over entry of foreign players into the sector also contributed to the delay in the growth of organized retailing. Foundation for organized retail in India was laid by Kishore Biyani of Pantaloon Retails India Limited (PRIL). Following Pantaloon's successful venture a host of Indian business giants such as Reliance, Bharti, Birla and others are now entering into retail sector.

A number of factors are driving India's retail market. These include: increase in the young working population, hefty pay-packets, nuclear families in urban areas, increasing working-women population, increase in disposable income and customer aspiration, increase in expenditure for luxury items, and low share of organized retailing. India's retail boom is manifested in sprawling shopping centers, multiplex-malls and huge complexes that offer shopping, entertainment and food all under one roof.

But there is a flip side to the boom in the retail sector. It is feared that the entry of global business giants into organized retail would make redundant the neighbourhood kiryana stores resulting in dislocation in traditional economic structure. Also, the growth path for organized retail in India is not hurdle free. The taxation system still favours small retail business. With the intrinsic complexities of retailing such as rapid price changes, constant threat of product obsolescence and low margins there is always a threat that the venture may turn out to be a loss making one.

A perfect business model for retail is still in evolutionary stage. Procurement is very vital cog in the retail wheel. The retailer has to fight issues like fragmented sourcing, unpredictable availability, unsorted food provisions and daily fluctuating prices as against consumer expectations of round-the-year steady prices, sorted and cleaned food and fresh stock at all times.

Trained human resource for retail is another big challenge. The talent base is limited and with the entry of big giants there is a cat fight among them to retain this talent. This has resulted in big salary hikes at the level of upper and middle management and thereby eroding the profit margin of the business. All the companies have laid out ambitious expansion plans for themselves and they may be hampered due lack of requisite skilled manpower.

But retail offers tremendous for the growth of Indian economy. If all the above challenges are tackled prudently there is a great potential that retail may offer employment opportunities to millions living in small town and cities and in the process distributing the benefits of economic boom and resulting in equitable growth.

DEFINITION AND SCOPE OF RETAILING MANAGEMENT

The word retail is derived from the French word "retailer", meaning "to cut a piece off" or "to break bulk". In simple terms, it implies a first-hand transaction with the customer. Retailing can be defined as the buying and selling of goods and services. It can also be defined as the timely delivery of goods and services demanded by consumers at prices that are competitive and affordable. Retailing involves a direct interface with the customer and the coordination of business activities from end to end-right from the concept or design stage of a product or offering, to its delivery and post-delivery service to the customer. The industry has contributed to the economic growth of many countries and is undoubtedly one of the fastest changing and dynamic industries in the world today.

ECONOMIC BASIS OF RETAILING

The role of retailing in our economic life is related to the values created in the retailing process and the marketing functions performed by retailing organizations as they produce such values.

CONCEPTS OF RETAILING MANAGEMENT

The terms "retailing," "retailer," and "retail store" are popularly used interchangeably and in a befuddled manner. Several questions may indicate the confusion that prevails. Is a sale "retail" because it was consummated in a retail store? Does a retail sale necessarily involve a small quantity of goods, a higher price than in a wholesale transaction, or a particular kind of merchant who effects the transaction? When a consumer buys from a business firm claiming to be a wholesaler and obtains a price lower than the ordinary retail price, is the consumer purchasing at retail or wholesale?

The variety of uninformed answers to such questions points to the need for considering the meaning of important retailing terms as authoritatively recognized. Carefully formulated definitions are a necessity for meaningful discussion and analytical study, for proper classification of quantitative data, and for various legal purposes, including matters of taxation and coverage of establishments under wage and hour legislation.

RETA]ILING AND RETAIL SALE

Retailing is an activity word and denotes selling at retail. Among authorities who have given the most serious study to the question, the consensus is that the only clear, sound criterion for distinguishing retailing from other business activity is the *status or motive of the purchaser. Thus, a retail sale is one in which the buyer is an ultimate consumer,* as opposed to a business or institutional purchaser, *and the motive is personal or family satisfaction stemming from the final consumption of the article being purchased,* in contrast with purchases for resale or for business, industrial, or institutional use. It is, however, impractical to obtain data pertaining to all such transactions. Insurmountable difficulties would be encountered in distinguishing retail sales from sales to business firms when a business user of a commodity makes a purchase of a small quantity of an item in a regular retail store and at the same price as paid by the ultimate consumer; consequently, such sales to business users are usually regarded as retail in character.

Retail Establishment

The composite of its transactions gives an establishment its principal character. A *retail establishment* is, therefore, *a single or separate place of business, principally engaged in the performance of marketing functions, wherein or out of which sales are made primarily to ultimate consumers.* In borderline cases such as are encountered in attempts to classify split-function establishments (*i.e.*, those that sell partly at retail and partly at wholesale), the classification is usually effected on the basis of the rule of more than 50 per cent of the dollar volume of business. Thus an establishment is considered as retail if more than one-half of its dollar volume of business consists of sales to ultimate consumers.

Retail Store

Most retail establishments are *stores* or *places of business open to and frequented by the general public, and in which sales are made primarily to ultimate consumers, usually in small quantities, from merchandise inventories stored and displayed on the premises.* Some retail establishments are operated by non-store retailing organizations. The major types in this category consist of mail order establishments, offices that serve as headquarters for house-to-house selling companies, and facilities from which vending machine operators conduct their businesses.

Retailer

Any person or business firm can own and operate a retail store or a retail establishment. The very great majority, however, are operated by retailers. *Retailers are merchant middlemen who are engaged primarily in selling to ultimate consumers.* Unlike manufacturers or farmers who may operate retail establishments, retailers specialize in retailing activities. They stand in the channel of distribution between manufacturers, farmers, or wholesale middlemen and ultimate consumers; they buy and assemble stocks of merchandise which they own and hold at their own risk and attempt to resell them at a profit.

Differences in Concepts

It is evident that distinct conceptions Underlie proper use of the terms *retailing, retail establishment, retail store,* and *retailer.* Retailing, the broadest conception, is the activity of selling to consumers for personal or household use. While most of this activity takes place through stores, it may be engaged in by anyone—for example, a farmer selling vegetables door to door, a wholesaler selling to a personal acquaintance, or a manufacturer selling direct to consumers by mail. Such retailing activities are not included within the scope of operations of retail establishments, which constitutes the basis for all Census of Business data presented in this part of the text.

On the other hand, many retail stores make some sales which are essentially wholesale because the goods are purchased by businesses for purposes of resale or for business use. Most retail stores are operated by retailers, merchant middlemen selling primarily to consumers, but this is not universal, for some are owned and operated by manufacturers, consumers, governmental agencies, and others.

PRODUCTIVE CHARACTER OF RETAILING MANAGEMENT

Retailing organizations add values to commodities principally through the creation of place, time, and possession utilities and, to a limited extent, by the creation of form utility. Place utility is added by bringing goods from wholesale markets to conveniently accessible stores and, in some cases, by providing delivery service to consumers. Time utility is provided by anticipating consumer wants and storing goods from time of receipt until time of consumer purchase. Retailers make a substantial contribution to possession utility by transferring the ownership from business organizations that have no use for goods other than trading, to ultimate consumers for whom value in use is high. Many kinds of retail stores engage in form utility production as is illustrated by food preparation in eating places, meat preparation and packaging in food stores, and the operation of drapery and clothing alteration workrooms in department stores. For the most part, however, the creation of form utility by retailers is incidental rather than the principal attribute of the organization.

MARKETING FUNCTIONS PERFORMED BY RETAILERS

In the process of creating economic values, most retailers perform all basic marketing functions, at least to some extent. *Buying* is an important function of merchants since they serve as purchasing agents and assemblers for their customers. This may be relatively simple or exceedingly complex. Some small appliance stores without repair service departments may have fewer than twenty different merchandise items in stock, and all of these may be obtained from one or two local wholesale distributors. In a modern supermarket there may be as many as 4,000 to 6,000 or more different items purchased or assembled from several hundred manufacturers and wholesale middlemen. At the extreme, a few large department stores carry more than 1 million different items in a wide variety of departments, and their buyers assemble merchandise from thousands of wholesale sources in almost all trade classifications. *Selling* is the basic reason for the operation of stores. In stores that sell merchandise of high unit value and low replacement frequency, major reliance is often placed on personal selling so that the product line can be interpreted to the consumer and selling can be adapted to circumstances that vary appreciably among individuals. Almost, all classes of stores engage in some form of advertising. Those that sell predominantly convenience or standardized goods tend to rely heavily upon non-personal selling effort, making sales from visual displays that permit self-selection by consumers.

The significance of the *transportation function* varies considerably. Small retailers in convenience goods lines tend to rely upon wholesalers for long-distance spatial movements from farms or factories to the local market and from the wholesaler to the retail store. Large retailers, especially chain and department store organizations, often arrange for transportation of merchandise from distant sources to their local warehousing facilities and operate their own transportation equipment for moving goods from warehouses to individual stores or departments. Consumers have tended to assume the transportation function in store-to-household movements of merchandise, as use of automobiles has increased and retail trade has become more decentralized within metropolitan areas. Delivery service remains of great significance, however, for stores that serve a large trading area or sell heavy or bulky merchandise.

The historical significance of the *storage* function is suggested by the designation retails "store." In an early era, when transportation and communication services were slow and uncertain, the major function of retailers was that of maintaining a storehouse of merchandise, but modern developments have placed more emphasis upon the retailer's role as a distributor or seller. Storage remains, however, a key function and its importance varies in relation to stock turnover which may be more than 50 times per year for meat markets but as low as once per year for some jewelry stores. The significance of storage varies also with special facilities that often must be provided. For example, while food-store turnover is high, the investment for all of the various types of refrigeration equipment required for a modern supermarket may amount to more than $50,000.

Many large retailers are concerned with *standardization* in that they set product specifications for items manufactured or packaged under their own brand names. Food stores often prepackage meat and fresh fruits and vegetables in standard units of sale. Some retailers confine their *financing* activities to providing an investment in fixtures, equipment, and inventory; but this is often supplemented by credit arrangements with wholesalers, manufacturers, and financial institutions. Many retailers finance purchases by ultimate consumers through charge account and installment sale credit. For some retailers like department stores that sell on credit, this function has assumed tremendous significance, so that much more may be invested in receivables than in merchandise inventories. Since retailers are merchant middlemen, they assume the *risk* associated with ownership of various assets including receivables and inventories. This is especially hazardous in fashion merchandising where the wants of consumers change seasonally and within seasons. Every retailer must analyse the needs of consumers by collecting and interpreting *marketing information* if his merchandise offerings are to be in harmony with their buying wants and the goods are not to stagnate upon his shelves.

The degree to which the total performance of any given marketing function is assumed by the retailer, is divided among other marketing institutions, or is assumed by consumers through self-performance of marketing activities, varies from time to time and with different kinds of business. The costs incurred and the values contributed by retailers thus shift from time to time, as some functions increase in importance and others decrease.

TOTAL RETAIL TRADE STRUCTURE

Some appreciation of the magnitude of the total retail trade structure and changes therein may be gained from a consideration of the dollar and physical volume of sales of all retail establishments, as related to trends in population growth, disposable income, and number of stores in operation.

Volume of Sales

Over some three decades covered by the Census of Business data in total sales of retail establishments fluctuated greatly with business conditions. In current dollars there was a decline from 1929 to 1939—years which, respectively, are regarded as highly prosperous and reasonably normal for the pre-World War II period. In more recent times, however, volume increased to such extent that 1958 sales in current dollars were 4.2 times the 1929 level.

Much of this variation is due to changing price levels. After adjustment by an appropriate price index to calculate *physical volume* in dollars of constant value, it is apparent that sales actually increased between 1929 and 1939. The long-run increase was much more moderate than indicated by data in current dollars. Physical volume in 1958 was 2.3 times that of 1929. This is, nevertheless, an increase that would have been regarded staggering in any preceding comparable period.

Much of the increase is due to expanded market opportunities. The physical volume of sales *per capita,* while relatively stable in short periods such as 1929-39 and 1948-58, increased markedly in the long run, being 60 per cent higher in 1958 than in 1929. This increase has been made possible by higher levels of real per capita purchasing power.

While varying somewhat from one census to another, the number of stores has been much more stable than sales volume, whether measured in current or constant dollars. During the 1930's, when the nation experienced its worst period of depression, the number of stores increased, but in the following years, marked by war conditions and high levels of prosperity, there was very little change in numbers, even though total physical volume of sales increased substantially.

In recent years the trend has been for an increase in the scale of store operations. Physical volume of sales per establishment in 1958 was more than twice that of the 1939 level. Such a development has resulted from enhanced efficiency in utilization of personnel and capital resources in retailing as a whole and in certain kinds of business in particular.

CLASSIFICATION OF RETAIL STORES

The same term, retail store, is used to refer to the vast R. H. Macy and Company department store in New York City and to the smallest cigar and newsstand operated in the lobby of a public building. Such a varied structure of retail institutions limits the extent to which it is possible to generalize about the totality. For proper understanding and evaluation of this structure and changes therein, it is essential to break it down into significant components through meaningful classifications, each of which may be studied by itself and in comparison with other segments with which it comes into competitive conflict or which may be deemed as socially or economically desirable alternatives.

It is possible to classify retail stores in an almost unlimited variety of ways, as illustrated by the outline of various alternatives. All of these classes are meaningful for some purposes, but it would be an endless and repetitious task to discuss all of them in detail.

OWNERSHIP CLASSES

Analysis of retail stores in terms of ownership classes has long been of great interest because this approach involves numerous competitive and other implications. Such a breakdown reveals what groups have an entrepreneurial interest in retailing and which tend to dominate the institutional structure. Certain legislative and tax questions are involved. Certain regulatory and tax legislation tends to preserve or fortify the status of some ownership classes while placing handicaps or limitations on others. Type of ownership often reflects differences in operation, especially with respect to financial structure, method of procuring merchandise, and the degree to which retail store operations are integrated with the performance of wholesaling and manufacturing functions.

Single-unit Independent Stores

Over a long period of years, the independent retailer who operates a single store has dominated the retailing structure. The importance of this ownership class is indicated by the fact that such stores have comprised 86 to 90 per cent of total retail establishments enumerated in the various Censuses of Business from 1929 to 1958. Even though "typical" independent merchants operate smaller stores than their chain competitors, they dominate in total sales volume. Over the same period, sales of single-unit independents have amounted to about 66 to 70 per cent of sales of all retail establishments. With only limited exceptions, single-unit independents are relatively small, family-type enterprises that operate solely or almost altogether on the retail level. In view of the visual prominence of chain retailers, as reflected by conspicuousness in shopping centers and advertising media, the persistence of the independent is indeed remarkable.

Chains or Multiunit Retailers

The major competitor of the independent is the chain. Multiunit or chain stores comprise about 10 per cent of all retail establishments counted in the Census of Business. Prior to World War II, the proportion of chain retail stores was somewhat higher, the decline being accounted for by the operation of larger scale establishments. Relatively, sales volume of chain organizations has been fairly stable in the long run, amounting to about 30 to 34 per cent of total retail trade, with some increase in competitive position in more recent years. About one-third of the total business of chains is done by fairly small multiunit organizations (ten stores or less) whose sympathies and outlook are in most respects more closely akin to the independent than to the large chain system. All but a small part of multiunit stores are owned by *retailers,* as opposed to manufacturers and other ownership classes.

Manufacturer-owned Stores

In certain lines of trade, independent and chain retailers compete with manufacturers who have integrated their operations forward in the distribution channel by the use of their own retail outlets.

Several reasons account for this practice. First, some manufacturers have opened stores in the belief that complete control over the entire marketing channel constitutes their most profitable alternative. This motive accounts for the presence of various well-known, manufacturer owned chains in the men's clothing, shoe, candy, and millinery lines of trade. Second, some manufacturer-owned stores are used to supplement other forms of distribution. Three of the best-known tire manufacturers operate company-owned retail outlets, but in no case do these constitute the company's sole outlets for tires and related automotive and household products. Such locations are usually established only in communities where there is an expectation of an unusually large volume of sales or where suitable independent outlets are not available. Third, a limited number of manufacturer-owned stores serve as experimental stations for testing product innovations or for developing merchandising methods or techniques that may be adapted for use by regular retailers. Finally, some manufacturers utilize their own retail establishments at factory locations in order to dispose of off-selected, rejected, or "stale" merchandise that is not salable through regular channels.

Expansion of retailing activities by manufacturers is limited by two major principles. First, manufacturer-owned stores are feasible only for well-financed companies that produce a relatively full line of related products, or products which are of relatively high unit value. In the absence of this condition, adequate sales volume cannot be obtained in a single retail establishment. As a corollary of this principle it has become apparent that successful manufacturer-owned stores usually function as merchant middlemen to some extent. Leading stores owned by men's clothing and tire manufacturers sell many items which are purchased from outside sources. Such goods are bought to round out the merchandise line, thus increasing sales volume per establishment and enhancing the efficiency of operation.

Second, many manufacturers who might prefer to develop some retail outlets are restrained by independent wholesalers and retailers, who object to such ventures as introducing unfair methods of competition. On certain occasions, the animosity of retailers has been so vociferous that attempts have been made to prohibit by legislation the operation of retail stores by manufacturers. Integration in marketing channels is now widely accepted, so that such public restrictions appear highly improbable. Fear of incurring "ill will" of regular outlets remains sufficiently strong, however, that it deters many manufacturers from engaging in retailing.

It is probable that the total of manufacturers' sales distributed through their owned retail stores does not exceed 2 per cent of the total of all manufacturers' sales distributed through all channels. To the extent that manufacturers make supplementary purchases from other sources, their retailing activities differ little from those of other multiunit retailers, except with respect to the major merchandise line of their own manufacture.

Farmer-owned Stores

Another ownership class consists of farmers, some of whom maintain roadside establishments or leased facilities in public retail markets. The character of such establishments often results in a misleading impression that they involve, principally or entirely, direct farmer-to-consumer marketing. It is practically impossible for farmers to operate a *regular* retail establishment *on a continuing basis* solely by the sale of their own produce. When an investment is made in physical facilities or when market space is leased, it is almost always necessary for the farmer to buy many items from other farmers and from regular wholesale sources. Experience has revealed that the typical farmer cannot afford to devote time and energy to retailing and expect the same returns that are afforded to him by concentrating on agricultural production and marketing his output through regular wholesale trade channels. Genuine direct retailing of farm produce is confined largely to seasonal and sporadic efforts. There is, for example, a considerable volume of roadside marketing during the home canning season for fresh farm produce. There is also evidence that farmers are most likely to resort to retailing as a desperation measure when prices are low or declining rapidly. So long as wholesale prices are adequate to cover the costs of agricultural production and afford the farmer a fair living, he is not likely to engage in the complex of activities necessary for satisfactory retailing.

Government-owned Stores

In a socialist commonwealth the government would own and operate business organizations for the benefit of the state. In the United States, however, the organization of practically all productive facilities reflects the democratic ideal of private competitive enterprise. Nevertheless, there are exceptional circumstances in which governmental units engage in retailing. Certain state governments maintain liquor stores: While such stores constitute an important source of government income, that cannot be considered as the motivating factor. The state has the alternative of levying excise taxes of any reasonable amount and could probably obtain the same or greater revenue on alcoholic beverages distributed through orthodox retail channels. State operation must then be viewed primarily as a device to effect social control of the distribution of alcoholic beverages. Another form of government stores consists of commissaries, post exchanges, and similar establishments often used in connection with military installations, for the purpose of providing a special type of "fringe benefit" to employees on military bases. It is estimated that all classes of government operated stores account for only about 1 per cent of total retail sales volume.

Consumer Cooperatives

A consumer cooperative is a marketing organization owned and operated for the mutual benefit of consumero-wners, who have voluntarily associated themselves for the purpose. Such an organization is an attempt to substitute joint or cooperative efforts of consumers for those of private enterprise. Properly speaking, *consumer* cooperation does not embrace cooperative dealings in industrial or business goods, such as farm supplies or equipment. There are, however, many farm cooperative associations that also handle consumer goods, and thus serve the farmers' interests as individual consumers, although such organizations are primarily concer-ned with the advancement of the interest of farmers as owners and operators of profit-making agricultural enterprises. The modern consumer cooperative movement dates from 1844 when a group of poverty-stricken English weavers opened a crude store in Rochdale. Out of their experience a set of basic principles was developed and these have governed most consumer cooperatives throughout the world. These so-called "Rochdale principles" highlight the character of consumer cooperation and distinguish it from retailing as carried on by private business organizations. In brief, they are as follows:

- *Membership is open to all* adult persons, without regard to political or religious affiliations or social status;
- *Democratic control* is achieved by providing all members with one vote, regardless of amount of capital stock owned;
- *Limited interest is paid* on capital investment in accor-dance with the view that capital is to be regarded as the servant, not the master, of the organization;
- *Sales are made at prevailing market prices* to accumulate a surplus to be distributed in lump sums to patrons;
- Services are limited, as exemplified by the policy of *selling only for cash*;
- Any surplus accruing from the spread between prevailing market prices and cost of merchandise and store operation is paid to members in proportion to their volume of purchases as *patronage dividends*;
- Consumer cooperatives are supposed to adhere to a policy of *religious and political neutrality*;
- Certain percentages of earnings are usually set aside for purposes of *education* in order that alleged benefits and ideals can be spread among non-members, thus expanding the scope of operations and influence. While such "principles" have been widely observed, some cooperative organizations have found it expedient to depart from them. For example, some have tried to attract a wider membership by selling at unusually low prices, offering some types of credit service, and others have worked actively for political candidates who favour consumer cooperation and by stimulating legislation favorable to the cooperative programme.

In certain European countries, consumer cooperation has achieved notable success, especially in England, Scotland, Wales, Sweden, Norway, Finland, Denmark, Switzerland, and Holland. By way of contrast, in the United States*strictly consumer* cooperative establishments (*i.e.*, excluding the operations of those primarily engaged in selling feed, farm supplies, and petroleum products for farm business use) account for only a small fraction of 1 per cent of total retail sales volume.

Considerable controversy about consumer cooperatives has resulted from the fact that "earnings" or "savings" distributed as patronage refunds are not treated as profits for purposes of income taxation. This, it is often alleged, gives the cooperative an unfair advantage compared to private enterprises that pay income taxes on all profits. Consumer cooperatives, on the other hand, have obtained judicial support for the view that patronage dividends are a refund of purchase price rather than profits, and they point out that they comply with income tax laws, the same as any other business, on profits paid to shareholders as a return on capital investment and on all other profits not distributed on the basis of patronage. In any event, the tax advantage is a relatively minor one which gives this type of organization little or no pricing advantage, even though it may operate to increase the amount of annual patronage refund accumulated on a member's total purchases. In the light of more than a century of experience with consumer cooperation, some explanation must be offered for the negligible part of this ownership group in the United States. For one thing, cooperatives in Europe achieved notable success in a competitive environment characterized by small, inefficient, tradition-bound, retail shops. In the United States, their success has been limited because consumers have had the opportunity to patronize chains and other limited-service retailers who have succeeded in attaining all types of economies sought by cooperatives. Second, in most European countries, the population has been more homogeneous in terms of heritage, social status, and religious affiliations, which has been conducive to cooperative effort.

In our country, the population of urban areas usually reflects a variety of occupations, social interests, and cultural values. This has made it difficult to assemble large groups of people who are favorably inclined to the cooperative movement. Third, under economic conditions favorable for the masses, the American consumer has had a higher level of real income, has felt much less need to "pinch pennies," and has preferred to shop in a wide variety of stores which afford him an exceedingly wide range of choice of novel and unusual merchandise as well as basic necessities. Indeed, the consumer cooperatives which have achieved most notable success in this country have tended to be the ones which have sought to serve their owner-patrons by having better or superior stores rather than by emphasis upon savings or economy alone.

When due consideration is given to the efficiency of our mass distribution retailing organizations and other circumstances that have limited cooperative development, it appears certain that consumer cooperatives will not become a significant competitive factor in our retail trade structure. Consumer cooperatives are, nevertheless, of considerable and continuing marketing interest due to various factors, including the following: distinctive ownership arrangement; idealistic objectives including operation for the economic benefit of patrons; rather substantial concentration in one line of trade, food stores; and conspicuous success in some localities, for example, northern Minnesota and Wisconsin, the Washington, D.C., area, and certain university communities such as Berkeley, California, and the Hyde Park area of Chicago.

EXTENT AND NATURE OF THE LINE OF GOODS HANDLED

Classification of stores on the basis of the extent and nature of the line of goods handled is useful because size, location, and, to a degree, merchandising methods are greatly affected by this factor. Three broad classes of stores are discernible:

General Merchandise Stores

General merchandise stores handles such an extensive variety of goods that they cannot be classified into some kind of business grouping designated by the name of a principal type of commodity. Stores within this broad group are of several distinct types, including general stores, department stores, dry goods stores, and variety stores. *General stores* are found chiefly in areas of scattered and isolated population, often as the only retail outlet in a small town or at some rural location. Such stores are usually small and non- departmentized. Among the principal commodities commonly sold are groceries, hardware, dry goods, notions, toilet goods, staple lines of apparel and furnishings. A gasoline pump and very limited automobile service facilities are often a part of such businesses. The general, store was once a very significant type of outlet but has greatly declined in importance due to population growth, urbanization, and increases in automobile use and highway improvements which have made larger shopping districts more accessible to rural residents.

Department stores are usually large urban retail institutions that handle a wide variety of lines, such as women's ready-to-wear and accessories, men's and boys' clothing, piece goods, small wares, and home furnishings. Merchandise is segregated into separate departments for purposes of promotion, service, accounting, and control. Because department stores normally serve a large trading area, they are usually located in downtown areas or in major secondary shopping districts of large cities. The distinguishing feature of department stores is *variety* of shopping goods offerings, organized departmen-tally. When the department store is operated on a sufficiently large scale, individual departments are as large as or larger than ordinary specialty stores and are characterized by breadth of assortment as well as variety.

Dry goods stores are similar to department stores in terms of merchandise handled, although home furnishings are often absent. They are classified separately because they do not meet certain department store classification criteria, including sale of all required merchandise lines, large scale operation, or departmental organization.

As the name implies, *variety stores* handle many different kinds of merchandise, mostly of low unit value. They were the first important type of institution to emphasize self-service methods of retailing. Operations are characterized by giving merchandise maximum open display, rather than by providing active personal selling assistance by salespeople. The role of the salesperson is that of maintaining the stock in order and handling the transaction for the consumer. These stores are still popularly known by their historical connotation, "5 and 10 cent stores," even though this term is no longer descriptive due to extension of price lines and greater emphasis on shopping goods. Originally, they were essentially convenience goods stores. They are generally situated at points of heavy concentrations of consumer traffic, and most of them are units of chain organizations.

Single-Line Stores

An extensive variety of one line of merchandise that is *related in sale or use* is the basis for classification as a single-line store. Such stores are usually designated in terms of the principal line of goods, such as groceries, drugs, hardware, men's clothing, furniture, or jewelry. In a men's clothing store, for example, a consumer expects to find all kinds of men's apparel including hosiery, shoes, underwear, shirts, neckware, suits, coats, and hats. Large assortments of any one of these kinds of merchandise are found only in fairly large clothing stores. Thus it may be said that the basis for the single-line store is related variety; wide assortments are dependent upon a scale of operation that permits an extensive inventory investment. When single-line stores operate on a very large scale, they are usually departmentized. This is especially true in the supermarket and chain drugstore fields, as well as in the furniture and apparel trades. Stores handling men's, women's, or family apparel and organized on a departmental basis are commonly known as "departmentized specialty stores." This gives rise to some confusion because the word "specialty" in this case is used to distinguish such stores from regular department stores rather than to denote the type of limited variety characterizing small specialty stores.

Historically, single-line stores tended to replace general stores as small communities grew in size. While their variety of merchandise is ordinarily much more limited than in stores of the general merchandise group, it is much more extensive than in the case of specialty stores.

Specialty Stores

This term refers to stores which handle an extremely limited variety of goods. In some trades, practically all establishments are of this highly specialized character. Examples include automobile dealers, gasoline service stations, florists, and book stores.

In other instances the specialty store handles only part of a line of goods customarily sold by single-line stores. Single-line grocery stores compete with specialty stores such as baked-goods establishments, dairy stores, and meat markets. In the clothing field single-line stores divide the market with specialty stores such as shoe stores, millinery shops, lingerie establishments, maternity dress shops, and furriers. Because specialty stores confine their offerings to a narrow range of items, they have more extensive assortments than single-line stores of comparable, size. A men's shoe store, for example, is a highly specialized operation in which the consumer expects to find a wide range of styles, colours, and prices in his size. The operation of a specialty store should not be confused with the sale of specialty goods.

The term "specialty" when used to designate a store implies limited variety of goods. These may be convenience goods as illustrated by cigar stands, they may be shopping goods such as apparel items, or they may be specialty goods such as automobiles, vacuum cleaners, or collectors' items as, for example, rare postage stamps. Specialty stores often have relatively simple buying problems in that most or all merchandise is drawn from one or few suppliers in the same trade. They have a competitive advantage over single-line stores in terms of assortments, but have a more limited opportunity for related, item selling. Specialty stores, for the most part, operate in well-established shopping districts.

Kind of Business Groupings

Single-line and specialty stores are not separately classified in Census tabulations, and it would probably be impossible to provide quantitative information about each of these two classes. For purposes of business use it is more desirable to classify both single-line and specialty stores within kind-of-business classifications. With the exception of the general merchandise group, all stores included in this table may be considered as single line or specialty. It is easy to distinguish certain single-line operations, such as grocery stores, from specialty establishments like meat markets or candy stores.

In other cases, such distinctions are not possible. One women's dress shop may handle a large variety of apparel, and be classified as a women's clothing store; another may specialize to the extent of selling only cotton dresses within a narrow price range, but still be grouped in the same classification.

Classification by Location

Classification of stores according to location indicates the extent to which retail trade is concentrated or dispersed, and it is indicative of consumer buying habits. Stores are found in

- Rural buying centers;
- Small cities or towns, in their downtown areas or in neighbourhood locations;
- Urban areas in a wide variety of specific types of locations. The distribution of retail establishments and sales volume corresponds rather closely with the distribution of population and disposable personal income among the largest metropolitan areas, other metropolitan areas, and the remainder of the country. Somewhat fewer

establishments are to be found in the largest metropolitan areas than would be expected on the basis of population and income, due to the location of many stores of unusually large size in such areas.

Sales volume is greater in the largest areas than would be expected on the basis of population, because of a tendency of major shopping goods stores to draw trade beyond the boundaries of the metropolitan area; it is less, however, than would be expected on the basis of income distribution, owing to a tendency for families of unusually high incomes (and with relatively low propensity to consume) to be concentrated in the largest population areas. The local character of retailing is well illustrated by the fact that outside of the 189 major metropolitan areas are to be found 43.0 per cent of the retail establishments, 32.7 per cent of the sales volume, 38.2 per cent of the population, and 30.3 per cent of the disposable personal income.

Retail trade has tended to become more localized than was formerly the case. Since 1929 the proportion of the total population residing in metropolitan areas has increased substantially, but the proportion of retail sales accounted for by such areas has remained constant.

As a result, per capita retail sales in non-metropolitan areas have risen faster than in metropolitan areas, and non-metropolitan areas have become relatively more important as trade centers than would be expected on the basis of their population importance. Among the plausible explanations for this situation are the following conditions:

- Changes in food purchasing patterns, reflecting increasing purchases of food store products for home use by farm families, and diminishing importance of home production for home use;
- Growing importance of brands as standards of value and increasing widespread distribution of most branded items of merchandise;
- Changes in consumer tastes and shopping habits which have tended to increase the number of items purchased on a local, or convenience, basis;
- General decline of the attractiveness of shopping in the central retail districts of major cities.

The local nature of retailing is also demonstrated by the dispersion of sales volume within metropolitan areas. Between 1954 and 1959 the proportion of retail trade transacted within the main city of the ten largest metropolitan areas declined from 61.0 to 54.8 per cent while the proportion of total sales in the remainder of such areas (consisting primarily of suburban communities which accounted for most of the population growth of the period) increased from 39.0 to 45.2 per cent..

Consumer Service Establishments

Any broad examination of the retailing structure must include some consideration of the hundreds of thousands of service establishments that market primarily to the ultimate consumer.

While such establishments are not included in the Retail Trade portion of the Census of Business, they operate on the same plane of distribution and are similar to retail stores in most other respects; moreover, service establishments that market to the general consuming public are recognized as being of the same essence as retail stores, for purposes of administering the Fair Labour Standards Act and have been so judged by federal courts. The sale of services produced upon the premises is the predominant characteristic of so-called "service establish-ments." Many, however, sell tangible commodities as well, either as part of the process of rendering a service (as supplies or parts used in shoe or automotive repair) or on a merchandising basis (as hair preparations sold in barber shops or bowling equipment and supplies sold in bowling places).

The magnitude of the structure of consumer or "retail" service establishments is suggested by the data. Such establishments, for the most part, can be classified according to the various bases previously outlined for retail establish-ments. In terms of ownership or location, for example, the same classifications used for retail stores are appropriate for consumer service establishments. By line or kind of business, however, most partake of the attributes of specialty stores, as opposed to single-line or general merchandise establishments, due to the lack of variety of offerings at a given place of business.

Other Classifications

The foregoing discussion of classifications of retail stores has revealed many varied characteristics of our retailing structure. It has not been sufficiently detailed, however, to present all significant institutional developments. Consequen-tly, additional classifications in connection with analyses of small- and large-scale retailers, department stores, chain stores and voluntary chains, supermarkets, planned shopping centers, discount houses, mail order companies, house-to-house selling organizations, and vending machine operations.

THE RETAIL PARTICIPANT GROUPS IN A RETAILER'S ENVIRONMENT

Central to the retailer's marketing concept is the customer. To satisfy customer needs and wants an organization must comprehend the nature of their relevant customer base. Useful for this purpose is the segmentation of the customers into logical groups, for example geographic regions or purchase frequency.

STAFF

The majority of interactions between staff and customers have until recently required at least one physical exchange of communication in the presence of both parties. Improvements and the increased availability of telecommunications technologies has enabled more of these communication exchanges without the need for either party to see, or hear speech from, the other party. Such a change in communications operational procedures often provides reduced transaction costs for the retailer, though it does require a revision of staff operations and training to successfully support the customer transactions.

Shareholders

Persons owning shares in a retailer require information on the operation and strategy of the organization to be able to monitor the investments. In the pre-online era, the shareholder was restricted to information from printed annual reports, the annual general meeting, direct mail and telephone enquiries made to the retailer.

Now, with the Web, the shareholder may interact with the retailer by monitoring the retailer's web site for breaking news, by exchanging e-mail correspondence with retailing staff, and by exchanging comments with other shareholders through online newsgroups.

Suppliers, Partners and Dealers

Operation of retail activities is not done in isolation. Retailers require business suppliers and stakeholders to provide merchandise supplies, financial systems, logistics, legal advice and ancillary services. Online architecture made up of the Internet and electronic data interchange systems enable the business suppliers and partners to keep the stakeholders informed of activities with a minimum of delay and thereby permit quicker responses and feedback.

Community

The community is composed not only of current and prospective shoppers but also individuals and groups that will exert influence upon others who will in turn determine the operating environment of the retailer.

Growth in community awareness of environmental, ethical and social welfare issues leads to greater attention being paid to business operations. Members of the community seek to acquire information on the activities of retailers and any potential negative effects on the environment, such as the use and disposal of packaging waste.

Organizations can use Internet information facilities (*i.e.* web pages or newsgroups) to provide public relations communications to emphasize positive corporate environmental issues and counter negative impressions held by the community.

From interactions with these five retail participant groups, the retail organization may anticipate positive or negative outcomes that will be quantitative or qualitative. Quantitative outcomes in the business environment are most readily revealed as the number of units sold, the revenue figures generated, returns on investment and company share price. Not as easy to measure, though still essential to the successful operation of a business, are qualitative outcomes. Examples of qualitative outcomes include customer loyalty, client satisfaction, employee loyalty, corporate image and supplier confidence.

Categorizing e-retailing Business Models

For the e-retailer to integrate the needs of the five retail participant groups, adapt to the merchandise mix offered and still meet the business objectives, the e-retailer may select from a variety of business models. Initially, the e-retail business models are categorized by 'distribution channel', that is, how the customers will access the retailer's merchandise mix. Following this, the business models may be categorized by the 'revenue stream' used to maintain the sales activity for the retailer.

DISTRIBUTION CHANNELS

The logistics for the retailer and prospective customer to establish contact and achieve an exchange of merchandise for payments have not always required a physical store. Apart from the physical bricks and mortar store, the retailing channel is also achievable through 'direct retailing' and online through a 'virtual retailer'.

Virtual Retailer

The introduction of commerce on the World Wide Web gave rise to the development of a new retailing form, the pure Web-based retailer, also known as a 'virtual retailer' or 'pureplay e-retailer'. Perhaps the best-known virtual retailer is Amazon, which started selling books over the Web in 1995. The virtual retailer enables Internet users to participate in retailing activities previously restricted to store-based retailers, *i.e.* product and price comparisons and payment systems, but in a speedier and more convenient manner.

Bricks and Mortar Retailers

With the establishment of the virtual retailer came a renaming of the traditional retailer to accommodate the e-commerce environment. Retailers retaining a physical store presence are now termed bricks and mortar retailers. A significant difference between the virtual retailer and the bricks and mortar retailer is the ability of the prospective bricks and mortar retail customer to physically inspect store merchandise before making a purchase and exiting the store.

Direct Retailers

'Direct retailers' have utilized a variety of distribution methods to provide a retail space for the customer. Examples of direct retailers have included catalogue marketing since the 1800s, *e.g.* the Sears catalogue; door-to-door selling, *e.g.* Avon since the 1960s; telephone shopping since the 1970s, *e.g.* Lands End (www.landsend.com); and 24-hour television shopping since the 1980s, *e.g.* QVC (www.qvc.com).

Categorizing Hybrid Retailers

Marketers today are not restricted to just bricks and mortar, direct and virtual categories of retailing. In between these categories are the three hybrid forms of retailing: the 'clicks and bricks retailer', the 'catalogue retailer' and the 'digital retailer'.

Clicks and Bricks Retailer

The clicks and bricks retailer has a physical store for consumer shopping and also conducts Web-based retail operations through the Internet. In the majority of cases, such a retailer originally transacted business as a bricks and mortar retailer, *e.g.* Harrods, then adopted the Web for additional sales coverage. In other cases, an established direct retailer or virtual retailer, *e.g.* Dell computers, will establish a store-based retail outlet to provide potential customers with the opportunity to physically examine merchandise.

As such, the retailer counters one of the leading objections to online purchases - the inability to personally view and inspect items before making a purchase.

Catalogue Retailer

Portal-based catalogue-marketing companies have been very successful in meeting their marketing and sales objectives. By developing web sites that are online representations of printed brochures and catalogues, the catalogue companies are able to widen their distribution network without replacing or alienating their postal clients.

The positive outcomes in this channel are reduced distribution costs; the expansion of the potential customer base; and speedier, more convenient, feedback to prospective clients.

Digital Retailer

Consumer access to the Internet has provided a logical environment for the distribution and exchange of items that are deliverable in a digital form. Currently, popular digital items sold by retailers over the Internet include recorded music and computer software. While visiting a digital retailer's web site, the Internet user may sample such items, *e.g.* hear the music or trial software, before making a purchase decision. Once happy with the sampled digital product, the Internet customer may download the complete digital product and arrange for payment.

REVENUE STREAMS

Customer-centred e-retailing business models are often categorized by the revenue stream achieved by the online retailer. The four revenue business models are based on advertising, merchandise sales, transaction fee and subscriptions.

Advertising-based e-retailing

The retailer generates revenues by selling advertising space on their web site. As one of the original revenue models of the Internet, portals such as Yahoo! have charged third parties a flat fee for placing an advertisement on their web page or charge for each visitor who clicks on the advertisement.

This is known as the 'click-through' rate to a third party's web site. A few years ago this service caused complaints from Web users about invasion of privacy, to which Double Click responded with a revised Privacy Policy that has placated much of this criticism and maintained the organization's competitive advantage.

Merchandise Sales e-retailing

As with the traditional bricks and mortar retailer, this revenue business model produces revenue from the sale of the retailer's merchandise over the Web, *e.g.* Sanity (www.sanity.com.au) selling recorded music.

Transaction fee e-retailing

Similar to the concept of brokerage, retailers may charge a third party for the marketing of merchandise to the retailer's customers. The most successful Internet example of transaction fee e-retailing is eBay (www.ebay.com), where the auction facilitator receives a fee once the successful bidder has finalised an online auction using eBay's online technology.

Subscription e-retailing

An adaptation of direct marketing, the subscription-based e-retailing revenue model allows consumers to access merchandise facilities, usually in a digital form, and through a subscription, *e.g.* the *New York Times* (nytimes.com) for Web-based archival news stories.

ASSESSMENT OF THE FIT BETWEEN ORGANIZATIONAL OBJECTIVES AND THE BUSINESS MODELS

In selecting the business model suited to a retail operation, the retailer will initially assess their marketing and sales objectives for the three principal retail channels: bricks and mortar, direct retailers and virtual retailers. Note that objectives are *samples* and not an exhaustive list.

Scoring the Retailer's objectives for Customers

The potential for a retail channel to meet the individual objectives for customers is assessed on a scale of 1 to 5. A retail channel with little potential to meet an objective scores 1 increasing to 5 for a retail channel with a high potential to meet the customer objectives.

The structure of each retail channel and the method of accessing the channel's target audience provide advantages for communicating certain information and appealing to certain human senses. For communicating information that appeals to the customers' senses of sight, sound, touch, taste and smell, there is currently no better medium than the face-to-face interaction possible in a physical retail store. This conclusion is reinforced by the 20/25 score for the bricks and mortar retailers. Restricted to audio and static visual images, direct retailers cannot provide moving images of new products or a tactile experience for a customer and this resulted in a score of 16/25. Encouragingly, research into direct retailing shows that such customers often retain the retailer's marketing correspondence to be reread in the future. Such correspondence may include details (*e.g.* retailer achievements) often overlooked while browsing in a retail store or un-clicked on the retailer's web site.

Though computer software and hardware facilities for the Web are improving to encompass audio, video and tactile reproductions of the real world, the experience is still not a replacement for the communication facilities and immediate feedback of the store environment. As an advantage over the direct retailers, the virtual retailer's ability to include moving video and online search facilities enables improved demonstration ability for merchandise offered, giving the virtual retailer a score of 18/25.

Globalization created by the Internet means that many retail names formerly restricted to domestic markets have become internationally recognized brands. While some retailers have attempted to establish a physical bricks and mortar presence in overseas markets, the logistical costs and unique requirements of the overseas locations has for some retailers resulted in major losses and eventual withdrawal from the overseas market.

Direct retailers have utilized the well-established international postal and courier systems for decades. With little more than a sales orientation, many direct retailers have accepted orders from overseas customers, packaged the orders and passed the distribution responsibility to transport groups such as DHL (www.dhl.com) or FedEx (www.fedex.com). The transport groups arrange pickup of the packaged merchandise, export documents, customs clearances, final delivery and, in some cases, payment clearances. For a small direct retailer, such international sales provide new market revenues without a major investment in logistics infrastructure, *i.e.* a specialized international shipping group. A drawback for the direct retailer is not being known by potential customers in other parts of the country and overseas. Many of us have turned to the phonebook to look for a supplier, but what if you don't have every phonebook in the world? The answer is turn to the World Wide Web and use of search engines. The Internet has given every person with access to the Web an access to every virtual retailer, as testified by the meteoric growth of Amazon (www.amazon.com) from being the seller of books to a few avid readers to becoming one of the largest book and video retailers in the world, and all this exclusively online. Worldwide access to the Web is now so entrenched that successfully established direct retailers such as Lands End (www.landsend.com) established sophisticated order-taking web sites and integrate sites into the retailer's marketing and distribution plans as an added retail channel.

Scoring the Retailer's Objectives for Staff

The potential for a retail channel to meet the retailer's objectives for staff is assessed on a scale of 1 to 5. A retail channel with little potential scores 1, increasing to 5 for a retail channel with a high potential to meet the individual staff objectives. The same score of 15/15 for staff objectives? It is because that, no matter what retail channels a marketer uses, staff must be prepared to provide the finest service possible within the constraints and advantages of that channel. Consider negative perception of a prospect should they ask a question concerning the exchange policy of the retailer's staff (face-to-face, by mail or through a web site) only to receive the reply 'I don't know' and without the follow up 'but I will find out and get back to you by (x period)'. Quality support systems are also essential in all retail channels because it is the retailer's personnel who receive the ire of annoyed prospects when an electronic system (*e.g.* web site or ordering facility) fails.

Scoring the Retailer's Objectives for Shareholders

The potential for a retail channel to meet the retailer's objectives for shareholders is assessed on a scale of 1 to 5. A retail channel with little potential scores 1 increasing to 5 for a retail channel with a high potential to meet the individual shareholder objectives. The immediacy of response and round-the-clock access of the Internet places the virtual retailer in an enviable position for providing shareholders with detailed information as demonstrated by the 15/15. Unlike the brief summaries of financial and business information conventionally available in an annual report, Web-based documents may incorporate interactive graphics and video to display information for more impact upon the shareholders.

Not all shareholders will be retail customers and therefore exposed to the marketing communications provided by both bricks and mortar and direct retailers. To inform their shareholders these retailers traditionally use printed media and call-centre responses to shareholder enquiries, therefore giving both retail channels a score of 9/15. Though effective, such methods have high labour costs and are slower to update when compared with information storage and retrieval from Web-based retailing.

Scoring the Retailer's Ofor Suppliers, Partners and Dealers

The potential for a retail channel to meet the retailer's objectives for suppliers, partners and dealers is assessed on a scale of 1 to 5. A retail channel with little potential scores 1, increasing to 5 for a retail channel with a high potential to meet the individual supplier, partner and dealer objectives. Using the series of objectives and totalling the scores for each retail channel, the maximum potential score is 15.Synchronizing data records between the retailer and their suppliers, partners and dealers is essential to avoid such errors as:

- Missed or duplication of orders;
- Misdirected correspondence to personnel or addresses that have changed;
- Non-compliance with legislation (*e.g.* government reporting schedules);
- Missed targets (*e.g.* end of month summaries or sale dates).

Direct retailers have honed their record systems to finalize sales and associated records in the absence of physical customers to score a total of 10/ 15. When disputes with customers and suppliers do occur, it may take time for the direct retailers to consult and correlate the electronic and manual record systems. Bricks and mortar retailers also pay a great deal of attention to the daily summarizing of financial exchanges. Though important, third-party contact records (*e.g.* contact names at suppliers or shipping agents) may not be updated as regularly nor carry the same level of priority customer interactions and this lessens the overall score to 9/15. By the nature of their operational environment, virtual retailers depend upon efficient real-time data exchanges through the Internet network, which itself depends upon detailed and automated record-keeping of transmitted information. Such an improved information exchange with the relevant parties gave the virtual retailer a higher score of 13/15, assuming e-retailers and their third-party partners regularly update and utilize the pertinent data over the Internet.

Scoring the Retailer's Objectives for the Community

The potential for a retail channel to meet the stated retailer's objectives for the community is assessed on a scale of 1 to 5. A retail channel with little potential scores 1, increasing to 5 for a retail channel with a high potential to meet the individual community objectives. An integral component of modern marketing plans is keeping the community informed about the direction and intentions of the retailer. For each retail channel, there are alternative communications media to carry messages to the relevant community. The current communications media available to the bricks and mortar and direct retailers include print (*e.g.* newspapers) and broadcasting (*e.g.* television). Though extensive, such media may not reach every community person who has a stake in bricks and mortar and direct retailer channels and this restricts the total scores to 8/15 and 9/15 respectively. In communications to the community, the virtual retailers have an interactive advantage over the other two retail channels. The e-retailer's web site may incorporate a series of messages to support their objectives for the community in a more convincing manner. Helping to communicate these messages through the web site and achieving a score of 15/15, the retailer may include any of these online facilities:

- Hyperlinks to relevant web sites
- Live footage (webcams streaming video)
- Storage of printable documents (*e.g. Adobe Acrobat* format)
- Interactive games
- E-mail exchanges.

As shown, each of the retail channels - bricks and mortar, direct and virtual - have varying degrees of suitability to meet organizational objectives. By summing the scores for each objective and each channel, the retailer will identify the retail channel with the greatest opportunity for marketing plan success. To reiterate, the objectives for the five retail participant groups are *samples* and *not* an exhaustive list for all retailers; the unique environments facing the retailers may require them to add or remove objectives.

Taking the results for each set of sample objectives, the results are 59/85 for direct retailers, 61/85 for bricks and mortar retailers and 76/85 for virtual retailers, placing the virtual retailer in the most effective position to meet the sample of objectives for the five retail participant groups. This does not restrict the retailer to a single channel.

The growing consumer acceptance of electronic shopping is allowing traditional retailers to expand into multiple retailing channels. To do this and provide the greater likelihood of meeting the retailer's multifaceted objectives, the channels chosen should be in order of their scores, which for this set of objectives is virtual retailing, followed by bricks and mortar retailing and finally direct retailing. Concentrating on the virtual retailer, the next stage is to gauge how suitable merchandise is for this particular retail channel.

DYNAMIC ADJUSTMENTS IN CATALOG RETAILING

The inception and period of rapid early development of mail order retailing was associated with the concept of a new merchandising service to the non-urban population. In modern times, with contemporary conditions of communication, transportation, and urbanization, it is indeed remarkable that catalog retailing (as measured by Census of Business data for the period 1929-58) has been able to hold a stable share of total retail sales, thus growing at the same rate as all of retailing. This is attributed to certain dynamic, and in some cases distinctive, methods and policies adopted by the general catalog houses—in large measure for the purpose of capitalizing upon their advantages, minimizing their limitations, and adjusting to changing consumer preferences.

Sales promotion activities are efficiently organized. Mailing lists are prepared with care and efforts are made to keep them up to date. Careful tests are made of the success of different types of copy and appeals. Experienced copy writers know the language and the appeals which are most useful in reaching their clientele. In order to overcome the reluctance of buyers to purchase articles which they cannot see before the order is placed, mail order houses give a very liberal guaranty, covering as a rule both quality and price.

If the purchaser is dissatisfied with the commodity, it may be returned at the expense of the seller, and the purchase price is promptly refunded. The general catalog houses have a special brand problem. To attract business, as they do in part, on a price-appeal basis, they must purchase from suppliers at lowest prices. For this reason such houses do not generally carry very many nationally advertised, branded articles. They prefer to sell unbranded commodities or those which carry their own brand. It is usually necessary to brand the specialties which they sell, in order to identify them and give them a certain distinction. Hence it is common for catalog houses to purchase such articles as vacuum sweepers, gasoline engines, washing machines, farm implements, cosmetics and drugs from suppliers who manufacture to the specifications of the catalog firm and who attach to the goods the private brand of the mail order company.

In order to reach a larger number of potential customers, the major firms have opened a large number of catalog order offices which are located in storerooms in hundreds of small cities and in many suburban shopping centers of large cities.

No merchandise is available for sale over the counter in these establishments, but selected items and swatch and sample books are displayed for examination. Employees assist customers to make out and transmit orders. Many such order offices have teletype communication with a regional warehouse which services the area. Orders received prior to a certain time each day can be delivered to the customer's home on the following day in most cities, thus rivaling the speed of delivery service available from local stores. Similar catalog departments are also found in the regular retail stores operated by mail order companies. In the typical Sears' store, the catalog order desk is usually the largest sales volume department.

Some catalog companies have expanded their customer contact points by establishing order stations in retail establishments operated by other companies. Certain small-town and cross-roads stores have displayed the general merchandise catalogs of some companies for a number of years, and accept and process orders on a commission basis. More recently some variety chains and supermarket organizations have made similar arrangements with mail order firms. For example, in 1960, Ward's established catalog order stations in certain New York state supermarkets of Loblaw, Inc., thus giving Ward's sales outlets in areas where it had no retail stores, and providing the Loblaw organization with a 100,000 item increase in its offering of non-food merchandise lines. Another feature is the operation of telephone order offices.

While confined to larger cities in which there is a considerable potential volume of daily business, this development is one of increasing significance, accounting in 1960 for more than 30 per cent of all catalog sales volume at Sears'. The catalog customer can sit in her home, order by number from the catalog, have her order dispatched by teletype as explained above in connection with catalog order offices, and receive next-day delivery in many large cities.

As a consequence of such innovations, the historic *mail order business* has evolved into a more modern conception of *general catalog retailing*, characterized by efforts to bring to the consumer wanted merchandise at various points of sales contact, using means of communication and delivery which are appropriate to contemporary conditions.

Catalogue Selling by Store Retailers and Manufacturers

Mail order selling is used to some extent by specialty retailers and by certain manufacturers who sell direct to the consumer. It is also used in the direct marketing of some farm products with a special appeal, such as Smoked Virginia Hams, smoked turkeys, and gift packages of fruit. Such sellers usually do not have elaborate catalogs, but secure orders by advertising in newspapers and magazines, on radio and television broadcasts, and by direct mail addressed to the homes of consumers.

Goods so ordered are shipped by parcel post, express, truck, or ordinary freight. This type of selling brings many kinds of goods to the attention of a broad market. Items so sold are often of a novel or unusual character and are not available in local stores, especially in smaller communities. Some merchandise is sold direct to consumers by manufacturers who stress a price appeal.

While specialty mail order retailing is relatively expensive, since it usually involves substantial advertising and handling and shipping costs, many consumers are nevertheless influenced by an appeal which suggests that they save money by purchasing direct rather than from a retail store. Appeals of "lower prices," "greater values," or "substantial savings," have been used by most of the major book and record club companies that have a membership which is contacted by mail. Such savings are customarily offered in terms of "free" or "bonus" books, awarded when the member actually purchases a predetermined number of books at regular prices, in accordance with a membership agreement. Bonuses offered in this manner are largely due to low purchase prices negotiated with publishers when contracting for large numbers of copies and not to economies of selling and distributing to individual consumers on a mail order basis. Manufacturers and retailers who sell a narrow line of goods by the mail order method are subject to most of the disadvantages enumerated above in connection with general catalog houses. In addition, they usually lack the prestige enjoyed by a large nationally known organization. Hence, such selling is relatively unimportant, and there are no reasons to believe that it will ever be of much significance in other than a very narrow range of merchandise items. Catalog selling is also an important form of supplementary promotional effort among many regular *store retailers*, especially large department stores and departmentized specialty stores, who have a ready-made mailing list consisting of their regular charge account customers. This is especially significant for the promotion of gift merchandise during the Christmas shopping season.

MAIL ORDER AND CATALOG RETAILING

The number of firms operating exclusively on a mail order basis is relatively small, but this method of operation is sufficiently widespread to justify detailed consideration. Moreover, it represents a distinctive way of doing business and illustrates the effect of changing conditions upon retailing institutions.

TYPES OF ORGANIZATIONS

Four distinct types of organizations sell by mail. The most important are the general merchandise mail order houses which sell a great variety of consumer and farmer goods, carrying more items than are sold by any department store. Such companies are primarily retail institutions. They purchase the majority of their goods from manufacturers, although the two biggest companies in this field— Sears, Roebuck and Company and Montgomery Ward and Company—both control the manufacturing of many private brand items. A second type consists of specialty retailers. Kinds of business in which specialty mail order operations by retailers is of some signficance include books, home furnishings, apparel and apparel accessories, food, and automotive accessories. Manufacturers who sell by mail constitute the third type of mail order institution. Some such producers have found that their particular products can be sold directly to the consumer by mail without the use of wholesalers or retailers. The fourth type of mail order retailing is carried on by certain department and other large stores which accept orders by mail. Primarily confined to orders for merchandise currently advertised, this type of selling is a supplement to the receipt of orders over the telephone.

History of Mail Order Retailing

Mail order selling arose in a number of ways. Montgomery Ward and Company was founded in 1872 by a former clerk in Chicago who had also worked as a traveling salesman. The Patrons of Husbandry (the Grange) had established a number of cooperative stores and needed a wholesale connection. Mr. Ward saw the opportunity and started the business which still bears his name. The Grange stores were not generally successful so Mr. Ward's business was expanded into a mail order house to take advantage of good will among former members of the cooperative stores.

Sears, Roebuck and Company, the largest mail order firm, grew out of the efforts of Mr. Sears, a small-town station agent in Minnesota, to sell watches which had been shipped to his station on approval but rejected. The success of this venture led to a watch and jewelry mail order house in Minneapolis which was later moved to Chicago. The present largescale enterprise has grown from this small part..

Other general mail order houses had varied beginnings. Many have expanded from ordinary retail stores. Others started as specialty mail order houses and gradually expanded until they handled a more general line of merchandise. Probably the most important reason for the success of the mail order houses in the early stages of their development is to be found in the failure of country merchants to adjust to changing conditions. In the post—Civil War period the country general store was a dominant institution. Throughout the West and South, farmers and small-town residents raised their standards of living after the period of reconstruction. Cash farm income became larger and farmers became interested in the kinds of things bought by city people. Rural and small-town merchants, however, did not appreciate such changes and continued to stock only staple merchandise which had sold well for many years. Even if such merchants had realized the significance of environmental change, the limitations of their small, local markets would have made it impossible for them to rival the assortments of the evolving mail order institution.

Another factor contributing to the development of mail order retailing was the growth of rail transportation. This made it possible to place orders by mail and to deliver merchandise to scattered areas at reasonable cost and at relatively certain dates. The spectacular and consistent development of mail order retailing began, however, with the establishment of rural free delivery service. Farmers as a class began to subscribe for city daily papers. They were thus reached by style news and by information on various changing methods of life which before had come to their attention only indirectly. Later, the moving pictures and the rotogravure supplements of the newspapers exercised their effect in creating demand for many articles not previously included in the rural standard of living. Mail order retailing offered an opportunity for the purchase of these goods. Developments in catalog making made it possible to advertise goods effectively and to supply realistic photographs. Establishment of the parcel post system in 1913 made it possible to ship small packages more economically. Another factor in the growth of mail order houses was the recognition that this method of selling could take advantage of the economies of large-scale retailing. The larger mail order companies engaged in programmes of diversification as the country became more urbanized and opened many retail establishments of the department store type. Such stores now account for the majority of the business of both Sears' and Ward's, but mail order or catalog retailing continues to be a very large segment of their total sales volume.

Present Status of Mail Order Establishments

In 1958 there were 2,550 retail mail order establishments, of which 1,502 had paid employees and 1,048 were small units operated exclusively by proprietors and family members. Aggregate sales volume of these establishments amounted to $20 billions, or about 1 per cent of the sales of all retail establishments. There has been practically no change in the relative sales volume importance of mail order establishments over the period 1929-58. While the 2,550 mail order establishments operated in many lines of trade, more than 75 per cent of their sales was reported by only 35 large establishments handling a complete line of department store merchandise. More than one-half of these establishments are operated by two companies— Sears' and Ward's—thus indicating high concentration in this field.

COMPETITIVE POSITION OF GENERAL CATALOG HOUSES

The general merchandise mail order organizations have, in the main, the advantages and disadvantages of other large-scale retail enterprises. Due to the peculiar nature of their business, certain special conditions affect their competitive situation.

Advantages

As compared with single-line and general stores in the rural districts, mail order houses offer a more complete and varied line of merchandise. Their location in the larger cities gives a certain amount of prestige to their merchandise, especially in style goods. Prices, at least for many articles, are somewhat lower than those charged for corresponding articles in the rural communities.

Buying from a catalog is perhaps quicker and easier for rural people than going to stores in somewhat distant cities, and such shopping can be done at any time of day or evening that is most convenient. Convenience, moreover, is a strong appeal among urban customers who patronize catalog order offices or telephone order facilities maintained by leading mail order companies in large cities. Absence of pressure to buy, avoidance of the confusion of crowded stores, informative statements concerning products, guaranties, and a liberal returned-goods policy are other attractions. Because sales are made in all sections of the country and to different classes of consumers, sales are not greatly affected by local industrial depressions, as are those of local merchants.

Some general advantages enjoyed by all mail order vendors grow out of certain operating economies. Warehouses are located in parts of the city where rent is much lower than that which must be paid by the ordinary retailer. Expensive fixtures are unnecessary, for only equipment of the warehouse type is required. It is unnecessary to employ retail salespeople, for the catalog descriptions plus the reputation of the firm and price appeals effect sales. Hence, employees of the clerical and shipping department type are used and their work is scheduled to permit an efficient utilization of time—something difficult to accomplish in retail stores which must be staffed in accordance with daily and hourly variations in consumer traffic.

Disadvantages

Selling by catalogs is limited by the impossibility of examining merchandise in advance of purchase. For shoes, gloves, or clothing, it may be difficult for the buyer to secure the right articles without trying them on for size and fit. Many consumers hesitate to order products where size, colour, style, or texture are significant in choice making. An important limitation is inflexibility of the merchandising programme. Semi-annual catalogs published by Sears' and Ward's comprise between 1,000 and 2,000 pages. Plans must be made well in advance of the season as to the detailed composition of the line of goods and the manner in which they are to be featured and illustrated.

More important, prices must be determined months before catalogs are distributed, and the firm usually must live with its pricing decisions throughout the catalog season. While the catalogs contain statements that prices are subject to change without notice, and even though special sale catalogs are issued, the companies do not have the pricing flexibility of other forms of retailing.

They cannot mark down individual items of merchandise as the rate of sale becomes too slow or as costs decline; neither can they raise prices on individual items as demand increases or as wholesale costs rise. New items can be added or dropped only when new catalogs are prepared.

IMPORTANCE OF SMALL VERSUS LARGE-SCALE RETAILING

Just what constitutes small- or large-scale retailing has been debated vigorously with little resulting agreement. A precise dividing line is of dubious value for present purposes because it is easy to demonstrate that the most prevalent form of retail enterprise is the independently owned store that would be judged small by anyone's standards.

Scale of operations is reflected in part by legal form of organization and also by size of assets. Of all retailing firms, 91 per cent are unincorporated business-77.6 per cent sole proprietorships and 13.4 per cent partnerships. To this group may well be added corporations with total assets of less than $1,000,000. These categories of firms together account for 99.8 per cent of all firms classified in retail trade and account for some three-fourths of total sales volume. On the other hand, retailing corporations with assets of over $1,000,000 (most of which would be commonly regarded as large-scale enterprises) account for only 0.2 per cent of the total number of firms but handle about onefourth of total retail sales.

The data of retail *firms* are from a new series first published in 1960 and hence cannot be evaluated historically. From other sources it is apparent that large-scale retailing has increased somewhat in significance in recent years. Between 1948 and 1958, however, sales of multiunit establishments increased from about 30 per cent to 33 per cent of total retail sales. Most of this gain in the sales volume of chains was accounted for by companies operating 11 or more store units.

This group increased its proportion of total retail sales from 18.6 per cent in 1948 to 22.3 per cent in 1958—a gain of about 20 per cent in *share* of total retail trade. Independents or smaller retailers, nevertheless, remain dominant, accounting for all but a minute fraction of firms and some two-thirds to three-fourths of sales, depending upon what criterion one wishes to use to distinguish between small- and large-scale organizations. In service trades, where most firms are engaged in marketing on the retail or consumer level of distribution, the preponderance of small-scale operation is even more pronounced. Corporations with assets over $1 million represent only about 0.1 per cent of the firms and handle less than 15 per cent of total service trade sales.

SMALL-SCALE RETAILERS

Smaller independent stores, as a class of institutions, enjoy certain competitive advantages which favour the growth and development of organizations where management has the ability to capitalize opportunities. On the other hand, smaller organizations are subject to certain rather general disadvantages which limit the growth and development of weaker firms and which, by the same token, contribute to the expansion of larger scale enterprises. Knowledge of these considerations is essential in appraising the present and probable future competitive situation in retailing.

COMPETITIVE ADVANTAGES

One advantage contributing to survival ability is that throughout the independent store field *explicit costs of doing business are generally low* in relation to sales. These costs include out-of-pocket outlays and other items, like depreciation, carried on the accounting records as costs. Selling costs are low because the proprietor and other family employees often derive their compensation in the form of "profit" rather than salary payments which are charged against business income. Often the location of such stores enables them to pay low salaries to hired employees and to utilize rather unskilled part-time help. Rental costs tend to be low, partly because large numbers of such stores are located in neighbourhood or rural areas, also because ownership of store premises by the retailer is much more common among smaller independents than it is among chains or large-scale independent operators.

Second, *in many cases a small independent store is operated by one who devotes only a part of his time to the store.* Were it not for this advantage, it would be impossible for many small retailers to continue in business. Consider the problem of operating a store with about $25,000 annual sales volume. While gross profit margins vary considerably with different lines of trade, about 25 per cent is reasonably representative. This means that about 75 per cent of sales or $18,750 would be required to cover the cost of merchandise sold and that only about $6,250 would be available as gross profit, from which all expenses must be paid before there is any residual net profit. If reasonable allowance is made for operating expenses such as rent, advertising, store supplies, telephone, heat and light, and depreciation, it is apparent that such a merchant would have a difficult time in realizing enough personal income to afford a decent standard of living.

Nevertheless, more than 600,000 retailers in the sole proprietorship category (about one-half of the total in this group) report annual sales volume of less than $25,000. It is possible for many such merchants to continue businesses only because they may be engaged in some other gainful employment, either as salaried workers or as entrepreneurs in other enterprises, or because they are able to supplement store income with disability benefits or retirement income. When due consideration is given to this point, one must refrain from passing judgement on the economic justification of such stores merely on the basis of their small size. The advantages thus far mentioned may be thought of by some as uneconomic or even antisocial. Yet the fact remains that a store which can operate only with the help of unpaid members of the family, or one which exists only because the owner has other income, constitutes a definite part of our distribution system, and it does have the advantages mentioned. Moreover, in its limited way it may serve urgent needs of customers who find it convenient or otherwise desirable, while at the same time supporting in part or entirely many persons who might not otherwise be gainfully employed.

Third, and undoubtedly most important, is the advantage of *convenience of location.* One of the outstanding characteristics of smaller retailers is they are to be found nearly anywhere that trade occurs. Since most of them deal in convenience goods, they are located mainly with reference to homes of customers. Only rarely does one have to go far to find a small independent store, and numerous studies of patronage motives have revealed the importance of location as a fundamental reason why consumers buy from independent merchants. A fourth common advantage is the *opportunity for close personal contact that grows out of the size of smaller independent stores.* The ability of the owner-manager to establish and maintain friendly relationships with customers and cater to their personalized tastes is a strong argument for the well-being of the independent merchant. A corollary to this advantage is the *opportunity to develop a unique store personality.*

In one survey of informed trade opinion, lack of a well-defined character was cited as a common characteristic of independent stores while, at the same time, the opportunity to create an identity or image that differentiates a given independent store from all others of like type or size was recognized as the most outstanding single opportunity for betterment of competitive situation. Unfortunately, opportu-nity and realization do not always go hand in hand. A strong and distinctive store personality, brought about by an integrated approach to all aspects of customer contact activities, is developed only by merchants with energy, initiative, and ability.

Competitive Disadvantages

An outstanding limitation of smaller independents is their *buying handicap.* They cannot enjoy the lower prices which come from large scale purchases unless they join some form of group-buying organization, and even then they are rarely able to offset entirely this handicap. Wholesalers who must make small and frequent deliveries cannot offer the same low prices which they can give to the larger buyers who have both the storage space and the finances to permit quantity purchases.

Second, the smaller retailer is handicapped by the *absence of specialized employees.* Generally speaking, the entreprenuer must be his own personnel manager, advertising manager, sales manager, accountant, sales person, and, all too often, janitor as well. Lack of specialized skill is often of great importance in making wise selection of goods for resale, especially in fashion merchandising. The lack of the trained accountant and the important statistical information provided by him are serious weaknesses, yet they constitute, as was so well said many years ago, "the rudder which shows which way the ship goes."

A third competitive limitation is the *inability to advertise* on a scale comparable with chain store organizations or large-scale independent stores. Small stores often spend as large or even a greater proportion of their sales volume for advertising as their larger rivals, yet the dollar expenditures are necessarily small. This limits the small merchant's ability to utilize media with large circulation. Even in small cities where such merchants may be able to afford advertising space comparable with chain units, the limited funds and lack of specialized talent often result in ineffective layouts or poor copy. Fourth, the small independent is distinctly *limited* with respect to *ability to innovate or experiment.* A chain store can try out a new merchandising technique or idea in one unit, or a department store in one department, and if the results prove unfavorable, the loss may be easily absorbed by profits arising from other operations. The small merchant, however, does not have this favorable distribution of risks and usually must follow rather than lead in new developments.

Fifth, most smaller stores suffer from *inability to utilize personnel and capital resources efficiently.* Surveys of operating results conducted by various associations reveal that the smallest classes of stores have lower ratios of sales per employee than the medium-sized and larger stores in the same trade classification.

For example, in a 1959 survey of hardware stores, the ratio of sales per person employed was $23,145 for stores with sales under $50,000 as compared with $30,745 for those with over $200,000 annual volume. The ratio of total assets per $10,000 of sales was about one-fifth less for stores in the larger of these two sales volume classes.

Ratios of sales volume per square foot of store area also vary directly with the sales volume size of establishments in most lines of trade, demonstrating that space and other capital resources are utilized more efficiently in larger firms. This disadvantage makes it necessary for small retailers to employ unskilled personnel that can be hired for low wages and to use physical facilities in low-rent locations; these conditions, in turn, contribute to continuing low levels of operating efficiency in the smallest firms.

Another common though not universal disadvantage of smaller stores is *lack of managerial ability.* Although it is impossible to measure this alleged lack of ability, it is evident that a large number of independent store owners cannot boast of great business acumen.

Because of location, friendship, lack of competition from more capable merchants, or other favorable circumstances, these merchants have been able to stay in business. But this does not constitute proof that either the individual involved or that members of his class can continue to withstand newer types of competition. A question of serious import is whether small stores can attract efficient owners or pay the going rate for capable managers. There are reasons to believe that the general level of managerial ability has risen in recent years among independent stores generally, but this does not apply to the management of the smallest such establishments. If this is true, independent store operation may prove less attractive to young men of outstanding ability and thus add to the difficulties of existing independents in meeting competition from larger-scale institutions.

Failures and Survival Ability

Operation of a retail store, like that of other business enterprises, involves considerable risk. Many stores are closed each year because of inability to meet financial obligations. Even more are closed because the proprietor has not been able to secure the return on his capital and invested time to justify continuation of the enterprise. When a retailer ceases to operate his store, some disturbance of normal trade relationships usually occurs. Often closing-out sales are at price levels which, if met by competitors, result in loss to them. Landlords lose tenants. Supply houses may have to take back fixtures which are no longer new. A failure, rather than voluntary cessation of store operation, involves losses to creditors. It is therefore important to note the extent of failures, some of the common causes, and possible remedies.

Numerous studies have been made of failure rates among retailers and the basic causes thereof. The most comprehensive data on this subject are those collected by the well-known mercantile credit agency, Dun and Bradstreet, Inc. Records from this source indicate that about one-half or more of business failures are usually failures of small retailing businesses. This is explained not so much by the unusually hazardous character of retailing as it is by the fact that the number of small business firms engaged in retailing (including consumer service enterprises) is so much greater than in other business classifications. Failures in retailing occur particularly in the smallest sales-volume classes of stores and in the first two or three years of their operation.

Studies of the causes of retailing failures, based on the opinions of informed creditors as reported by Dun and Bradstreet, Inc., indicate that it is relatively rare for a retail business to fail because of reasons which are beyond the realm of managerial ability or control. About 85 to 90 per cent of retailing failures are attributed to inexperience, incompetence, or other factors related to management qualifications or performance, and this situation does not change much from one year to another. Yet, as one small merchant succumbs, another usually rises to take his place, as evidenced by continuing stability of total number of independent retailers over many years. While individual merchants, especially the less well qualified, are highly vulnerable, smaller merchants *as a class* demonstrate remarkable survival ability regardless of numerous failures.

An important underlying cause of retailing failures is *relative ease of entering the field without the experience or capital* necessary for successful operation. In retailing, more than in any other field, many persons with relatively little chance for success manage to get a start. To the extent that it is desirable for the door of opportunity always to be open to all, this is encouraging. But when the costs of failure are considered, it may be that entry is too easy.

Although many students of marketing and of social progress believe this last conclusion to be sound, no effective way of preventing the opening of stores by persons unlikely to succeed has yet been devised. Proposals urging more careful credit-granting by banks, wholesalers, and manufacturers have been made for years, but there is little valid evidence that credit is harder to secure than in the past except in periods when the supply of capital is unusually limited. Systems of licensing based upon examinations have been suggested, but it is not likely that the probabilities of success can be adequately measured by tests. If a license to open a store were required, some governmental agency would necessarily be charged with the responsibility of determining who should receive a license. It does not seem probable that any such agency could select from many applicants those with high probability of success. It must therefore be concluded that as yet the various attempts to reduce the failure rate of merchants have met with little success.

LARGE-SCALE RETAILING

The antithesis of the small-scale retailer is illustrated by a variety of specific kinds of stores—the metropolitan department store, large departmentized stores in the apparel and home furnishings trades, mail order companies, large supermarkets and discount houses, and multiunit or chain organizations of many kinds. Each of these types has its unique problems and advantages, but all of them have attributes in common, to the extent that they arise out of scale of operation or size of enterprise.

ADVANTAGES

One of the most important advantages of scale is the elaborate *division of labour* that results from specialization in effort. Size permits employment of experts for executive positions. Skilled buyers, advertising managers, accountants, statisticians, and personnel directors are all at the command of such big businesses.

Large firms can usually afford *extensive departmentization.* By carefully classifying merchandise and creating departments for the sale of particular lines of merchandise or for more specific appeal to differentiated groups of customers, management enjoys not only advantages of specialization on the part of buyers and salespeople but is also facilitated in discovery of profitable and unprofitable classes of goods and in a more accurate measurement of the efficiency of department or store managers.

A most important competitive advantage is *large buying power.* Since purchases are large and hence important to suppliers, large-scale retailers can often circumvent the wholesaler in an economical manner and, by so doing, can obtain the most favorable prices. Not only are large discounts from list prices secured when big quantities are purchased, but other concessions, such as advertising allowances, exclusive rights for distribution, or free goods, may also be obtained. While manufacturers' freedom to quote more favorable prices to large buyers has been somewhat limited by legislation, particularly the Robinson-Patman Act, large-scale retailers remain in a position to purchase on much more favorable terms than their smaller rivals on purely economic grounds. Further buying advantages are realized through ability to employ experts to perform this function.

The *financial strength* of large institutions often attracts investors and facilitates the acquisition of capital for expansion. Size is an advantage in making banking connections which may enable the borrower to secure loans on favorable terms. Large financial resources make it possible to take advantage of cash discounts offered by sellers and to attract vendors who may be led to offer especially favorable terms of sale.

Large retailers have the ability to *command the most favorable locations.* Many leases in retailing involve rental payments calculated as a per cent of sales volume. In such cases, the large firm, with a demonstrated capacity to generate substantial volume, is generally a preferred tenant. Shopping centre developers prefer to obtain leases from large, financially strong companies because such leases can be used as security in obtaining loans from banks, insurance companies, and other sources of capital for shopping centre construction.

Many large-scale retailers achieve operating economies or derive additional income from the *integration of other business activities* with retail merchandising. Many chains, department stores, and mail order companies have established their own warehouses which are operated on an efficient scale and in which are performed the distributive functions of the regular wholesaler, with the exception of personal selling activities which are largely eliminated between these two levels in the channel of distribution. Outright ownership or control of manufacturing plants is not uncommon among large organizations in the apparel, general merchandise, and food trades. Some retailing corporations have subsidiary companies which perform essentially a banking service by financing accounts receivables for the parent organizations. Real estate developments, particularly of the planned shopping centre type, are also integrated into the operation of some department store groups and food chains, usually by means of separately incorporated subsidiaries.

The *prestige* which results, in part at least, from the great size of the leading chain, department store, and mail order companies is a distinct advantage in attracting patronage. The reputation of such firms is well established, either because of a long history in a given location or the publicity associated with their operations on a widespread geographic basis. This prestige, when accompanied with integration, is particularly suitable for the promotion of private brands of merchandise.

All forms of large-scale retailing benefit from a certain amount of *risk distribution.* Customers are drawn from large areas or many different lines are sold. The organization can usually assimilate severe losses in some departments or operating units, without greatly impairing the profit making possibilities of the entire organization. Finally, *experimentation and research* represent types of activity which may prove most effective in increasing efficiency and which, while practical for the large retailer, may be too expensive to be undertaken by his smaller competitors.

Inherent Disadvantages

The unfavorable factors incident to large-scale retailing are less numerous than the advantages and for that reason may be stated much more briefly. This should not, however, lead to an underestimation of their importance, because it is these disadvantages that contribute a great deal towards explaining the significance of small-scale operation in our retailing structure. Furthermore, each of the various forms of large-scale retailing has some disadvantages that are peculiar to it, but which are not discussed at this point.

A major weakness of large companies lies in the *absence of close personal contact between the owners or general managers and the consuming public.* Most consumers meet only the rank and file of subordinate employees, rarely the owners or major executives. While the self-interest of routine workers, together with their training and supervision, may produce some measure of efficiency, hired managers usually function with less effectiveness than do the more able owners of small businesses with their sharpened personal interest in customers. Another disadvantage consists of *high overhead costs arising out of the complex organization structures* of large-scale enterprises. Some advantages of specialization are offset by lack of close contact between top management and subordinates and may have unfavorable effects upon efficiency. Larger concerns ordinarily have a much greater proportion of non-selling employees than smaller retail organizations. Much non-selling labour results from the need for costly methods of recording and checking the activities of the various divisions and maintaining the minute supervision necessary to fix responsibility, check performance, and minimize waste.

Legal Limitations

Belief in small business as a manifestation of the American way of life has had an important bearing upon the history of trade legislation. Numerous enactments have been designed to curb some of the buying power and other advantages of large organizations and to provide, thereby, legal methods of balancing the competitive situation between the large and the small. Noteworthy are the Robinson-Patman Act, and fair trade and unfair trade practices legislation designed to curb uneconomic price-cutting tactics.

The Robinson-Patman Act

The Robinson-Patman Act, a federal law enacted in 1936, represents an attempt to curb certain uneconomic advantages of large retailers, which they enjoyed merely because of large size and great purchasing power. Numerous instances are on record in which large-scale buyers have more or less compelled manufacturers to sell to them at prices much lower than paid by wholesalers who supply small independent merchants. Supporters of this legislation contend that such manufacturers must then charge wholesalers or independent retailers a higher than normal price to compensate for abnormally low prices given to large-scale buyers. To prevent unjustifiable differences in prices, the Act makes it unlawful for sellers to discriminate in price between different buyers (of the same type or class) on goods of like grade and quality where the effect of such discrimination may be substantially to lessen competition, to tend to create a monopoly, to injure, destroy, or prevent competition. In substance, the law provides that *only those price discriminations are allowed which are justified by differences in cost to the vendor* or when done *in good faith to meet the lower price of a competitor.* Thus, in many instances large retailers are deprived of the sizable discounts and other price concessions which they once enjoyed.

In some cases, however, a manufacturer may show that his economies in selling to large buyers are greater than the discounts given, but in general the effect has been to reduce the buying advantage of the large firms. Because of their great importance to resources, large retailers have been able to secure substantial advertising allowances. Numerous manufacturers follow a policy of advertising cooperatively with their retail outlets, with part of the cost paid by the manufacturers. This established practice usually works to the benefit of both parties and is above criticism. Objections arise not from the nature of the practice but from its abuse in the form of unjustified discrimination.

Chains and large department stores were able to secure substantial advertising allowances from many companies which did not grant such allowances to small independents. In essence, such discrimination amounts to a subsidization of the big retailer's advertising programme at the expense of independents who are not able to obtain comparable discounts. A second major provision of the Act attempted to prevent this kind of discrimination by *prohibiting advertising and all other forms of sales promotional or service allowances, unless they are made available on proportionally equal terms to all customers.*

It is perfectly legal for a manufacturer to give a large buyer an advertising allowance amounting, for example, to 3 per cent of such buyer's purchases, but it cannot do this *legally* without making the same percentage allowance available to all customers. Another practice curbed by the Act pertains to brokerage fees. Numerous manufacturers cannot support their own sales force and hence employ brokers who also serve other manufacturers. In performing the selling function for the manufacturer, the broker renders a valuable service for which he is entitled to reasonable compensation. Many large chains and department store buying offices set up subsidiary purchasing companies which were, in effect, *dummy* brokerage offices. Retailers required manufacturers to sell through these subsidiaries and grant to them the usual brokerage fee. In such an instance, the dummy brokerage office is not a representative of the seller, but rather an agent of the purchaser.

As a purchasing company seeking out sources of supply, it would be logical to expect that it should be compensated by the buyer rather than the seller. When an organization owned by a buyer obtains a brokerage fee from a seller whom it does not serve, this merely amounts to an unjustified price discrimination, because other purchasers must pay the manufacturer's factory price with perhaps a brokerage fee *added* rather than *deducted.* A third major provision of the Robinson-Patman Act was designed to *prohibit sellers of merchandise from paying brokerage fees to other than their own agents.* A broker may only collect a commission or fee when he acts as a bona fide third party, rather than as an employee of the buyer, for services rendered to the principal who pays the fee.

These provisions do not curb any *economic* advantages of large-scale retailers. To the extent that a seller can deal with a large buyer at lower costs of marketing than encountered when dealing with small independents, he can give a lower price. The large retailer can still obtain advertising allowances, but only if the allowances are made available to all of the vendor's customers on proportionally equal terms. It cannot obtain brokerage fees for itself, but this does not place it at a disadvantage with respect to small merchants. The effect of the Robinson-Patman Act has been substantially that of restricting *power* advantages of giant retailers, that is, benefits that they once enjoyed to a high degree because of ability to secure concessions by coercion. It does not penalize them through curbing any natural advantages they enjoy *because of ability to perform marketing functions in a more efficient and economical manner.*

State Pricing Legislation

In many states, laws have been enacted which limit pricing freedom, thereby restricting the price appeal and price-cutting tactics of some merchants, primarily in the large-scale classification. Other laws place restrictions on price discrimination in *intrastate commerce.* The best known of these are the so-called *fair trade* laws.

The first such law was enacted in California in 1931, for the purpose of putting a floor under the resale prices of the branded items of manufacturers that chose to operate under this type of law. Eventually, 45 states passed similar laws, and they were legalized in interstate commerce originally by the Miller-Tydings Act of 1937 and later also by the McGuire Act of 1952. For reasons explored at length, these laws became highly controversial in the 1950's. Constitutionality was challenged in the court systems of most states, and judicial opinion was approximately equally divided regarding the constitutionality of such laws, either in entirety or in regard to some major provision. In 1961 some

26 states still had fully operative fair trade laws with respect to non-signers. Fair trade laws permit the manufacturer of a branded item to set the minimum, or in some cases the actual, price which must be observed by retailers in reselling such merchandise. To establish a resale price under the state laws, a manufacturer must ordinarily obtain a contract with one retailer who agrees to maintain the resale price. In most states, the price is then binding on all other retailers as soon as they are notified of the agreement. Fair trade legislation has been described by opponents as "handicap competition."

It has been compared with a cross-country race in which handicaps are placed on the swiftest, to assure equality of opportunity for retail contestants of varying strengths vying for consumer acceptance in the market place. Protagonists, on the other hand, attribute to it all the qualities that make for healthy competitive business enterprise. Regardless of the intent, these laws have been widely utilized in only a few lines of trade. Although effectiveness has been limited, they have enabled some small merchants to compete on more nearly equal terms, in sale of fair-traded items, with price-cutting competitors.

While fair trade laws are only permissive, that is, they merely allow a brand owner to operate under them if he so elects, there are so-called *unfair trade practices acts* which are mandatory. Some 31 states have enacted such legislation and it was still operative in 1961 in 27 states where constitutionality has been upheld or uncontested. These laws directly prohibit sales below cost, or sales below cost plus some designated per cent of markup. Also, some 26 states have laws prohibiting "sales below cost" of specifically designated products (*e.g.*, cigarettes, liquors and malt beverages, dairy products) which are commonly used as "leaders" by price-cutting stores. About one-half of the states have specific *price discrimination laws* which are in essence state Robinson-Patman Acts. They prohibit price discrimination such as is forbidden in the federal law but apply, of course, only to transactions in intrastate commerce.

The net effect of the federal and state trade legislation has been to curb buying advantages incident to mass purchasing power and to render it more difficult for large retailers to engage in price-cutting practices designed to make consumers believe they have tremendous operating advantages over independent merchants. Large organizations, however, have not been the only price cutters. This practice has been important among some small independent merchants, and the laws apply to them with equal force. Because of limited buying power, somewhat higher operating costs, and less emphasis upon price appeal among independents as a class, the laws are to be regarded primarily as limitations to large-scale operations.

FUTURE OF E-RETAILING

'There is a Chinese curse which says, "May he live in interesting times". Like it or not, we live in interesting times.' Despite serious questions as to the origin of the phrase, that is, that the phrase is more likely to be of Western origin than Chinese itor, 2002), the sentiment 'living in interesting times' holds true now and will continue to do so for e-retailing. Changes in the retailing service exchange medium from bricks and mortar to an electronic medium have not endowed retailers with magical insights into the needs and buying processes of potential customers. This lack of consumer understanding was confirmed by the collapse of so many would-be Web e-retailers in the dot.com crash. What is needed is to consider the demands upon e-retailing from the point of view of the potential interaction between the web site and shopping browser. Huarng and Christopher (2003) suggested examining the issues that come into play during such interactions through the traditional consumer buying decision process.

CONSUMER BUYING DECISION PROCESS

A potential e-consumers buying decision process will follow the established stages of need recognition, information search, information evaluation, purchase decision and post-purchase behaviour.

Need Recognition

An e-retail web site is a combination of the traditional store display window, information desk, stocked display shelving, mood lighting/sound, promotional material that shout out specials, and the time-honoured *barker/spruiker* used to stimulate shopping interest. Such an e-retail site ought to elicit a need recogni tion response from any visitor to the site. A new or returning visitor should be treated to a combination of the four basic marketing elements - *price* (*e.g.* specials, discounts, interest free periods), *product* (*e.g.* new lines, clearance items, seasonal products, fashion and fad limited ranges), *promotion* (*e.g.* sales, seasonal specials, select shopper campaigns) and *distribution* (*e.g.* free delivery, lay-away, home installation) that accentuate the visitor's own need identification.

Technology within the web site, for example cookie files, captures data about the visitor's responses and what information was accessed. Such information then enables e-retailers to improve the rapport with the online customer by tailoring the site content to consumer demand. One positive application from such data collection is the inclusion of customer loyalty programmes that encourage return visitation to the e-retailer site and increased purchases.

Information Search

Improved telecommunications technology and general population access to the Internet have transformed user availability to customization of, and digestion of, large information volumes. Unlike the bricks and mortar retailer, an e-retail site has the facilities to make available such large volumes of information in a customized format to meet the immediate and potential queries of site visitors following the need recognition stage.

Without personal embarrassment or the self-consciousness of asking a stranger (*e.g.* a shopkeeper) what may be an obvious or foolish product-related question, the e-retail site visitor can access online product brochures, price comparisons, frequently asked questions (FAQs), suggested product applications, cleaning and repair information, and an efficient search engine technology, as well as asking for specialized information via the e-retailer's e-mail system.

Information Evaluation

When seeking to evaluate the collected information on products and services, the potential shopper will often turn to the experiences and advice of family, friends and persons who have already experienced use of such merchandise. Also, e-retailing gives the user added facilities to access evaluative experts and previous users of the merchandise in question to aid in the digestion and customization of all this information.

Many consumer groups act as such reference experts through the testing and personal evaluations of retailed products and then make these findings available to others. Experienced e-retailers encourage interactions between previous, current and future shoppers by way of:

- Online discussion groups.
- Suggesting site visitors rate the available merchandise.
- Suggesting site visitors express comments about this merchandise and the service exchange experiences.

Monitoring of the online discussions and visitor comments endows the retailer with invaluable knowledge regarding merchandise features and limitations that may be incorporated into promotional materials. To conclude, apart from all the benefits mentioned above, the e-retailer gains all this free information that would normally require expensive market research.

Purchase Decision

After a visitor to an e-retailer site has determined the merchandise to be appropriate for their needs, it is still not a certainty that this visitor will finalize a purchase. Commonly, an online customer nominates particular merchandise from an e-retail web site and places those items in the online *shopping cart* (also known as a *shopping trolley*) for the checkout, but later the customer discontinues the purchase process and leaves the e-retailer's site. This action of discontinuing an online purchase is termed 'abandoned cart syndrome;

- A lower level of education.
- Higher frequency of Web purchases.
- Greater concern of online data risk and fraud.
- Greater frequency of web site service problems.

- The use of shopping as a facility to see family and friends.
- High levels of concern about online retailers' tracking data.
- Younger buying groups.
- Shopping causing little arousal.
- Higher frequency of browsing for a later purchase.
- Higher fashion consciousness.
- Higher frequency of Web search for product information.

Although the e-retailer cannot yet duplicate the human interactions possible in a physical store setting, e-retailers may still empower customers in an attempt to reduce the incidence of online cart abandonment. One positive step to improve the e-retailer's customer interactions is streamlining the order process by:

- Making improvements in the e-retailer's site navigation.
- Incorporation of help links and interactive facilities to stimulate the shopper's arousal and fashion consciousness.
- Supplying the relevant merchandise information as needed.
- Greater use of online help facilities and screen prompts.
- Establishing chat rooms and customer discussion opportunities to share experience with family, friends and new acquaintances.
- Improved guarantees (including deliveries, data security, 30-day trials).
- Offline contact details (phone number, fax number, street address).

Post-purchase behaviour

The key to a retailer's survival and success whether offline or online is to generate repeat purchase behaviour. For a customer to return to a retailer that customer needs to have confidence in the retailer, but e-retailer confidence is often difficult to establish in light of online issues that have caused customers to make complaints and/or never return to the e-retailer. According to Cho *et al.* (2002), the online issues that often alienate customers and lead to complaints are the failure to meet customer *expectations* in relation to:

Merchandise offerings.

The e-retailer's store-front technology (this includes, but is not limited to, the web site) that integrates:

- Usability of the technology;
- The technology failing to carry out a function.

The e-retailer's information sources (the policies).

Payment/settlement issues;

- Agreed conditions (including delivery timing).

To reduce the chance of customer expectations being unfulfilled, e-retailers will compensate for the lack of a face-to-face exchange by making available more information details than would otherwise be considered in a bricks and mortar environment. Dealing with each of the Cho *et al.* (2002) points, we suggest the following responses:

Merchandise offerings -

- Define all dimensions of the size options, colour variations, and accessories provided. One suggestion is to include the supply of actual colour swatches to reduce the colour errors often attributed to variations on computer colour monitors.

The e-retailer's store-front technology (this includes, but is not limited to the web site) -

- Provide sufficient technology to cope with peak buying periods such as St Valentine's Day and Mother's Day.
- Keep redundant backup to take over when systems fail.
- Offer facilities to store (file) partial orders for future use should the customer be interrupted and/or wish to continue the shopping process in the near future.
- Provide improved access facilities for the disabled/impaired computer user. Facilities may consist of:
  - Selectable larger display fonts;
  - Voice recognition commands;
  - Spoken responses embedded in the web pages;
  - Written descriptions of displayed images (these can be read out to the non-sighted user even if they can't see the picture).
- Alerts given by the e-retailer's site to advise users:
  - Pending specials;
  - Replenishment of merchandise that was out of stock;
  - Arrival of special orders.
- Such alerts can reach the user through e-mail, phone short message service (SMS), automated faxing or other communications technologies.

The e-retailer's information sources (the policies) -

- Information is to be detailed (even exhaustive), accurate and timely (not noticeably out of date).
- Information is to be easy to find on the e-retailer site.
- Links to relevant or 'just interesting' sites shall establish the e-retail not only as an appropriate purchasing site but as a point of reference or portal for future enquiries in this area; thereby achieving a great milestone: being bookmarked as a favourite site in the user's Web browsing software.
- A continued customer relationship should be maintained after a purchase by:
  - Continued updates on the relevant and near-relevant issues by e-mail or newsgroup (for example, a customer purchases an

electric grill and then receives a monthly recipe; the e-retailer keeps the contact and the customer's satisfaction in the purchase is supported);

– Space may also be sold to sponsors seeking to promote their products.

Payment/settlement issues -

- Not all customers want to reveal their personal details and movements to online parties. To aid these potential customers, e-retailers can now provide alternatives for the customer in the shopping cycle to minimize risk. In Australia, a purchaser using the Wishlist retailer (www.wishlist.com.au) may opt to have their online purchases delivered to a participating BP petrol service station rather than to their home address. In this way the customer picks up the merchandise at a time that suits and conceals their personal address details while still gaining the advantages of shopping online.
- Most courier organizations (*i.e.* DHL and FedEx) used by e-retailers have facilities for the purchaser to trace and track the merchandise while it is in transit. The e-retailer receives proof the item is 'on its way' and the client achieves the peace of mind of 'seeing' where the item is any time they go online.

THE HYBRID RETAILER: THE MOST LIKELY WINNER IN THE FUTURE OF RETAILING

Retailers today are not restricted to just bricks and mortar, direct and virtual categories of retailing but often opt for a hybrid business model. Hybrid retailers, sometimes referred to as 'multi-channel retailers', appear to be taking the greatest advantage of e-retailing opportunities.

In a study by Haeberle (2003) multi-channel retailers were identified as generating 72 per cent of Web-based sales in 2002, 5 per cent up from 2001, and 18 per cent up from the Web sales of 2000. Using profitability as a success measure, multi-channel retailers and particularly those established in the market as catalogue brands, made the greater impact as e-retailers. The Haeberle (2003) study found that, in 2002, 92 per cent of those retailers for whom catalogue was the primary sales channel were profitable. That compares with 80 per cent of bricks and mortar-based retailers and 50 per cent of Web-based retailers in the study.

When John Lewis bought the UK arm of Buy.com, the takeover gave Buy.com financial credibility while Buy.com gave one of the 'Old Men' of UK retailing street credibility (Editor, 2001). Though the purchase of a virtual retailer by a bricks and mortar retailer was nothing new, it was an early example of a continuing trend as virtual retailers ran out of operating capital. These new players in the retailing arena are faced on one side by the downwards pressure on prices to stay competitive and on the other by fearful investors who remember all too clearly the dot.com crash at the end of the first millennium.

Retailer adaptation: a key to survival and growth

Long-standing bricks and mortar retailers are not only looking at a Web presence as the means to becoming e-retailers. To improve the relationship with their customers, retailers are adopting new electronic systems that complement their physical store presence. Sears in the US (www.sears.com) uses a system termed 'buy online, pick up at the store', where the customer places and pays for an order with a credit card at the Sears web site, Sears.com, but, departing from other Web stores' procedures, picks up the merchandise from a local Sears store. An e-mail is then used to advise the customer about stock availability at the time of the order and when the merchandise is ready for store collection.

Misunderstanding or ignoring a market position of strength is a failing that leads to the demise of some retailers. The availability of a new distribution channel is not an automatic indication of future success. Consider the US retailer Egghead (was www.egghead.com), which in the early 1990s had strong market presence with around 250 stores across the country. The retailer was well respected by its consumer market, had a solid brand image and was profitable. Long before most other retailers, Egghead created an online presence for its technology-minded customers in 1994.

Effectively, this entry into a new distribution channel made Egghead one of the first multi-channel retailers. But, as Lightfoot (2003) described, Egghead did not leverage its unique multi-channel position; rather, it decided to abandon all of its offline stores in 1998 and exclusively sell online, evolving into a virtual retailer.

Regrettably, following a series of problems, *e.g.* much-publicized hacking attacks on Egghead's web site, technical failures in the e-commerce technology, failing customer loyalty and internal management problems, Egghead went the way of many dot.coms and exhausted its cash reserves and filed for bankruptcy in 2001 (Thornton and Marche, 2003).

On the positive side for customers, the Egghead assets (including brand name and customer base) were sold to Amazon in 2001. To Amazon's credit, the new owner honoured the privacy policy of the previous Egghead clients as noted in the statement:

Please note that if you are a returning Egghead.com customer, Egghead.com will not disclose any existing account information to Amazon.com, so you will need to re-enter all information necessary to complete a transaction. For information about how Amazon.com treats the information you give us, see Amazon.com's Privacy Notice.

WHAT CAN YOU EXPECT TO SEE AND HEAR IN E-RETAILING?

Improved customer education, availability of information and increasing legislation have given rise to a new type of customer for this new millennium. Our new customers are more demanding, have a higher expectation and are increasingly adversarial in their service exchanges with retailers. Part of the retailer response will be to empower the customer to tailor their own service exchange in the physical store and online. Metro, an organization that already markets hardware systems to retailers, has suggested a series of scenarios in a future retail store to provide technologies that make shopping encapsulate greater individualization, reliability and convenience (Metro Group, 2003a).

Greater Individualization

Just as Web browsing technology learns and recalls a user's preferences for colour, fonts and items for inclusion, future stores will match their offering to learned customer experiences. Once the customer is identified to the store through a loyalty card or personal *radio frequency identification* (RFID) tag, the store's 'electronic personal shopping assistant' (EPSA) technology will record the shopper's preferences for merchandise, delivery (*i.e.* home delivery, parcel pick-up) and method of payment. To save the customer time, the store system would forewarn the customer of difficulties (including stock outages) and then make suggestions for alternative merchandise that is either in stock or pending (*e.g.* new season's stock).

Greater Reliability and Convenience

New store technology will improve reliability for both customer and retailers. When a customer selects an item and adds this to their shopping trolley, the EPSA will read the merchandise's RFID tag and present the details to the shopper via shopping trolley mounted visual display. No longer will the customer be disadvantaged by the omission of shelf pricing or getting to the checkout only to be told that the product is 'not on the system' and needs a delaying price check. Through the use of the unique RFID tag being identified by EPSA, the customer will be advised of these details at the point of merchandise access - the shelf or bin stocking the merchandise. Once the price information absence is detected, the retailer's system can search or calculate the price before the checkout is reached.

Aiding the retailer, this technology will indicate low- or out-of-stock situations at the shelf as customers place the item into their trolley, long before the item is removed from the inventory system at the checkouts. Staff will have a perpetual inventory rather than depending upon physical stock updates. Retailers use a *planogram* to determine what merchandise is displayed where and in what quantities throughout a store. Shoppers become familiar with their favourite stores but what do they do when a new merchandise line is added to the store and they are unsure where it is located? What is needed is a personal guide or in the future an EPSA to direct customers through the store like a global positioning system (GPS) directs a car through traffic.

Fig. The new Shopping Trolley will Record the Selected Merchandise and Advise the Customer of the Details, Including Price and Running total Expenditure

Merchandise Tracking

With delivery problems representing one of the main elements holding back the growth of e-shopping, merchandise tracking may be one of the essential development areas for the future. Early developments in bricks retailing followed research by Bernard Silver and Norman Woodland in the early 1950s. As a result, the bar code became a world standard for tracking and recording the movements of retail stock (Anonymous, 2003).

A standard bar code is made up of dark (predominantly black) vertical bars broken up with light (predominantly white) spaces. To read the bar code a beam of light is passed over the code where the dark bars absorb the light and the spaces reflect it. The scanner (also known as a reader or detector) then turns the reflected light into electrical pulses that may be recorded on a data file. While an excellent product identification system, bar codes have a significant and obvious limitation, that is, they need to be scanned to register stock movement.

Fig. A Sample of a Bar Code

Stock may enter or be removed from the retailer's premises and if the bar code is not scanned with a reading laser, the stock is not identified and recorded so its movement is unknown. The solution is to have the stock *speak* up and identify *itself* to the retailer's electronic inventory management system. The stock speak? How? By adding to, or replacing the bar code with a miniature RFID tag. RFID tags are tiny (about one quarter of a square millimetre), carry between 64 and 96 bits of information and have a life of at least ten years. They are inexpensive (as low as one cent per unit) and can be energized and activated by radio waves from a scanner/receiver in close proximity, or can be hooked up to a battery. After being activated by the transmitter's power, the RFID tag then passes the information to the retailer's stock system.

RFID tags have already been trailed and applied in a variety of applications. McDonald's (www.mcdonalds.com) and KFC (kfc.com) are trialling RFID tags; the US Department of Defence will be incorporating RFID tags to improve the management of inventory through hands-off processing; Nokia is incorporating the tags in some of its mobile phones; theme parks are providing them on wristbands to identify the positions of children; and the European Central Bank is considering incorporating the tags on new Euro notes to reduce counterfeiting and track illicit monetary flows.

Some bricks retailers have already piloted RFID tags. Privacy concerns have since led to Wal-Mart (www. walmart.com) and Benetton (www.benetton.com) dropping trials and orders of the tags. Privacy becomes an issue when you consider that although the RFID receivers were conceived to detect the movements of the tagged merchandise, they are in effect able to track the movements of the customer carrying the tagged merchandise within a shopping district that contains multiple RFID scanners/receivers. Consider that, if an organization has more than one member store in the company's group (*e.g.* a supermarket, a bottle shop and a variety store all owned by one organization) in the same shopping mall, radio triangulation by the RFID receivers triggered by the merchandise's RFID radio signal could detect the move of merchandise and, therefore, the shopper from one store to another and so on. The data from these movements could also interpret how long the shopper spent at various spots in the mall and all this data is collected *without* the shopper having given their permission. It is an *ethical* dilemma that will be debated for some time. Despite the debate, bricks retailers such as Tesco are pushing ahead with RFID tags for tracking supply-chain movements and for further trials in-store. As we argue below, the potential benefits are substantial, so we expect the development to diffuse into e-retail tracking as shoppers become more accustomed to it. As the number of applications for RFID tags increases retailers may expect to fulfil management and marketing objectives, including:

- *Reduced retail fraud and theft*- RFID tags will track products for clothing, grocery items, electrical merchandise and recorded music to reduce shrinkage.
- *Asset supply-chain control*- RFID tags will track the movement of goods from one process centre to another, *e.g.* delivery dock and warehouse.

This is not limited to the selling inventory but includes organizational assets that have in the past left the premises without authorization or without being entered in a log book, *e.g.* storage pallets and shopping trolleys.

- *Inventory control-* RFID tags will transmit inventory relevant information, *e.g.* batch number, unit code, number of items on the property and consumer-related merchandise information such as product category, size and colour.
- *Intelligent packaging-* RFID tags can be linked to a sensor that recognizes any tampering or deterioration of the merchandise while in transit and when that damage behaviour occurred. This damage may relate to a non-deliberate deterioration error, *e.g.* food storage temperature being outside the recommended range. Equally, the sensor would detect malicious actions of third parties upon the merchandise, *e.g.* when a sealed lid on a container is removed and a subsequent replacement is made to disguise the tampering activity.

For customers, the expected benefits from a retailer using RFID tags are:

- *Speedier checkout process-*In combination with intelligent shopping carts/trolleys, shoppers would have all their purchases totalled automatically as the individual product RFID tags are read by the shopping cart and the totals provided at the checkout point for payment.
- *Security-* Manufacturers will introduce RFID tags into the components of final products so that if the components are removed they can be tracked. Consider the theft of car parts from a whole vehicle; in the past the panels would be almost impossible to detect and trace once removed from the original car.
- *Tracking-* 'Where are the b—y car keys?' Consumer RFID tag readers will become available to learn the tag codes of products that the consumer wishes to inventory. An immediate benefit is being able to locate the proximity of individual RFID tagged items, such as the ever-elusive car keys.
- *Preparation and care-* RFID tags provide the opportunity to include preparation and care information that will be understood by future appliances. Potential applications in this vein are:
- For allergens - home health systems that are programmed for the individual's health requirements will 'listen' to the RFID tags of grocery items. The tags may contain all the ingredients of the grocery items, even the complicated chemical codes, and notify the home health system of potential allergens that could be harmful to the customer/householder.

- For clothing - RFID tags would alert the washing machine that the fabric is not machine washable or should be dry cleaned only.
- For frozen foods - RFID tags would alert the freezer display panel that the food is near or at its expiration date.
- For frozen foods - RFID tags would pass cooking instructions to the microwave or convection oven to avoid over- or under-cooking.

In-store interactive electronic kiosks

Multi-channel e-retailers are not restricted to the sale of physical merchandise in bricks and mortar establishments, but may also market digital products and services that were previously limited to virtual retailers. Through the use of interactive kiosks, retailers will be able to offer such services as:

- Detailed product information;
- Price checks;
- Recipes and product application suggestions;
- Tickets for events;
- Reservations for events and activities;
- Self-checkout to make purchases;
- Personalized and targeted promotions;
- Photo-finishing - this is a growing segment as customers bring in their digital camera cards and have the kiosks transfer the images to final photos;
- Internet access;
- Customer loyalty programmes;
- Banking and financial services;
- Maps and direction services;
- Human resource services, *e.g.* recruitment.

Interactive kiosks generate extra revenue and, because the customer is self-servicing, the variety of service exchanges is increased without added staff and subsequent drains on profits.

Greater use of Electronic Payments

The advent of the cheque made it possible for consumers to make purchases for items that cost more than the cash funds they carried on their person. A cheque could only be written up to the amount of funds the customer had in, or could deposit into, the financial institution issuing the cheque prior to the cheque being cashed by the retailer. To improve on the flexibility of the cheque and to make purchases using the financial institution's funds (up to a predetermined limit) the store and bank credit card became a popular alternative to the cheque.

To make a payment by credit card necessitates the retailer obtaining a payment authorization from a financial clearance centre and the customer's identification being validated by a signature or personal identification number (PIN). All this takes time and depends upon the retailer's authorization equipment being operational. Now that consumers are carrying their own mobile technology, *e.g.* cellular mobile phones, there is an opportunity for the consumer to contribute to the transaction verification process.

Fig. Interactive Kiosks Come in a Variety of Styles

The consumer may pay for the goods by sending an SMS message to a specific phone number that verifies that a payment should be made to the retailer for the specific merchandise. Other mobile phones permit the transmission of an inferred (IR) transmission to the retailer's equipment to again verify that this payment is to be passed to the customer's charge or mobile phone account.

Widening the application of wireless device payments, Royal Philips Electronics and Visa announced an alliance to encourage and develop chip technology that does not require any physical contact with other devices. With this technology consumers will be able to pay for merchandise by waving the new smart card in front of a sensor in the retailer's store (Shim, 2003). For both retailer and customer it means reduced payment delays and improved customer satisfaction.

A further development in progress by the major credit card companies at the time of writing is 'pay-as-you-go', which should enable consumers who do not have access to credit to e-shop.

Audio Visual Shopping Trolley

As seen in the section Greater reliability and convenience, the electronic personal shopping assistant will increasingly support shoppers as they negotiate a bricks store, and we argue below that the development should lead to future benefits for e-retailers and e-shoppers. Linked to a future shopping trolleymounted touch screen, an EPSA will provide shoppers information on current store merchandise, in-store events, specialized product demonstrations/ taste testing and, of course, store specials.The audio visual shopping trolley will act as a two-way shopping data vehicle presenting benefits to customers and retailers. Benefits to customers from using the EPSA-linked shopping trolleys are:

- A quicker shopping trip for those customers who do *not* enjoy the shopping experience.
- Personalization of the product offering and related information.

- Recall of frequently purchased items to reduce the chance of forgetting items.
- Reduced embarrassment in asking for item locations.
- Reduced delays by transmitting special orders to specific departments before arriving at those sections, *e.g.* special cuts of meat from the meat department.
- Suggested recipes for a grocery item on special or in bulk.

Management equally receives benefits from EPSA-linked shopping trolleys through greater control over their operations resulting from improved knowledge and awareness of stock issues. Advantages to the future e-retailer will be:

- Real time inventory levels.
- Better understanding of customer shopping habits and profiling.
- Promotion of specialized or seasonal merchandise direct to the customers with the greater likelihood of making a purchase.
- Shelving that recommends cross-sells and up-sells to increase sales volumes.
- Improved feedback to suppliers on what sells and daily traffic patterns for demonstrations and gondola-end displays.
- Alerts for corrective action being needed in dramatic situations, *e.g.* staffing issues with long queues of customers at checkouts or other sections of the store.

The future of e-retailing is, as is the case for most estimates of the future, encouraging, but the format is uncertain. What can be said with certainty is that success and profitability will revolve around an historical truism: when the retailer knows the customer, the customer will continue to know the retailer and that translates into repeat sales and profits. The solution is in adopting the appropriate technology to meet the needs of customers.

9

Production and Service Processes

SERVICE PROCESSES

Because of their diversity, services have traditionally been difficult to define. The way in which services are created and delivered to customers is often hard to grasp since many inputs and outputs are intangible. Most people have little difficulty defining manufacturing or agriculture, but defining service can elude them.

Here are two approaches that capture the essence of the word.

- A service is an act or performance offered by one party to another. Although the process may be tied to a physical product, the performance is essentially intangible and does not normally result in ownership of any of the factors of production.
- Services are economic activities that create value and provide benefits for customers at specific times and places, as a result of bringing about a desired change in—or on behalf of—the recipient of the service.

More humorously, service has also been described as "something that may be bought and sold, but which cannot be dropped on your foot." Services make up the bulk of today's economy, not only in the United States and Canada where they account for 73 per cent and 67 per cent of the gross domestic product (GDP), respectively, but also in other developed industrial nations throughout the world. Figure shows how service industries contribute to the economy of the United States relative to manufacturing, government, agriculture, mining, and construction. The service sector accounts for most of the new job growth in developed countries. In fact, unless you are already predestined for a career in a family manufacturing or agricultural business, the probability is high that you will spend your working life in companies that create and deliver services. As a nation's economy develops, the share of employment between agriculture, industry, and services changes dramatically. Figure shows how the evolution to a service-dominated employment base is likely to take place over time as per capita income rises. Service jobs now account for 76 per cent of private sector payrolls in the United States, with wages growing at a faster pace than in manufacturing jobs. In most countries, the service sector of the economy is very diverse and includes a wide array of different industries, ranging in size from huge enterprises that operate on a global basis to small entrepreneurial firms that serve a single town.

It comes as a surprise to most people to learn that the dominance of the service sector is not limited to highly developed nations. For instance, World Bank statistics show that in many Latin American and Caribbean nations the service sector accounts for more than half the gross national product (GNP) and employs more than half the labour force. These countries often have a large "underground economy" that is not captured in official statistics. In Mexico, for instance, it has been estimated that as much as 40 per cent of trade and commerce is "informal." Significant service output is created by undocumented work in domestic jobs or in small, cash-based enterprises such as restaurants, laundries, rooming houses, and taxis.

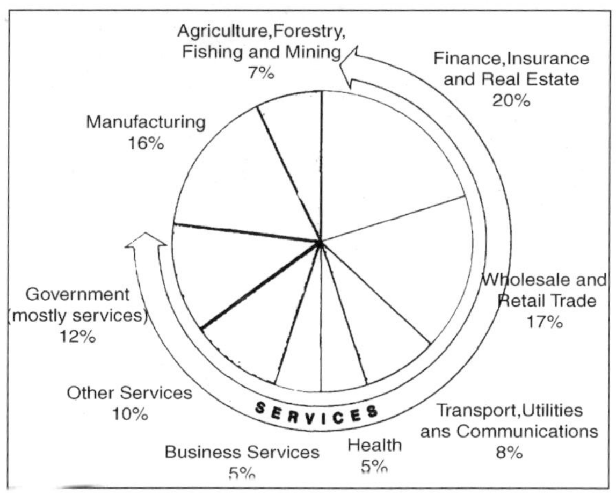

Fig. Services in the Economy: Share of GDP by Industry

Service organisations range in size from huge international corporations like airlines, banking, insurance, telecommunications, hotel chains, and freight transportation to a vast array of locally owned and operated small businesses, including restaurants, laundries, taxis, optometrists, and numerous business-to-business ("B2B") services. Franchised service outlets—in fields ranging from fast foods to bookkeeping—combine the marketing characteristics of a large chain that offers a standardised product with local ownership and operation of a specific facility.

Some firms that create a time-sensitive physical product, such as printing or photographic processing, are now describing themselves as service businesses because speed, customisation, and convenient locations create much of the value added. There's a hidden service sector, too, within many large corporations that are classified by government statisticians as being in manufacturing, agricultural, or natural resources industries. So-called internal services cover a wide array of activities including recruitment, publications, legal and accounting services, payroll administration, office cleaning, landscape maintenance, freight transport, and many other tasks. To a growing extent, organisations are choosing to outsource those internal services that can be performed more efficiently by a specialist subcontractor. As these tasks are outsourced, they become part of the competitive marketplace and are therefore categorised as contributing to the service component of the economy. Even when such services are not outsourced, managers of the departments that supply them would do well to think in terms of providing good service to their internal customers.

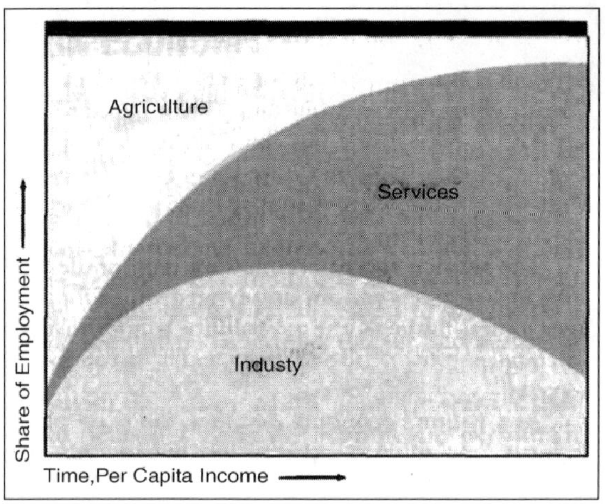

Fig. Changing Structure of Employment as an economy Develop

Governments and non-profit organisations are also in the business of providing services, although the extent of such involvement may vary widely from one country to another, reflecting both tradition and political values. In many countries, colleges, hospitals, and museums are publicly owned or operate on a not-for-profit basis, but forprofit versions of each type of institution also exist.

MARKETING SERVICES VS. PHYSICAL GOODS

The dynamic environment of services today places a premium on effective marketing. Although it's still very important to run an efficient operation, it no longer guarantees success.The service product must be tailored to customer needs, priced realistically, distributed through convenient channels, and actively promoted to customers. New market entrants are positioning their services to appeal to specific market segments through their pricing, communication efforts, and service delivery, rather than trying to be all things to all people. But are the marketing skills that have been developed in manufacturing companies directly transferable to service organisations? The answer is often no, because marketing management tasks in the service sector tend to differ from those in the manufacturing sector in several important respects.

BASIC DIFFERENCES BETWEEN GOODS AND SERVICES

Every product—a term used in this book to describe the core output of any type of industry—delivers benefits to the customers who purchase and use them. Goods can be described as physical objects or devices and services are actions or performances. Early research into services sought to differentiate them from goods, focusing particularly on four generic differences, referred to as intangibility, heterogeneity, perishability of output, and simultaneity of production and consumption.

Although these characteristics are still cited, they have been criticised for over-simplifying the real world environment. More practical insights are provided in figure, which lists nine basic differences that can help us to distinguish the tasks associated with service marketing and management from those involved with physical goods. It's important to note that in identifying these differences we're still dealing with generalisations that do not apply equally to all services. We classify services into distinct categories, each of which presents somewhat different challenges for marketers and other managers.

We also need to draw a distinction between *marketing of services* and *marketing goods through service.* In the former, it's the service itself that is being sold and in the latter, service is added—usually free of charge—to enhance the appeal of a manufactured product.

Customers do not Obtain Ownership

Perhaps the key distinction between goods and services lies in the fact that customers usually derive value from services without obtaining permanent ownership of any substantial tangible elements. In many instances, service marketers offer customers the opportunity to rent the use of a physical object like a car or hotel room, or to hire the labour and skills of people whose expertise ranges from brain surgery to knowing how to check customers into a hotel. As a purchaser of services yourself, you know that "while your main interest is in the final output, the way in which you are treated during service delivery can also have an important impact on your satisfaction.

Service Products as Intangible Performances

Although services often include tangible elements—such as sitting in an airline seat, eating a meal, or getting damaged equipment repaired—the service performance itself is basically an intangible. The benefits of owning and using a manufactured product come from its physical characteristics. In services, the benefits come from the nature of the performance. The notion of service as a performance that cannot be wrapped up and taken away leads to the use of a theatrical metaphor for service management, visuali

service delivery as similar to the staging of a play with service personnel as the actors and customers as the audience. Some services, such as rentals, include a physical object like a car or a power tool. But marketing a car rental performance is very different from attempting to market the physical object alone. For instance, in car rentals, customers usually reserve a particular category of vehicle, rather than a specific brand and model. Instead of worrying about styling, colours, and upholstery, customers focus on price, location and appearance of pickup and delivery facilities, extent of insurance coverage, cleanliness and maintenance of vehicles, provision of free shuttle buses at airports, availability of 24-hour reservations service, hours when rental locations are staffed, and quality of service provided by customer- contact personnel. By contrast, the core benefit derived from owning a physical good normally comes specifically from its tangible elements, even though it may provide intangible benefits, too. An interesting way to distinguish between goods and services is to place them on a scale from tangible dominant to intangible dominant.

Customer Involvement in the Production Process

Performing a service involves assembling and delivering the output of a combination of physical facilities and mental or physical labour. Often, customers are actively involved in helping create the service product, either by serving themselves or by cooperating with service personnel in settings such as hair salons, hotels, colleges, or hospitals. Services can be categorised according to the extent of contact that the customer has with the service organisation.

People as Part of the Product

In high-contact services, customers not only come into contact with service personnel, but they may also rub shoulders with other customers. The difference between service businesses often lies in the quality of employees serving the customers. Similarly, the type of customers who patronise a particular service business helps to define the nature of the service experience. As such, people become part of the product in many services. Managing these service encounters—especially those between customers and service employees—is a challenging task.

Greater Variability in Operational Inputs and Outputs

The presence of personnel and other customers in the operational system makes it difficult to standardise and control variability in both service inputs and outputs. Manufactured goods can be produced under controlled conditions, designed to optimise both productivity and quality, and then checked for conformance with quality standards long before they reach the customer.

However, when services are consumed as they are produced, final "assembly" must take place under real-time conditions, which may vary from customer to customer and even from one time of the day to another. As a result, mistakes and shortcomings are both more likely and harder to conceal. These factors make it difficult for service organisations to improve productivity, control quality, and offer a consistent product.

As a former packaged goods marketer observed some years ago after moving to a new position at Holiday Inn:

- We can't control the quality of our product as well as a Procter and Gamble control engineer on a production line can.... Wlien you buy a box of Tide, you can reasonably be 99 and 44/100ths per cent sure that this stuff will work to get your clothes clean. When you buy a Holiday Inn room, you're sure at some lesser percentage that it will work to give you a good night's sleep without any hassle, or people banging on the walls and all the bad things that can happen in a hotel.

Not all variations in service delivery are necessarily negative. Modern service businesses are recognising the value of customising at least some aspects of the service offering to the needs and expectations of individual customers. In some fields, like health care, customisation is essential.

Harder for Customers to Evaluate

Most physical goods tend to be relatively high in "search attributes."These are characteristics that a customer can determine prior to purchasing a product, such as colour, style, shape, price, fit, feel, and smell. Other goods and some services, by contrast, may emphasise "experience attributes" that can only be discerned after purchase or during consumption. Finally, there are "credence attributes"—characteristics that customers find hard to evaluate even after consumption. Examples include surgery and auto repairs, where the results of the service delivery may not be readily visible.

No Inventories for Services

Because a service is a deed or performance, rather than a tangible item that the customer keeps, it is "perishable" and cannot be inventoried. Of course, the necessary facilities, equipment, and labour can be held in readiness to create the service, but these simply represent productive capacity, not the product itself.

Having unused capacity in a service business is rather like running water into a sink without a stopper. The flow is wasted unless customers are present to receive it. When demand exceeds capacity, customers may be sent away disappointed, since no inventory is available for backup. An important task for service marketers, therefore, is to find ways of smoothing demand levels to match capacity.

Importance of the Time Factor

Many services are delivered in real time. Customers have to be physically present to receive service from organisations such as airlines, hospitals, haircutters, and restaurants. There are limits as to how long customers are willing to be kept waiting and service must be delivered fast enough so that customers do not waste time receiving service. Even when service takes place in the back office, customers have expectations about how long a particular task should take to complete—whether it is repairing a machine, completing a research report, cleaning a suit, or preparing a legal document. Today's customers are increasingly time sensitive and speed is often a key element in good service.

Different Distribution Channels

Unlike manufacturers that require physical distribution channels to move goods from factory to customers, many service businesses either use electronic channels or combine the service factory, retail outlet, and point of consumption at a single location.

In the latter instance, service firms are responsible for managing customer-contact personnel. They may also have to manage the behaviour of customers in the service factory to ensure smoothly running operations and to avoid situations in which one person's behaviour irritates other customers who are present at the same time.

MANAGING PEOPLE AS PART OF THE SERVICE PRODUCT

The more involved customers become in the service delivery process, the more visible service personnel and other customers become. In many people-processing services, customers meet lots of employees and often interact with them for extended periods of time. They are also more likely to run into other customers. After all, many service facilities achieve their operating economies by serving large numbers of customers simultaneously.

When other people become a part of the service experience, they can enhance it or detract from it. Direct involvement in service production means that customers evaluate the quality of employees' appearance and social skills, as well as their technical skills—concerns that are important for human resource managers and front-line supervisors. And because people also make judgements about their fellow customers, managers find themselves trying to shape customer behaviour, too. Service businesses of this type tend to be harder to manage because of the human element. Susan enjoyed the comments made by other students in her marketing class. But at the food court, lazy customers had failed to clear their table. Even though they had already left, their behaviour still detracted in a small way from the experience of Susan and her friends.

The poor attitude and appearance of the employee at the dry cleaner compounded the problem of delays in cleaning Susan's suit and may lead to the loss of her business in the future. As a manager, how would you get customers to clear their tables after eating at the food court? How would you make the staff at the dry cleaner more friendly?

REQUIREMENTS FOR THE SERVICE PROCESS LIFECYCLE

Services are becoming more and more important in today's economies. This applies not only for pure services such as transportation, etc. but also for material products that are augmented by services such as maintenance, consulting, training, etc. By augmenting products with services, enterprises stabilise their revenues. Often, services are used by the customer as a substitute for owning or using goods. This allows enterprises to concentrate on their core competencies and outsource non-strategic activities to service providers.

Thus, service orientation allows increasing the division of labour. The interest in services has grown rapidly and led to the term services science. Many attempts to characterise services exist and there is a long-lasting debate about the characteristics of services. Most definitions see a service as the value provided to the customer through a set of interactions and impacts on the input from the customer. Thus the service process is the detailed specification of a service. Service processes intensely interact with the customer. Production processes differ from service processes: The customer only perceives the output of a production process: he selects it and pays for it. The service process is implemented and executed by the service provider.

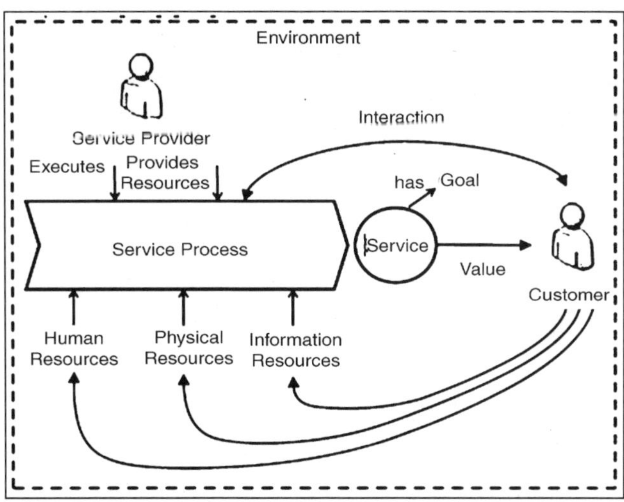

Fig. Service Processes in a Service System

The input to the service process from the customer may be in form of information, belongings or even the person of the customer itself. The service and service process are designed to reach a goal which has been defined by the stakeholders, especially the customer and the service provider. The service, its goal, the service process, the customer, the service provider and the resources are embedded into an environment which is source of legal compliance requirements, etc.. All together they constitute a service system.

Services processes and the services provided by them have a number of special properties. These properties do not require a completely different business process lifecycle but extensions to the standard phases of the life cycle. Therefore this thesis analyses these properties and identifies the requirements resulting from these properties.

The thesis starts with a discussion of related work. Then the special properties of service processes and services are identified and analysed. Based on this analsis, the requirements for the lifecycle of service processes are identified. A conclusion and outlook on further work is given at the end of the thesis.

RELATED WORK

There are a number of approaches for structuring the lifecycle of service processes. The newest and most advanced one proposes a structure for lifecycle of service. Its eight stages are based on the phase model developed in. Four of the eight stages are assigned to service design, the other to service management. Service design contains the definition of the design attributes, setting the design performance standards, the generation and evaluation of the design concepts and the development of the design details.

Service management contains the implementation of the design, the measurement of the performance, the assessment of customer satisfaction and the identification of steps for improving the performance. However, important steps such as testing and deployment are missing. Furthermore, the structure of the lifecycle is not deduced from the properties of services. A very often cited approach is the one from Lovelock et Wirtz. Nine topics relevant to service design are separated by the line of interaction that separates the customer from the service provider and the line of visibility that separates the actions visible to the customer from those that are not. Although this approach offers a very detailed support during service design, it does not cover the other phases of the software process lifecycle.

It is based on the so-called service blueprinting. In the approach of Meier and Massberg an integrated view of the service life cycle is developed and a configurator for services presented. However, the process-oriented nature of services is neglected. A method for the conceptual design of services is presented in. They are created by determining the attributes of abstract objects belonging to 9 classes: customers, goals, input, outputs, processes, human enablers, physical enablers, information enablers and environment.

Furthermore, there are approaches that only support one phase of the service process lifecycle. The operation phase of service processes is discussed in. The application of an composite product development process to the development of service processes is shown in.The approach of Cauvet and Gwladys is strongly modelling oriented. It shows how to compose business processes from socalled business services. However, only the design phase is considered.

SERVICE PROCESSES AND THEIR PROPERTIES

There are a number of crucial differences between service and business processes. First, there are intense interactions with the customer: Service processes show long encounters, during which customers interact directly. There may be duties of the customer that are critical for success or failure of the service process. For example, it may be necessary that the customer provides some information to allow the further proceding of the process.

It is important to emphasise that a service process must describe the interaction between customer and service provider. A second important property is, that service processes differentiate two areas, front stage and back stage. The front stage contains the activities of the customer and the service provider's activities that are visible to the customer. The back stage contains the activities not visible to the customer. The third important property is, that service processes need to represent the handover of resources and information from the customer to the service provider and the restitution vice versa. Furthermore, service processes are often cross-organisational. A top-level service process that is responsible for providing the service to the customer coordinates a number of sub processes.

SERVICES AND THEIR PROPERTIES

Services show a number of special properties that strongly influence the design and the whole lifecycle of service processes. These are the inseparability of production and consumption, the lack of suitability for storage, and the perishing of services. The inseparability of production and consumption means, that a service can only be produced in the moment it is needed.

This inseparability has a far-reaching consequence: you cannot put services on stock. Therefore, a service can not be measured in its quality before it is produced. Thus, you have to "trust" the provider of service that he will provide the service in the quality promised. This is trust may be established, if you already cooperated with the service provider. However, in most cases you do not know the service provider in advance. Therefore, you have to create surrogates for trust. An surrogate are certificates confirming that the service process has been appropriately set up to provide a high quality service. For example, if your computer does not work, you look for a service provider who has been certified by the computer's manufacturer to be capabable to perform the repair. Furthermore, the inseparability of production and consumption also increases the necessity for service recovery and back up mechanisms. In the case of service failure there is no possibility to quickly replace the failed service by a service from the stock. Therefore, service recovery and backup mechanisms should be available to remedy the service process and to minimize the effects on the customer. Thus, customer irritation and possible high direct and indirect costs by penalties and reduced customer loyalty can be avoided.

The second important property of a service is, that not only the service itself is important for the customer but also the potential to provide it. That means not only the repair of computer is important but also the possibility to hand in the computer for repair at certain times and the capability of the service provider to repair the computer in a defined amount of time. This potential of the service provider is described as service level agreement. The level of service availability strongly influences the pricing of the service. The service provider has to keep ready resources to provide the service if requested. Therefore cost are created even if the service is not requested and these costs have to included in the price of the service.

SERVICE AS A PROCESS

Marketers don't usually need to know the specifics of how physical goods are manufactured— that responsibility belongs to the people who run the factory. However, the situation is different in services. Because their customers are often involved in service production and may have preferences for certain methods of service delivery, marketers do need to understand the nature of the processes through which services are created and delivered. Furthermore, they should be involved in any decisions to change the nature of a given process if that change will affect customers. A process is a particular method of operation or a series of actions, typically involving multiple steps that often need to take place in a defined sequence.

Think about the steps that Susan went through at the hair salon: phoning in advance to make an appointment, arriving at the store, waiting, having a shampoo, discussing options with the cutter, having her hair cut and styled, tipping, paying, and finally leaving the store. Service processes range from relatively simple procedures involving only a few steps—such as filling a car's tank with fuel—to highly complex activities like transporting passengers on an international flight. The characteristics of the processes that might be used in a particular service operation necessarily reflect the nature of the business. Within certain constraints, the choice of processes may also be shaped by customer expectations and preferences. Looking at the processes *currently* used is only part of the story, since alternative processes may be available for exploration.

As indicated by our service decision framework, it's important for marketers to understand:

- Whether the service is directed at customers themselves or at their possessions,
- Whether service entails delivery of tangible or intangible actions,
- The sequence in which different elements of service delivery need to be organised, and
- The role played by information.

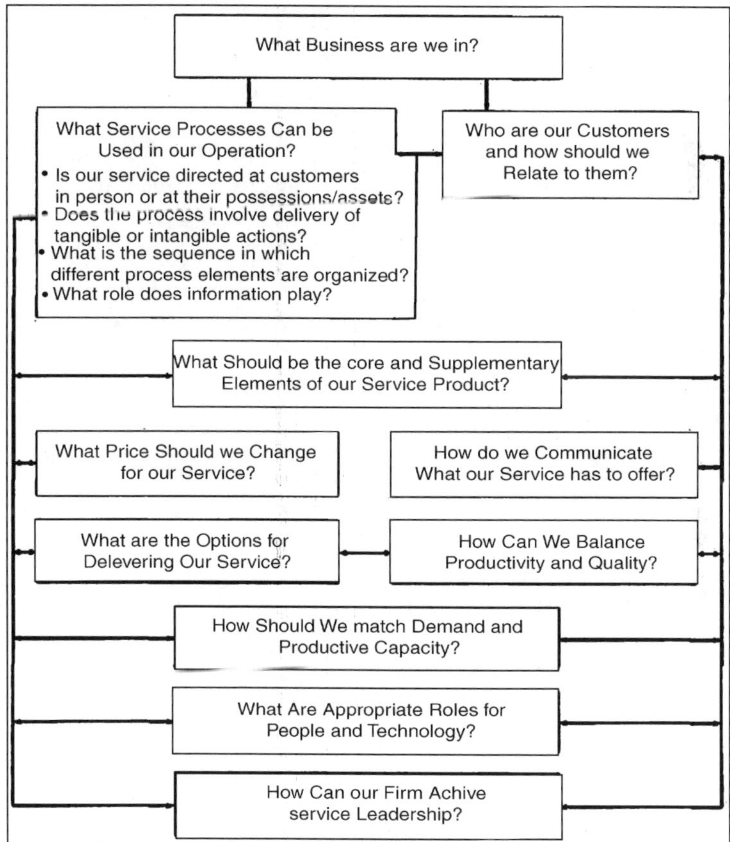

Fig. Service Decision Framework as it Relates to Processes

The answers to be gained from such analysis can help managers to identify the service benefits offered by the service product, consider options for improving productivity and quality, clarify how customer involvement relates to design of service facilities, evaluate alternative channels for service delivery, and determine if there will be problems in balancing demand for the service against our organisation's productive capacity. Finally, understanding these service processes helps managers to evaluate the strategic roles that might be played by people and technology.

CATEGORISING SERVICE PROCESSES

A process involves transforming input into output. But what is each service organisation actually processing and how does it perform this task? Two broad categories are processed in services: people and objects. In many cases, ranging from passenger transportation to education, customers themselves are the principal input to the service process. In other instances, the key input is an object like a malfunctioning computer or a piece of financial data.

In some services, as in all manufacturing, the process is physical and something tangible takes place. But in information-based services, the process can be almost entirely intangible. By looking at services from a purely operational perspective, we see that they can be categorised into four broad groups.

Table shows a four-way classification scheme based on tangible actions either to people's bodies or to customers' physical possessions and intangible actions to people's minds or to their intangible assets.

Table. Understanding the Nature of the Service Act

	Who or What is the Direct Recipient of the Service?	
What Is the Nature of the Service Act?	People	Possessions
Tangible Actions	*(People Processing)* Services directed at people's bodies: Passenger transportation Health care Lodging Beauty salons Physical therapy Fitness centers Restaurants/bars Haircutting Funeral services	*(Possession Processing)* Services directed at physical possessions: Freight transportation Repair and maintenance Warehousing/storage Janitorial services Retail distribution Laundry and dry cleaning Refueling Landscaping/lawn care Disposal/recycling
Intangible Actions	*(Mental Stimulus Processing)* Services directed at people's minds: Advertising/PR Arts and entertainment Broadcasting/cable Management consulting Education Information services Music concerts Psychotherapy Religion Voice telephone	*(Information Processing)* Services directed at intangible assets: Accounting Banking Data processing Data transmission Insurance Legal services Programming Research Securities investment Software consulting

Each of these four categories involves fundamentally different forms of processes, with vital implications for marketing, operations, and human resource managers. We refer to the categories as people processing, possession processing, mental stimulus processing, and information processing. Although the industries within each category may appear at first sight to be very different, analysis will show that they do, in fact, share important process-related characteristics.

As a result, managers in one industry may be able to obtain useful insights by studying another one and then creating valuable innovations for their own organisation.

- People processing involves tangible actions to people's bodies. Examples of people-processing services include passenger transportation, haircutting, and dental work. Customers need to be physically present throughout service delivery to receive its desired benefits.
- Possession processing includes tangible actions to goods and other physical possessions belonging to the customer. Examples of possession processing include airfreight, lawn mowing, and cleaning services. In these instances, the object requiring processing must be present, but the customer need not be.
- Mental stimulus processing refers to intangible actions directed at people's minds. Services in this category include entertainment, spectator sports, theater performances, and education. In such instances, customers must be present mentally but can be located either in a specific service facility or in a remote location connected by broadcast signals or telecommunication linkages.
- Information processing describes intangible actions directed at a customer's assets. Examples of information-processing services include insurance, banking, and consulting. In this category, little direct involvement with the customer may be needed once the request for service has been initiated.

PEOPLE PROCESSING

From ancient times, people have sought out services directed at themselves. To receive these types of services, customers must physically enter the service system.

Because they are an integral part of the process, they cannot obtain the benefits they desire by dealing at arm's length with service suppliers. They must enter the service factory, which is a physical location where people or machines create and deliver service benefits to customers. Sometimes, of course, service providers are willing to come to customers, bringing the necessary tools of their trade to create the desired benefits in the customers' choice of locations. If customers want the benefits that a people-processing service has to offer, they must be prepared to cooperate actively with the service operation. For example, Susan cooperates with her hair stylist by sitting still and turning her head as requested.

She will also have to be part of the process when she visits the optometrist for her next eye exam. The level of involvement required of customers may entail anything from boarding a city bus for a five-minute ride to undergoing a lengthy course of unpleasant treatments at a hospital. In between these extremes are such activities as ordering and eating a meal; having one's hair washed, cut, and styled; and spending some nights in a hotel room. The output from these services is a customer who has reached her destination or satisfied his hunger or is now sporting clean and stylishly cut hair or has had a good night's sleep away from home or is now in physically better health. It's important for managers to think about process and output in terms of what happens to the customer because it helps them to identify what benefits are being created. Reflecting on the service process itself helps to identify some of the non-financial costs—such as time, mental and physical effort, and even fear and pain—that customers incur in obtaining these benefits.

POSSESSION PROCESSING

Often, customers ask a service organisation to provide treatment for some physical possession— which could be anything from a house to a hedge, a car to a computer, or a dress to a dog. Many such activities are quasi-manufacturing operations and do not always involve simultaneous production and consumption. Examples include cleaning, maintaining, storing, improving, or repairing physical objects—both live and inanimate—that belong to the customer in order to extend their usefulness. Additional possession-processing services include transport and storage of goods; wholesale and retail distribution; and installation, removal, and disposal of equipment—in short, the entire value-adding chain of activities that may take place during the lifetime of the object in question.

Customers are less physically involved with this type of service than with peopleprocessing services. Consider the difference between passenger and parcel transportation. In the former you have to go along for the ride to obtain the benefit of getting from one location to another. But with package service, you drop the package off at a mailbox or post office counter and wait for it to be delivered to the recipient. In most possession-processing services, the customer's involvement is usually limited to dropping off the item that needs treatment, requesting the service, explaining the problem, and later returning to pick up the item and pay the bill. If the object to be processed is something that is difficult or impossible to move, like landscaping, installed software, heavy equipment, or part of a building, the service factory must come to the customer, with service personnel bringing the tools and materials necessary to complete the job on-site. The service process could involve applying insecticide in a house to get rid of ants, trimming a hedge at an office park, repairing a car, installing software in a computer, cleaning a jacket, or giving an injection to the family dog. The output in each instance should be a satisfactory solution to the customer's problem or some tangible enhancement of the item in question. In Susan's case, the cleaners disappointed her because her suit wasn't ready when promised.

MENTAL STIMULUS PROCESSING

Services that interact with people's minds include education, news and information, professional advice, psychotherapy, entertainment, and certain religious activities. Anything touching people's minds has the power to shape attitudes and influence behaviour. So, when customers are in a position of dependency or there is potential for manipulation, strong ethical standards and careful oversight are required.

Receiving these services requires an investment of time on the customer's part. However, recipients don't necessarily have to be physically present in a service factory— just mentally in communication with the information being presented.There's an interesting contrast here with people-processing services. Passengers can sleep through a flight and still arrive at their desired destination. But if Susan falls asleep in class or during an educational TV broadcast, she will not be any wiser at the end than at the beginning! Services like entertainment and education are often created in one place and transmitted by television, radio, or the Internet to individual customers in distant locations.

However, they can also be delivered to groups of customers at the originating location in a facility such as a theater or lecture hall. We need to recognise that watching a live concert on television in one's home is not the same experience as watching it in a concert hall in the company of hundreds or even thousands of other people. Managers of concert halls face many of the same challenges as their colleagues in people-processing services. Similarly, the experience of participating in a discussion-based class through interactive cable television lacks the intimacy of people debating one another in the same room. Because the core content of all services in this category is information based, it can easily be converted to digital bits or analog signals; recorded for posterity; and transformed into a manufactured product, such as a compact disc, videotape, or audiocassette, which may then be packaged and marketed much like any other physical good. These services can thus be "inventoried" because they can be consumed at a later date than when they were produced. For instance, Susans Spanish videotape can be used over and over again by students visiting the language lab.

INFORMATION PROCESSING

Information processing, one of the buzzwords of our age, has been revolutionised by computers. But not all information is processed by machines. Professionals in a wide variety of fields also use their brains to perform information processing and packaging. Information is the most intangible form of service output, but it may be transformed into more enduring, tangible forms as letters, reports, books, tapes, or CDs. Among the services that are highly dependent on the effective collection and processing of information are financial services and professional services like accounting, law, marketing research, management consulting, and medical diagnosis.

The extent of customer involvement in both information and mental stimulus processing is often determined more by tradition and a personal desire to meet the supplier face to face than by the needs of the operational process. Strictly speaking, personal contact is quite unnecessary in industries like banking or insurance. Why subject your firm to all the complexities of managing a people-processing service when you could deliver the same core product at arm's length? As a customer, why go to the service factory when there's no compelling need to do so? Susan appears comfortable dealing at arm's length with both her bank and her insurance company, using a self-service ATM for her banking transactions and receiving mail communications from her insurance company. Habit and tradition often lie at the root of existing service delivery systems and service usage patterns. Professionals and their clients may say they prefer to meet face to face because they feel that in this way they learn more about each other's needs, capabilities, and personalities. However, experience shows that successful personal relationships, built on trust, can be created and maintained purely through telephone or e-mail contact.

SERVICE ENCOUNTERS: DIFFERING LEVELS OF CUSTOMER CONTACT

A service encounter is a period of time during which customers interact directly with a service. In some instances, the entire service experience can be reduced to a single encounter, involving ordering, payment, and execution of service delivery on the spot. In other cases, the customer's experience includes a sequence of encounters. This can mean an extended process that may be spread out over a period of time, involve a variety of employees, and even take place in different locations. Although some researchers use the term "encounter" simply to describe personal interactions between customers and employees, realistically we also need to think about encounters involving interactions between customers and self-service equipment.

As the level of customer contact with the service operation increases, there are likely to be more and longer service encounters. We've grouped services into three levels of customer contact, representing the extent of interaction with service person nel, physical service elements, or both. You'll notice that traditional retail banking, telephone banking, and home banking by Web site are all in different locations on the chart. High-contact services tend to be those in which customers visit the service facility in person. Customers are actively involved with the service organisation and its personnel throughout service delivery. All peopleprocessing services are high contact. Services from the other three process-based categories may also involve high levels of customer contact when, for reasons of tradition, preference, or lack of other alternatives, customers go to the service site and remain there until service delivery is completed.

Examples of services that have traditionally been high contact but can be low contact today because of technology include retail banking, purchase of retail goods, and higher education. Medium-contact services entail less interaction with service providers. They involve situations in which customers visit the service provider's facilities but either do not remain throughout service delivery or else have only modest contact with service personnel.

The purpose of such contacts is often limited to:

- Establishing a relationship and defining a service need,
- Dropping off and picking up a physical possession that is being serviced, or
- Trying to resolve a problem.

Low-contact services involve very little, if any, physical contact between customers and service providers. Instead, contact takes place at arm's length through the medium of electronic or physical distribution channels—a fast-growing trend in today's convenience-oriented society. Both mental stimulus-processing and information-processing services fall naturally into this category. Also included are possession-processing services in which the item requiring service can be shipped to the service site or subjected to "remote fixes" delivered electronically to the customers' premises from a distant location. Finally, many high-contact and medium-contact services are being transformed into low-contact services as customers engage in home shopping, conduct their insurance and banking transactions by telephone, or research and purchase products through the World Wide Web. Advertising for low-contact, Web-based services often promotes speed and convenience. For instance, Wings pan Bank.com contrasts the old and new approaches: "In the 60 seconds it takes to find a parking spot at your old bank, you can get an answer on your loan application.... leave your car in the garage. Your new bank's in the den".

MANAGING SERVICE ENCOUNTERS

Many services involve numerous encounters between customers and service employees, either in person or remotely by phone or e-mail. Service encounters may also take place between customers and physical facilities or equipment. In low-contact services, customers are having more and more encounters with automated machines that are designed to replace human personnel. To highlight the risks and opportunities associated with service encounters, Richard Normann, a Paris-based Swedish consultant, borrowed the metaphor "moment of truth" from bullfighting.

Normann writes:

- We could say that the perceived quality is realised at the moment of truth, when the service provider and the service customer confront one another in the arena. At that moment they are very much on their own.... It is the skill, the motivation, and the tools employed by the firm's representative and the expectations and behaviour of the client which together will create the service delivery process.

In bullfighting, what is at stake is the life of either the bull or the matador. The moment of truth is the instant at which the matador deftly slays the bull with his sword—hardly a very comfortable analogy for a service organisation s intent on building long-term relationships with its customers! Normann's point, of course, is that it's the life of the relationship that is at stake. Contrary to bullfighting, the goal of relationship marketing is to prevent one unfortunate (mis)encounter from destroying what is already, or has the potential to become, a mutually valued, long-term relationship.

Jan Carlzon, the former chief executive of Scandinavian Airlines System, used the "moment-of-truth" metaphor as a reference point for transforming SAS from an operations- driven business into a customer-driven airline. *Carlzon made the following comments about his airline:*

- Last year, each of our 10 million customers came into contact with approximately five SAS employees, and this contact lasted an average of 15 seconds each time.Thus, SAS is "created" 50 million times a year, 15 seconds at a time. These 50 million "moments of truth" are the moments that ultimately determine whether SAS will succeed or fail as a company. They are the moments when we must prove to our customers that SAS is their best alternative.

CRITICAL INCIDENTS IN SERVICE ENCOUNTERS

Critical incidents are specific encounters between customers and service businesses that are especially satisfying or dissatisfying for one or both parties. The critical incident technique (CIT) is a methodology for collecting and categorising such incidents in service encounters.

Conducting such an analysis offers an opportunity to determine what incidents during service delivery are likely to be particularly significant in determining whether or not customers are satisfied. The types of encounters classified as critical incidents differ depending on whether the service is high or low contact in nature.

SERVICE AS A SYSTEM

The types of relationships a service business has with its customers depend to a great extent on the level of contact customers have with the firm.

Whether a service is high, medium, or low contact becomes a major factor in defining the total service system, which includes:

- The service operations system,
- The service delivery system, and
- The service marketing system.

Parts of this system are visible to customers; other parts are hidden in what is sometimes referred to as the technical core, and the customer may not even know of their existence. Some writers use the terms "front office" and "back office" in referring to the visible and invisible parts of the operation. Others talk about "front stage" and "backstage," using the analogy of theater to dramatise the notion that service is a performance. We like this analogy—sometimes referred to as "dra- maturgy"—and will be using it throughout the book. The extent to which theatrical elements exist depends largely on the nature of the service process.

SERVICE OPERATIONS SYSTEM

Like a play in a theater, the visible components of service operations can be divided into those relating to the actors and those relating to the stage set. What goes on backstage is of little interest to customers. Like any audience, they evaluate the production on those elements they actually experience during service delivery and on the perceived service outcome. Naturally, if the backstage personnel and systems fail to perform their support tasks properly in ways that affect the quality of front stage activities, customers will notice.

For instance, restaurant patrons will be disappointed if they order fish from the menu but are told it is unavailable or find that their food is overcooked. Other examples of backstage failures include receiving an incorrect hotel bill due to a keying error, not receiving course grades because of a computer failure in the college registrar's office, or being delayed on a flight because the aircraft has been taken out of service for engine repairs. The proportion of the overall service operation that is visible to customers varies according to the level of customer contact. Since high-contact services directly involve the physical person of the customer, customers must enter the service "factory" or service workers and their tools must leave the backstage and come to the customers' chosen location. Examples include roadside car repair by automobile clubs and physical fitness trainers who work with clients at their homes or offices.

Medium-contact services, by contrast, require customers to be less substantially involved in service delivery. Consequently, the visible component of the service operations system is smaller. Low-contact services usually strive to minimize customer contact with the service provider, so most of the service operations system is confined to a remotely located backstage; front stage elements are normally limited to mail and telecommunications contacts. Think for a moment about the telephone company that you use. Do you have any idea where its exchange is located? If you have a credit card, it's likely that your transactions are processed far from where you live.

KNOWLEDGE MANAGEMENT IN SERVICE ENCOUNTERS

The concept of Knowledge Management (KM) has attracted the attention of researchers over the last decade since it is considered an important tool to achieve innovation and sustainable competitive advantages. Nonaka noted that in highly uncertain economies the only sure source of lasting competitive advantage is knowledge. Several studies found that firms that adopt knowledge management practices perform better than competing firms that do not. Knowledge management practices have been implemented in a wide range of industries including manufacturing, consulting, tourism, and call centers. Extensive research has demonstrated the importance of customer-employee interactions in customers' evaluation of overall quality and/or satisfaction with services.

Research has also identified:

- The relationships between consumer satisfaction and service quality,
- Perceived control,
- Emotional contagion,
- Perceived employee effort,
- Perceived fairness, and
- Service recovery efforts.

However, the impact of knowledge management practices on consumer evaluations of service has received less research attention. Sigala proposes that organisations need to implement Customer Relationship Management (CRM) strategies to enhance profitability and customer loyalty. Recent research suggests that both CRM and KM are directed towards the same goal: continuous improvement of processes to meet customer goals. Initiatives emerging from this effort have been labeled as 'customer knowledge management' (CKM) or 'knowledge-enabled CRM'. Croteau and Li note that an organisation's KM capabilities are an important factor affecting CRM impact. However, recent studies indicate an underutilisation of KM practices in the hospitality/tourism industry. There is substantial evidence of the impact of knowledge management practices in building strong relationships with customers, and enhancing customer satisfaction and organisational performance.

However, no prior studies have investigated the influence of KM practices in a service encounter context. KM begins with an understanding that knowledge is broadly classified as explicit knowledge and tacit knowledge. Each has very particular characteristics, discussed more fully later in this thesis, that influence KM. This thesis commences analysis at this foundational level to ask how consumer reactions differ when service providers use one or the other form of knowledge. More specifically, this study examines the influence of KM practices on consumer satisfaction and consumers' repurchase intentions. This study focuses strictly on the dyadic interaction between service provider and customer – the service exchange. KM practices outside these bounds are not within the scope of this study. Therefore, the focus of this thesis is on the influence of two fundamental knowledge management components, namely tacit and explicit knowledge, on consumer reactions.

LITERATURE REVIEW

CRM (Service Relationships)

Service relationships occur when customers have repeated contact with same service provider. Service relationships refer to instances where service providers know their customers personally and expect to see them again in future. Three distinguishing characteristics of service relationships are: reciprocal identification, expected future interaction, and a history of shared interaction between customers and service providers.

Over time customers and service providers get to know each other and develop a history of shared interaction on which they rely to complete a transaction. In this study, this conceptualisation is adopted to suggest that returning customers seek evidence of reciprocal identification and their history with the service organisation. When these elements are evident, customers will be more confident and, consequently, satisfied with the nature of their relationship with the service provider. Customers discern evidence of reciprocal identification and shared history by observing frontline service provider behaviours.

When the service provider recognises the customer and suggests that the customer occupy the same room, this indicates the quality of the relationship to the customer, leading to greater satisfaction. This action by the service provider reassures the customer that the service organisation 'mutually identifies" with the customer and that the service provider 'knows about' the customers previous transactions with the organisation. Service organisations have recognised this important component of customer relationships and have installed processes – knowledge management processes – to manage the interaction. Sigala notes the importance of an information and communication technology system that is well-integrated with KM and relationship management principles to maximize the benefits of a CRM process. The collection, storage, and dissemination of information and data within organisations have been examined in the area of knowledge management and is discussed more fully later in this thesis.

Service Product

Recent research in services marketing has shifted conceptual and analytical focus from a *goods-dominant (G-D)* to a *service-dominant (S-D) logic*. G-D logic refers to goods or products as the main focus of economic exchange and *services* as an add-on that enhances the value of a good. Contrarily, S-D logic refers to *service* as a process of doing something using one's resources to benefit another party, and is identified as the primary focus of a service oriented economic exchange. In a service transaction, therefore, the focus is on the creation of value rather than products. Value estimations by customers are idiosyncratic and are based on customers' specific needs. This service-centric and processdriven logic shifts the locus of value creation from service providers to a collaborative process of co-creation between customers and service providers.

This shift in analysis from service delivery to value creation adds emphasis to the role of the frontline service provider. Lusch propose that service provider competencies are essential to value creation. Following this conceptualisation, this study connects the literatures on knowledge management to customers' satisfaction with a service. As earlier noted, the knowledge and skills of the service provider are essential to value creation. Within the bounded area of a dyadic service interaction, the knowledge and skills of a front line service employee are considered an intangible component of the service. Research has noted that intangible components, especially service provider behaviours, have an important role as indicators of relationship strength. Customers estimate they have a stronger relationship with a service organisation when the service provider demonstrates knowledge of the customer's preferences. However, the manner in which this knowledge or understanding is demonstrated has an effect on customer evaluations. Whether the service provider relies on tacit or explicit knowledge will influence consumers' satisfaction with the service.

Explicit and Tacit Knowledge

Knowledge has been classified as personal or shared and public, practical or theoretical, hard or soft, internal or external, and foreground or background; however, the classification of knowledge as tacit or explicit is the most widely accepted categorisation. "Explicit" or codified knowledge is transmittable in formal, systematic language. "Tacit" knowledge, on the other hand, has a personal quality which makes it difficult to formalise and communicate. Importantly, tacit knowledge is deeply rooted in individual action, commitment, and involvement in specific circumstances. Jasimuddin differentiates tacit knowledge and explicit knowledge based on eight features.

Explicit knowledge represents knowledge that can be:

- Articulated;
- Codified in a tangible form;
- Documented and transmitted, stored in the printed and the electronic media;
- Stored in external databases;

- Available in organisational repositories;
- Is easily available to anyone in the organisation;
- Is transferred from the "giver" to the "receiver" indirectly through information technology; and,
- Is not owned by individuals.

Herrgard suggests that tacit knowledge is the unarticulated knowledge that exists in human beings acquired by individual processes like experience, reflection, internalisation, or individual talents. The presence of personal elements makes tacit knowledge valuable, rare, inimitable, and non-substitutable. This thesis suggests that when service providers employ tacit knowledge in the value creation process, the characteristics of tacit knowledge increase the value of the service product to the customer. The use of tacit knowledge will strengthen customers' judgements of the quality of the relationship with the service provider. Contrarily, when the service provider refers to documentation, databases, or other sources of information in the value creation process, customers are likely to discern lower levels of relationship with the service provider and consequently influence their overall judgements of satisfaction and value in the exchange. Explicit knowledge management is not context specific, as service employees simply reuse the knowledge provided by the organisation. In high relationship service contexts, employees possess unique customer-provider dyadic knowledge based on past transactions with the customer and do not depend on knowledge made available to them by the organisation.

Therefore, when consumers perceive the service provider is using tacit knowledge management practices in a service exchange they are more likely to perceive the service to have:

- More personal meaning for them;
- A higher relationship value; and
- Are more likely to trust the service provider's assistance in value creation leading to higher satisfaction and behavioural intentions.

Based on the following hypothesis is proposed:

- H1. Tacit knowledge management practices will have a stronger impact on consumer satisfaction than explicit knowledge management.

Mediation of Fairness and Control

The positive influence of perceived control and perceived fairness on consumer satisfaction and behavioural intentions has been demonstrated in a number of studies. Researchers have mostly studied control and fairness as important antecedents of customer satisfaction and behavioural intentions. However, not much attention has been given to study the antecedents of control and fairness, other than studies related to service failure and service recovery. This study proposes that service providers' knowledge management practices have a significant impact on control and fairness perceptions of customers. Further, when consumers perceive high control and fairness in the service exchange they are more likely to evaluate the service positively.

Control and KM

Scholars have suggested that people are more likely to feel and behave more positively when they perceive high control in any environment. Empirical studies have found a significant positive relationship between perceived control and human physical and psychological well-being. In a service encounter any situational or interpersonal characteristic that enhances customers' perceived control will positively affect customer satisfaction and behavioural intentions. Suprenant and Solomon explained "personalised service" in service encounters as a service provided based on the recognition of specific unique requirements of a customer as an individual over and above his/her status as an anonymous service recipient.

Personalisation was proposed by scholars as a significant determinant of perceptions of control and customer satisfaction. Researchers recommend that service organisations adopt effective KM practices to provide personalised service experiences that fulfill customers' unique needs and enhance customers' perceptions of control of the service value creation process leading to higher satisfaction and behavioural intentions.

Suprenant and Solomon suggests that "programmed personalisation" consisting of routine actions to make each person feel like an individual and not just another customer may not necessarily lead to higher customer satisfaction. However "customised personalisation" will increase customers' confidence that they will obtain the best alternative, one that fulfills their unique needs and influence their satisfaction evaluations. More specifically, in a high relationship oriented service, customers will perceive higher control of the value creation process when service providers employ knowledge about customerspecific preferences developed through prior transactions. When customers observe service providers using tacit knowledge to assist in building their desired service product, they feel more in control. The use of tacit knowledge indicates to customers that the service provider will provide the required service components based on their awareness of the consumers' preferences. Higher perceptions of control lead to higher satisfaction and behavioural intentions.

Therefore, the following hypotheses are proposed.

- *H2a*: Perceived control will mediate the relationship between knowledge management practices and satisfaction.
- *H2b*: Tacit knowledge management practices will have a stronger impact on perceived control than explicit knowledge management practices.

Fairness and KM

Appropriate KM practices ensure customers desired levels of perceived control over the value creation process. However, KM practices may not always influence customers' perceptions of control over the value creation process. For example, when in order to create a suitable product a service provider performs certain value adding processes obscured from customers' direct observation, customers are unlikely to perceive control over the processes. In this instance, service provider behaviours indicate the quality of the interaction to the customer. Research has shown that when service providers demonstrate courtesy, consideration, impartiality, and appropriate knowledge collectively termed fair behaviours, customers are reassured of the service providers' service intentions. As noted earlier, when service providers demonstrate knowledge about the customers' preferences, this is important to establishing relationship quality in the minds of the customer with effects on satisfaction. In the absence of perceptions of control over the processes, appropriate demonstration of customer and product knowledge reassures customers of both, their value to the organisation and that they will receive their desired product. Recently, scholars have proposed more focus on CRM strategies to seek, gather, and store the right information to provide personalised and unique guest experiences.

In a service encounter when consumers perceive that service providers are effectively using knowledge management to assist them create the desired service product customers are more likely to perceive the service exchange process to be fair. Customers in a service relationship who perceive that their service provider employs tacit knowledge to assist in the value creation process will report higher levels of perceived fairness. As noted earlier, the adoption of tacit knowledge in interactions indicates a stronger relationship and adds value to any interpersonal interaction. Further, reliance on tacit knowledge reassures the customer of the service intentions of the service provider – that the customer will receive the best 'deal' possible due to expected future interactions, shared history, and reciprocal identification. Since explicit knowledge is codified and external to the service provider, it is less likely to reassure customers of reciprocal identification and a shared history.

Therefore the following hypotheses are formulated:

- *H3a*: Tacit knowledge management rather than explicit knowledge management practices will have a stronger impact on perceived fairness.
- *H3b*: Perceived fairness will mediate the relationship between knowledge management practices and satisfaction.

METHODOLOGY

Sample and Procedure

Participants included 36 staff members and 110 management students from two management departments at a Northeastern university in United States. Since no significant differences were found, the student and non-student samples were combined making the overall sample size 146. Fifty two per cent of the sample was female and the average age was 26 years. The study attempts to attain diversity in sample demographics to overcome one major limitation of an experimental study, namely the limited generalizability of findings to a population.

Deliberate sampling for heterogeneity was adopted in this study by recruiting both student and non-student sample, to increase external validity of the findings of this study. Participants were randomly assigned to either a tacit or explicit knowledge management experimental condition. Researchers have demonstrated the ecological validity of videos in general, and also in simulating service settings. Moreover, video clips have been shown to have high predictive validity in a number of different settings, including interpersonal interactions. Knowledge management practices were manipulated using two video scenarios.

The experiment was conducted in a hotel setting. Before watching the video, participants were asked to imagine they were in a hotel, where they had stayed in the past. The video showed a front desk clerk enacting the two experimental conditions. The video was made from the point of view of the camera - the front desk clerk looks and speaks directly into the lens of the camera as if the respondent were being addressed. In the first video scenario, the front desk clerk uses tacit knowledge to assist the customer. In the second video scenario, the front desk clerk uses explicit knowledge to help the customer. To control for gender effects, both male and female front-desk clerks were used in the study. Respondents were randomly assigned to watch one of the two video scenarios. After watching the video, respondents completed a survey questionnaire consisting of Likert type scale items. A between subject analysis of variance and an analysis of covariance design in SPSS 17.0 was utilised to test the hypotheses. The dependent variables measured were satisfaction and behavioural intentions, and the mediating variables were perceived fairness and perceived control.

Knowledge Management Manipulation Check Item Generation

The success of the knowledge management manipulation was measured using two scales developed for this study. The scales measured tacit and explicit knowledge management. Items were generated for each scale based on the dimensions proposed by Jasimuddin. Face and content validity of the scales was ensured following Hinkin and Tracey's analysis of variance approach. Using ANOVA to assess each item, the results showed that 14 of 32 explicit KM items had significantly higher mean score on explicit KM construct than tacit KM construct. These 14 items were retained. Similarly, 14 items out of 32 were retained for the tacit KM construct. Cronbach's alpha for perceived tacit KM scale was.95. A sample item is, "The service provider helped me using knowledge off the top of his/her head." Cronbach's alpha for perceived explicit KM scale was.92 indicating adequate reliability. A sample item is, "The service provider used external sources to retrieve information, in order to help me."

Measures

Satisfaction was measured with three items adapted from a three-item satisfaction scale developed by Lee A sample item is, "I am satisfied to do business with this hotel." Cronbach's alpha was.94. Behavioural Intention was measured with three items adapted from a three item behavioural intention scale developed by Lee. A sample item is, "I will definitely use this hotel again." Cronbach's alpha was.93. Perceived control was measured with three items adapted from a perceived control scale developed by Namasivayam. A sample item is, "The service encounter had everything that was essential for the service I needed."

Cronbach's alpha was found to be.85. Perceived fairness was measured with eight items adapted from:

- Truxillo
- Bauer, and
- Colquitt.

A sample item is, "Overall, I believe that the service process was fair." Cronbach's alpha was found to be.81. All items were measured on a scale of 1 to 7.

Analysis

ANOVA was used to test the influence of knowledge management practices on consumer satisfaction, behavioural intentions, perceived fairness, and perceived control. The hypothesised mediation effects of perceived control and perceived fairness on the relationship between knowledge management and dependent variables were tested using ANCOVA.

RESULTS

Manipulation Checks

To examine the effectiveness of the knowledge management manipulation, participants completed the perceived tacit and explicit knowledge management scales developed for this study. Results indicate that respondents in the tacit KM condition perceived higher tacit KM than respondents in the explicit KM condition. Similarly, results also indicate that respondents in the explicit KM condition perceived higher explicit KM than respondents in the tacit KM condition providing support for the effectiveness of the manipulations.

Table. Correlation Matrix (N = 138) (Listwise Deletion)

	KM	Fairness	Control	Satisfaction	Behavioural Intentions
KM					
Fairness	.27**	(.81)			
Control	.15+	.45**	(.85)		
Satisfaction	.36**	.73**	.57**	(.94)	
Behavioural Intentions	.34**	.60**	.52**	.82**	(.93)

Note: Cronbach's alphas reported on the diagonal in prentheses.

1KM: 1 = Tacit KM; 0 = Explicit KM

**p <0.01

*p < 0.05

+p < 0.1

Table presents the correlation matrix. The correlations are all in the desired direction. Significant correlations were found between KM practices and perceived fairness, satisfaction, and behavioural intentions. Although the correlation between KM and perceived control was in the desired direction, the relationship was not significant.

Therefore, the correlations indicate that the respondents reported higher perceptions of fairness, satisfaction, and behavioural intentions in the tacit KM condition compared to the explicit KM condition. Additionally, positive correlations were found between perceived control, perceived fairness, satisfaction, and behavioural intentions.

Table. Means and Standard Deviations

Variables (N = 141)	Fairness (N = 144)	Control (N = 145)	Satisfaction Intentions	Behavioural (N=146)
Explicit KM	3.6(.59)	3.3(.85)	3.4(.88)	3.4(.94)
Tacit KM	4.0(.57)	3.60(.87)	4.1(.85)	4.1(.84)

Table reports the means and standard deviations for all variables of interest. The means reported in Table show patterns as expected. The means of perceived control, perceived fairness, satisfaction, and behavioural intentions were higher in the tacit knowledge management condition than explicit knowledge management condition.

Tests of Hypotheses

The analyses included gender of service employee, gender of respondents, and age as control variables. Age and gender of respondents did not have any influence on outcomes and are therefore not discussed further in this thesis. Since employee gender was found to influence the outcomes, employee gender was used as a covariate in further analyses. The dependent variable, consumer satisfaction, was first subjected to an analysis of variance to compare the tacit and explicit knowledge management conditions.

Therefore, hypothesis 1 is strongly supported. Hypothesis 2a proposes the mediating effect of perceived control on the relationship between KM practices and customer satisfaction. Hypothesis 2b predicts that KM will have a positive effect on perceived control. Baron and Kenny propose several necessary steps to test mediation. First, the independent variable (KM) should have a significant effect on the dependent variable. As reported earlier, KM significantly affects consumer satisfaction. Second, the independent variable (KM) should significantly affect the mediator; this requirement was marginally supported. Therefore, hypothesis 2b is partially supported as well. Third, an analysis of covariance was conducted with perceived control as covariate to test the third and fourth requirements for mediation. Results show that control was significantly related to satisfaction. Results indicate that although KM has a significant relationship with satisfaction the size of the relationship reduces when control was partialed out, indicating a partial mediating effect. Therefore, hypothesis 2a is supported.

A similar procedure was followed to test hypothesis 3b which predicted that perceived fairness mediates the relationship between KM and customer satisfaction. The influence of KM on customer satisfaction was reported earlier satisfying step 1. There was a significant effect of KM on perceived fairness, satisfying step 2.

Results indicate that tacit KM had a greater impact on customer perceptions of fairness in the service exchange process, compared to explicit KM, supporting hypothesis 3a. When fairness was introduced as covariate in the model, fairness had a significant effect on satisfaction. The effect of KM on satisfaction is reduced when fairness was partialed out, indicating a partial mediating effect. Therefore, hypothesis 3b is supported.

DISCUSSION

The results show that tacit, rather than explicit, knowledge management has a greater influence on customer satisfaction and behavioural intentions in a service encounter. This shows the importance of tacit knowledge management in value creation especially in a high relationship-oriented service context. When customers' perceive that the service provider is using tacit knowledge they are more likely to believe that service providers possess knowledge of the customer's preferences. Use of tacit knowledge strengthens the customer-service provider relationship. In these conditions, customers are more likely to trust the service provider's assistance in value creation resulting in positive evaluations of the service exchange.

Moreover, a partial mediation effect of perceived control on the relationship between KM practices and customer satisfaction was also found in the study.

The results clearly indicate that when service providers use tacit knowledge during a service exchange customers are more likely to perceive higher control in the value creation process compared to when service providers use explicit knowledge. Use of tacit knowledge by service providers ensure the customers that service providers possess knowledge about customer-specific preferences developed through prior transactions.

Therefore, the use of tacit knowledge by service employees provide an indication to customers that the service employee will provide the appropriate service components to assist customers in building their desired service product. This assurance enhances customer perceptions of control in the service exchange process as they are certain that they will be able to create the desired service product. Consequently, higher perceptions of control lead to positive service exchange evaluations. Although a partial mediating effect of control was found, the effect was weak.

Additionally, the effect of KM on control was not very high. The results clearly support the propositions made earlier that KM practices may not always influence customers' perceptions of control over the value creation process as often service provider perform certain value adding processes which customers might fail to observe, resulting in lower perceptions of control. In these conditions, customers look for fair service provider behaviours which indicate the quality of customer-service provider interaction. A mediating effect of perceived fairness on the relationship between KM practices and customer satisfaction was found in this study.

These results indicate that when service providers use tacit knowledge to assist customers in a service exchange, the customers consider the service exchange to be fairer compared to when service providers use explicit knowledge. Use of tacit knowledge indicates stronger relationships and adds value to the interpersonal interaction between customers and service providers. Reliance on tacit knowledge also assures customers about the service intentions of the service provider to provide the best service components possible to maintain the service relationship. More specifically, when customers believe that the service providers are adopting the appropriate procedures to maintain the customer-provider service relationship, customers are assured that they will be treated fairly.

These higher perceptions of fairness result in higher satisfaction levels and positive behavioural intentions. The correlation matrix, and means and standard deviations, provide evidence of the relationship between knowledge management and behavioural intentions, and satisfaction and behavioural intentions. The correlation matrix shows positive relationships between KM and behavioural intentions. Table shows means for behavioural intentions which are higher for tacit KM condition compared to explicit KM condition. Significant relationships were found between satisfaction and behavioural intentions.

Moreover, ANCOVA results clearly indicate that tacit rather than explicit knowledge practices have a greater influence on customers' behavioural intentions after controlling for employee gender. No separate hypotheses were formulated to test satisfaction-behavioural intentions linkages as the relationship is well established and current results replicate prior findings.

IMPLICATIONS

Managers need to understand the value of tacit knowledge and focus on the tacit knowledge that front-line workers possess. Front-line workers regularly interact with customers in service encounters and as a result service relationships develop. Based on their personal experiences, service providers build their tacit knowledge about customers' preferences and employ this tacit knowledge in future service encounters to strengthen customer-service provider relationship.

Therefore, managers need to install organisational systems that encourage frontline workers to develop and use tacit knowledge in service encounters. Moreover, managers need to understand that it is not always possible for front-line workers in a service setting to follow strict rules and regulations to assist customers. Each customer might approach a service provider with completely different requirements. Managers cannot provide front-line employees with solutions to every problem. Therefore, front-line employees have to use their tacit knowledge to handle customers' unique problems. Organisational leaders can take necessary steps to enhance the skills and knowledge of their front-line employees so that employees utilise tacit knowledge management in service encounters.

However, this study does not intend to suggest that tacit knowledge practices are uniformly better. Managers must make informed decisions about the appropriate knowledge practice in customer facing processes based on their organisation's strategic intent. If a repeat and loyal client base and a differentiated product are important facets of the organisation's strategy then tacit knowledge practices add value. If on the other hand, the organisation competes on the basis of volume or a low cost standardised or commoditised product, then explicit knowledge practices will add value to the strategic posture.

LIMITATIONS AND FUTURE DIRECTIONS

Although the study makes valuable contributions in the field of service management, it has limitations. The study utilises video clips to simulate the setting. The main disadvantage of this method is that subjects may not completely identify with the imaginary situation; however, studies have demonstrated the validity of using such methods. Future studies need to test the findings in field settings with actual knowledge management practices used by service providers. The studies can be done in settings such as airports, restaurants, supermarkets, and other service establishments to ensure broader generalizability of the results. Second, future studies can also test the relationships with a different sample. Although age and the student and non-student sample did not affect influence of knowledge management on outcomes, the current sample may not be entirely representative of the population.

The current study makes no attempt to generalise the findings to broader population. However field studies in future can enhance the generalizability of this study. Future field studies can be done with samples that include business travellers, and repeat customers in hotels, restaurants, banks, which may be more representative of the population. Additionally, an investigation of these relationships in different cultural contexts is also important. In some cultures, it might be considered as invasion of privacy if service providers assist customers utilising knowledge based on prior transactions. Third, future studies should compare the influence of knowledge management dimensions in high versus low relationship-oriented service.

It may be that in low relationship services customers prefer service providers to use explicit knowledge management practices, and their use of tacit knowledge may be considered "programmed" leading to negative evaluations. These propositions need to be tested in future studies. Fourth, this study manipulated knowledge management and gender of service providers. Although service provider gender emerged as a significant factor, no interactions between gender and KM practices were found. Gender of service providers was used as a control variable in the current study. Future studies can explore if service employee gender, customer gender, and knowledge practices interact. Further, studies can also investigate the influence of employee race, gender and knowledge management to see the impact on outcomes. Under what conditions is the interaction seen as most fair or satisfying?

This study used perceptions of control and fairness as mediators. Partial mediating effects of perceived fairness and control were found in this study. Future studies can investigate the three way interaction of control, fairness, and knowledge management. Other mediating variables such as trust and self-esteem need to be investigated. Service providers using tacit knowledge management and making sincere efforts to maintain relationships with their customers are likely to enhance customer self-esteem and customer trust with the provider and the organisation, which leads to positive evaluations. Although there was substantial evidence of the influence of KM on perceptions of control, the impact was not strong.

One explanation for the lower influence of KM practices on perceptions of control could be that customers often do not perceive direct control in a service exchange process. In this case, consumers focus more on the fairness of the procedures adopted by service employees to evaluate the exchange. These procedural fairness perceptions reestablish customer perceptions of control.

Therefore, future studies can investigate if certain KM practices, lead to higher fairness perceptions and whether such increase in fairness perceptions leads to perceptions of control and customers' satisfaction in an exchange.

The current study focused on one dimension, procedural fairness. Future studies can perform a detailed examination of the influence of knowledge practices on three dimensions of fairness: procedural, interactional and informational fairness. These investigations can help researchers and practitioners better understand the relationships between knowledge practices and customer evaluations of service exchanges.

STRATEGIES MANAGEMENT IN CUSTOMER SERVICE

The customer service study revealed that no specific tactic, technology, or mission statement is the key to effective customer service delivery. In fact, what is clear is that effective customer service delivery is organization specific, since services are designed around the targeted customers' desires and the frontline employees delivering the services.

The components of the process for producing effective customer service delivery include appropriately identifying and targeting the ideal customer, establishing a customer-focused vision that is consistent with the prioritized desires of the target customers, establishing the operational procedures and internal infrastructure that support customer service, continuously measuring customer and employee satisfaction, embracing change, and striving persistently to improve.

The customer service literature clearly demonstrates that both profit-seeking and public agencies that implement effective customer service strategies realise financial benefits, either through increased profits or through reduced costs associated with long-term, informed customers; customer referrals; employee retention; improved information exchange; and streamlined service delivery.

Child support enforcement, in this case, is like any other business. In order to implement effective customer service strategies and reap the benefits of good customer service, the Office of Child Support Enforcement (OCSE) agencies will need to implement the process of developing effective customer service.

In an effort to become "more results-oriented and responsive to customers," the Office of Child Support Enforcement (OCSE) contracted with Circle Solutions, Inc. to undertake a study of public and private sector practices and outcomes in customer service. The study included a review of customer service literature, a review of the annual reports and Web sites of 40 companies mentioned in the literature, telephone interviews with companies sited as leaders in customer service in the literature, and site visits to three agencies—two private and one child support agency.

Throughout the study, an advisory group of four State child support enforcement directors provided input and feedback. As a final product of the study, this report summarizes the literature on effective approaches to customer service delivery, highlights four promising practice case studies, conjectures about the transferability of these concepts to child support, and offers future research recommendations. Child support enforcement agencies can refer to this report as a guide for improving customer service, as a resource to learn the costs and benefits of effective customer service delivery, and to inspire future enquiries into effective customer service delivery.

In the 1990s, IBM conducted global research on the question, "What will keep CEOs and senior management awake at night as we begin the twenty-first century?" The study found that, regardless of the industry or geographic location, the most common response was a desire to generate a more customer-oriented culture or business vision.

Customer service is not merely customer relations or how nice frontline workers are to customers. Rather, satisfying or even delighting customers is the goal of excellent customer service. Because customers for different types of services have different needs, customer service strategies will differ and must be tailored to the target customer.

It improves trust and information exchange: In the public sector, including child support offices, good customer service generates satisfied or delighted customers. Satisfied customers lead to increased compliance, improved information exchange, improved relationships, increased trust, and, potentially, decreased workloads or costs. For instance, police departments across the Nation have embraced the concept of community policing. Through community policing, police departments incorporate a customer focus as well as an attitude of partnership with customers, to increase satisfaction and trust and even reduce fear of crime in the community. Customers actually participate in addressing crime and disorder problems, thus reducing the workload on patrol officers.

It saves money and increases profit: In the private sector, good customer service leads to satisfied or delighted customers, which generates customer loyalty, which produces increased revenues and reduced costs. For example, during the early 1990s, IBM transformed itself into a customer-driven organization. From 1994–1999, customer satisfaction increased by 5.5 per cent, revenue increased from $63 billion to over $80 billion, cost and expense savings equaled $7 billion, and stock prices improved over 1,000 per cent.

Upon becoming CEO of Greater Southeast Hospital, a private, non-profit community hospital, Tom Chapman refocused customer service strategy to save the faltering hospital. Instead of trying to attract more clientele outside the community or turning away the uninsured in the community it served, under Chapman's leadership, Greater Southeast sought to provide better customer service—improving the quality of life and creating community-specific services.

The emphasis shifted to treating people when it was cheapest—not in the emergency room but rather when their problems were minor—and to instituting preventative care.

He opened a clinic in the high school to address minor health issues and provide health education resources to teach students about prevention. Additionally, Mr. Chapman improved coordination with the local health clinic and obtained the specific technology from which patients served by the hospital would benefit. Before his arrival, Greater Southeast spent only $20,000–$30,000 a year on a blood pressure programme, although a single stroke victim could cost $30,000 to treat.

The public and private sector customer service literature concurs on the process for delivering great customer service, even if outcomes differ. The current literature supports an outside-in strategy of customer service, rather than the traditional inside-out model for providing services. In the private sector, profit and growth are the *outcomes,* not goals.

Profit and growth are generated by customer loyalty. Loyalty is generated by customer satisfaction. Customer satisfaction is the *goal* that companies should seek and focus on, because high customer satisfaction, as a matter of course, produces customer loyalty and subsequently profit and growth. At this point, the public and private sectors converge—customer satisfaction is the *goal*.

Customer satisfaction is achieved by providing valued services and products, where value is the positive difference between customers' actual experiences and their service delivery expectations. Productive employees also create value.

Employee productivity stems from employee loyalty, and loyalty is a product of employee satisfaction. Satisfaction is generated by high-quality support services (people, information, and technology) and by being empowered to provide value and resolve customer complaints.

This customer service culture must be supported by leadership that emphasizes the importance of each customer and employee. These leaders must be creative and energetic (not lofty or conservative), participatory and caring (not removed or elitist), that is, one who can be a coach, teacher, or listener (not just a supervisor or manager).

Such a leader demonstrates company values (rather than simply institutionalizing policies) and motivates by mission (rather than by fear).

Some components of this model are cyclical. A 1991 study of property and casualty insurance companies found that employees who felt that they were meeting customer needs had twice the job satisfaction level of employees who did not believe they were meeting customer needs. In that study, when a frontline service worker left the company, customer satisfaction levels dropped from 75 to 55 per cent.

In the customer service literature, five guiding principles are adopted by public as well as private agencies delivering excellent customer service:

- Embrace change and persistently strive to improve (be a learning organization).
- Continually ask the target customers what they want and then give it to them.
- Empower, support, and reward frontline personnel.
- Harness the power of information.
- Establish an enabling infrastructure.
- Identify the Target Customer.
  - Begin by identifying the target customers and by considering the point of purchase, point of service delivery or receipt, and point of consumption.
  - Cluster or segment target customers based on their common behaviours, knowing that targeting the wrong customers can have adverse effects on the organization.
  - Determine the priorities of various clusters of customers, knowing that the capabilities of the organization are crucial in addressing these priorities.
  - When possible, focus on customers with high current or future value. (Perhaps in child support this is a custodial parent with many children in the system.) This does not mean that other customers will not receive service, but it may mean that they will receive a different level of service. Consider the frequent flier programmes that airlines and hotels offer to their customers with high current and future value. This does not mean that other passengers will not receive services, but services may not be at the same level.
  - Discourage non-target customers, those who are not likely to be satisfied by the services, and those to whom it is expensive to provide services, which is a necessary part of a customer focus. A simple example is offered as an illustration. A fire department could discourage residents from contacting the department to remove cats from trees by charging a $20 fee for performing the service and by advertising their busy emergency call load. The equipment and time investment of sending a ladder truck and several firefighters may reduce the effectiveness of the department at responding to an emergency and may not be the most prompt means of accomplishing the task for the customer.
- Determine What Customers Want..
  - Determine what target customers want (not just what they need right now) by asking them in person or as part of a mail or

telephone survey or by using other mechanisms (*e.g.*, electronic tracking and researching marketing trends) to determine what they want. Be aware that advertising, word of mouth, and public relations influence customers'expectations. Meeting customers'basic needs or expectations does not always bring high levels of satisfaction. Exceeding expectations produces high satisfaction-therefore, determine customers'ideal desires.

- Determine how the target customers prioritize their "wants." Generally, customers want convenience, quality products and services, variety or selection, low prices, and protection or security. However, each organization must identify what is most important to its customers.
- Weigh how important the customer-identified"wants"are to the organization. Are the services something that the organization does, is capable of doing, or wants to pursue?
- Determine how well the organization can meet the customers'"wants"in comparison with competitors. The success of other companies at meeting and exceeding customer expectations changes a customer's frame of reference and increases a customer's expectations.
- Determine which"wants,"if performance delivery were to be improved, would most impact the organization's bottom line (profit, cost, loyalty, trust, or compliance).

• Establish an Organizational Culture Supportive of Customer Service.
  - Utilizing the information gathered, establish the company's customer-focused vision. The vision statement should be simple and may also identify what the company does not want to be. Some examples of simple vision statements include"Absolutely, Positively Overnight"by Federal Express and L.L. Bean's promise "Guaranteed. Period."
  - Live up to what is promised by concurrently developing and applying externally and internally oriented strategic service concepts that reflect the vision. If the organization does not implement both internally and externally oriented service strategies consistent with the vision, the organization will have good intentions but poor customer service (Thompson).
  - Continually reflect on the vision and goals and the way services are delivered to customers. Be creative about the mechanisms used to create and deliver new services. Be willing to change existing practices to integrate improvements.

• Implement an Externally Oriented Strategic Service Concept. The externally oriented strategic service concept establishes how the organization's service is designed, marketed, and delivered to target customers.

- Take into account the costs of providing services and ways to minimize those costs while implementing quality control. The service concept must be developed with the frontline worker at its centre. Determine the necessary financial, human, and technological resources necessary, as well as how the organizational structure and flow can enable the frontline worker to delight the customer and deliver the promised vision.
- Use advertising/educational strategies to set appropriate customer expectations.
- When planning, realise that control of information can take the place of assets. For instance, the Rural/Metro Fire Department in Scottsdale (AZ) has reduced the size of its crew and trucks because of technology that allows crews to view microfiche floor plans on the way to a fire. The added knowledge of the building layout allows fewer fire fighters to accomplish the same task that requires more firefighters when they do not have this advance knowledge.
- Provide a feedback loop for incorporating customer comments and complaints into the planning processes. Customer complaints are an invaluable resource and source of information without which organizations cannot be successful. Complaints brought to the organization are one of the most efficient and least expensive ways to obtain information about customer expectations of products and services. Complaints are a more direct means of obtaining information than conducting research studies of customer expectations, conducting transaction studies, or reviewing customer expectations in parallel industries. Another means of soliciting customer feedback that has been implemented by a number of service leaders is to interview lost customers-those who have switched service providers. (Perhaps in child support these customers were custodial parents who had been making timely payments but who stopped doing so.) Still other options are holding customer meetings, hosting social events, and attending seminars or conferences where customers are present. Ensure that the complaint resolution strategy supports the customer-focused vision. Most research shows, "...if customers believe their complaints are welcomed and responded to, they will more likely repurchase." British Airways found that 67 per cent of its complaining passengers fly again if their complaints are handled well. British Airways even implemented a creative

and convenient way to allow customers to complain by installing video booths at Heathrow Airport so that customers could immediately go into a booth and state a complaint, even during non-business hours. The videotapes are reviewed and addressed during business hours.

   – One final element of an externally oriented service strategy is to regularly measure customer satisfaction or delight in the products and services.

- Implement an Internally Oriented Strategic Service Concept.

The internally oriented strategic service concept establishes how the organization's internal processes will support the customer-focused vision. The premise behind the internally oriented strategic service concept is "...capable workers who are well trained and fairly compensated provide better service, need less supervision, and are much more likely to stay on the job. As a result, their customers are likely to be more satisfied...". A study by Sears in 1989 found that "employee turnover and customer satisfaction are directly correlated." Stores with high customer service ratings had a 54 per cent sales force turnover versus 83 per cent in stores with low customer service ratings. This is supported by examples throughout the literature. Taco Bell found that the 20 per cent of stores with the lowest employee turnover rates have 55 per cent higher profits (an outcome of customer satisfaction) than the 20 per cent of stores with the highest turnover rates.

A number of other studies provide convincing evidence as to why companies should avoid employee turnover. Merck and Co. found in 1990 that turnover costs were 1.5 times an employee's annual salary. Clearly this varies based on a number of cost factors (*e.g.*, workers compensation claims, hiring process costs, training costs, and lost business), but it is commonly noted that employee turnover is an expensive problem. Abt Associates studied an automobile dealer's sales and determined that it cost $36,000 to replace a salesperson with 5–8 years of experience with a salesperson with less than 1 year of experience. The economic costs of excessive employee turnover in one trucking company were analysed, and it was determined that the company could increase profits by 50 per cent by cutting driver turnover in half.

- Ensure that leaders of the learning organization exhibit the company values. Leaders must foster the creation and testing of new ideas and be unabashedly willing to change existing practices to integrate improvements.
- Identify employee groups important to implementing the externally oriented service concept. Frontline workers are of central importance.
   – Identify the characteristics and needs of the employee group(s) and how well those needs are met. This may include resources needed to successfully perform the job or needs can refer to

compensation, work environmental factors, or personal needs. Understanding employee needs helps an organization to develop successful processes as well as employee retention policies. Learn how targeted employees perceive the proposed customer services. An organization cannot change without the participation of its employees.

- Focus on recruiting employees who support the customer service vision. The costs of employing people who do not support the customer service vision are considerable. Forum Corporation research in the service industry showed, "...only 14 per cent [per cent] of customers who stop patronizing service businesses do so because they are dissatisfied with what they bought. More than two-thirds defect because they find service people indifferent or unhelpful." Oftentimes, the right employees are those that fit in with the corporate culture's customer service vision, not necessarily those with the most experience in the industry. Additionally, develop career paths that allow successful customer-oriented employees to remain on the frontline.
- Focus on training and employee development throughout employment. A study by Ryder Truck from 1988 through 1989 found that increased training meant lower employee turnover.
- Empower frontline employees to do what it takes to satisfy the customer. Management must support employee empowerment by clearly defining the parametres of the empowerment, while remaining flexible within the parametres. This will encourage creativity. Rules should be simple and few—Continental Airlines actually had an employee handbook burning party to signify the change from a procedural environment to one of empowered customer service. Also, in support of internal customers, the Department of Defence reduced its 230 pages of travel regulations to 17 pages.
- Ensure that management supports employee decisions and judgement calls, even if this means that the cost of satisfying customers initially increases. In positions of high customer contact, quality control is not met by increased supervision, but by the use of incentives to emphasize quality, making service providers highly visible to customers, and by building a peer group to instill a sense of pride and teamwork.
- In addition to skills and empowerment, equip frontline personnel with the technology, information, and internal resources to do what it takes to satisfy the customer. The literature is replete with examples of how incorporating the latest information technology can improve employee productivity. For example, Charles Schwab developed IWIN,

a system that allows an agent to identify and view electronically Charles Schwab literature to respond to customer questions received by telephone. Before this system was implemented, agents who were unfamiliar with the literature in question could not provide immediate and succinct answers to customer questions.

- Ensure that divisions and individuals within the organization communicate. Frontline employees and other employees need information and a support network. A customer should never have to tell one employee what another employee already knows.
- Develop cross-functional teams for operations and improvement tasks. First ask those who are doing the work for suggestions to improve productivity. The Social Security Administration nearly doubled its telephone-answering capacity by implementing automated features, utilizing additional technology to change the way employers' reports of wages are recorded, and cross training its employees to work outside their normal areas of responsibility during peak periods.
- Link all employees' compensation to (and offer rewards for) good customer service performance. Rewards can be money, status, praise, acknowledgement, or perks such as trips or special events. While Charles Schwab does provide monetary incentives based on the amount of money a broker team brings into the company, if the customer service survey for the quarter does not show strong customer service by the team, the reward is reduced or even eliminated for the quarter. This policy in a profit-seeking environment leaves no doubt that customer satisfaction is the primary goal.
- Finally, measure employee satisfaction regularly. Leaders in the service industry have employed such methods as toll-free numbers, periodic roundtable meetings, and surveys to collect employee satisfaction information.

CUSTOMER EXPECTATION OF SERVICE MANAGEMENT

As the consumer market segment of the Internet economy continues to grow, the role of customer service in the emerging logistics supply chain systems will continue to change. Therefore, the need to improve logistics customer service (LCS) to consumers is greater than ever before. Finding meaningful ways to meet consumer service expectations requires LCS programmes that strategically blend web site service activities (*e.g.*, online ordering procedures) with offline logistics supply chain activities (*e.g.*, order delivery).

This balance may be a key strategy in satisfying and maintaining loyalty relationships with online consumers. Yet very little is understood about the nature of web site-enabled LCS and the impact on online customer loyalty, although the level of e-logistics service expectations is often thought to be higher than that demanded by customers in brick-and-mortar environments.

The purpose of this study is to examine:

- The factors that determine the level of perceived LCS quality in the Internet-enabled logistics supply chain, and
- The impact of LCS quality on customer loyalty towards online retailers'web sites.

Internet-enabled logistics supply chain refers to the total logistics system of transportation, warehousing, inventory, order processing, information flow, and web site-enabled order processing procedures that drive the level of perceived quality of LCS in this system. Perceived LCS quality is defined as the level of expectation-minus performance gap and customer intended loyalty is defined as the tendency of online consumers to repurchase from the same web site, as reflected in repurchase intentions or intention to recommend a web site to peers. Following conventional practice, LCS was defined as the total output of the logistics system, but with emphasis on cognitive impact: perceived service speed and consistency of service speed, perceived availability of merchandise on the retailer's web site and in the supply chain, and perceived responsiveness of the retailer.

This study contributes to the literature on two levels. At the conceptual level, the study provides an empirical validation of the logistics customer service-customer loyalty linkage in the online environment. While this linkage has been widely established in traditional business-to-business markets, it remains to be established in the online environment where the impersonal and self-service nature of customer service may raise doubts about the validity of the LCS-customer linkage.

At the managerial level, the study suggests ways to create a consumer-oriented online logistics customer service strategy by identifying the relevant web-based and traditional supply chain logistics activities that are important in creating and maintaining loyalty relationships with online consumers. As with all service activities, not all web site features are likely to be relevant to consumer perception of online LCS quality. Moreover, different web site features are likely to play different roles in consumer perception of LCS quality. Thus, this study provides insight into which web site features should be emphasized in the different phases of the Internet-enabled logistics supply chain.

The following discussion presents an overview of the influence of web site design strategy on LCS quality assessment among online consumers. Using the consumer disconfirmation theory as a theoretical foundation, a conceptual framework is proposed including the hypotheses isolating influences of key web site design features on LCS quality, followed by the field study that was conducted to specifically examine the service encounter evaluation of 373 online transactions. Finally, analysis and findings are discussed followed by a discussion of the managerial implications and suggestions for future research.

VALUES AND ATTITUDES DIFFER ACROSS CULTURES

Values and attitudes help to determine what members of a culture think is right, important, and/or desirable. Because behaviours, including consumer behaviours, flow from values and attitudes, services marketers who want their services adopted across, cultures must understand these differences While American brands often have an "exotic" appeal to other cultures, U.S. firms should not count on this as a long-term strategy.

In the late 1990s, Wal-Mart found that the cachet of U.S. brands was falling in Mexico. The Mexican news media alerted consumers to shoddy foreign goods and some Wal- Mart customers turned to a spirit of nationalism. The retailer responded with an "Hecho en Mexico" programme similar to the "Made in the U.S.A." programme that was successful in the United States. In some situations it is more than a case of nationalism: Brand attitudes are negatively influenced by specific prejudices towards "dominating" cultures.

10

Enterprise Resource Planning

OVERVIEW

Information in large organizations is often spread across numerous homegrown computer systems, housed in different functions or organizational units. While each of these "information islands" can ably support a specific business activity, enterprise-wide performance is hampered by the lack of integrated information. Further, the maintenance of these systems can result in substantial costs. For example, many of the older programmes cannot properly handle dates beyond the year 2000, and they must be fixed at a steep cost or replaced. While the Y2K bug has been fixed over time, the lack of integration is a pervasive problem.

Consider, for example, Boeing, which relies on hundreds of internal and external suppliers for the millions of components needed to build an airplane. The goal of putting the right parts in the right airplane in the right sequence at the right time was managed at Boeing by four hundred systems that were designed in the sixties and were all but integrated. Information inconsistencies were prevalent and the systems were not synchronized. As a result, parts often arrived late, idling partially-built airplanes on Boeing's assembly lines. In 1997, as Boeing faced unprecedented demand for its aircraft, these problems became unbearable, and the company's manufacturing ground to a halt. Boeing was forced to shut down two of its major assembly lines and take a ₹ 1.6 billion charge against earnings. Boeing has since replaced these systems by an integrated Enterprise Resource Planning system based on commercial, off-the-shelf software. With the advent of E-Business and the need to leverage multiple sources of information within the enterprise, ERP software has emerged as a major area of interest for many businesses.

Back-office enterprise software has its roots in the 1960s and 1970s, as computing power became affordable enough for companies to automate materials planning through MRP and financial processing through payroll and general ledger software. MRP, short for Material Requirements Planning, was developed in the early 1960s at IBM and had become the principal production control paradigm in the U.S. MRP consists of a set of procedures that convert forecasted demand for a manufactured product into a requirements schedule for the components, subassemblies and raw materials comprising that product.

MRP is limited to controlling the flow of components and materials, and does not lend itself to more complete production control and coordination. The next generation of manufacturing software, known as MRP II, was developed to address this shortcoming and to further integrate business activities into a common framework. MRP II divides the production control problem into a hierarchy based on time scale and product aggregation.

It coordinates the manufacturing process, allowing a variety of tasks such as capacity planning, demand management, production scheduling and distribution to be linked together. However, even MRP II is primarily a specialized tool designed to serve the needs of the manufacturing function within a company. Its data and processes are not integrated with those in the rest of the enterprise, such as marketing, finance and human resources. ERP entered the scene to facilitate information sharing and integration across these different functions and to operate the enterprise more efficiently and effectively, using a unified data store and consistent processes.

WHAT IS ERP

ERP is a software architecture that facilitates the flow of information among the different functions within an enterprise. Similarly, ERP facilitates information sharing across organizational units and geographical locations. It enables decision-makers to have an enterprise-wide view of the information they need in a timely, reliable and consistent fashion. ERP provides the backbone for an enterprise-wide information system. At the core of this enterprise software is a central database which draws data from and feeds data into modular applications that operate on a common computing platform, thus standardizing business processes and data definitions into a unified environment.

With an ERP system, data needs to be entered only once. The system provides consistency and visibility or transparency across the entire enterprise. A primary benefit of ERP is easier access to reliable, integrated information. A related benefit is the elimination of redundant data and the rationalization of processes, which result in substantial cost savings. The integration among business functions facilitates communication and information sharing, leading to dramatic gains in productivity and speed. Cisco Systems, for example, harnessed ERP to help it become the market leader in the global networking industry. Cisco's ERP system was the backbone that enabled its new business model Global Networked Business based on the use of electronic communications to build interactive, knowledge-based relationships with its customers, business partners, suppliers and employees.

In the process, Cisco doubled in size each year and reaped hundreds of millions of dollars in both cost savings and revenue enhancements. Autodesk, a computer-aided design software company, reported a decrease in its order fulfillment times from two weeks to 24 hours after installing an ERP system. Similar examples abound in today's business environment. Based on the promise of tightly-integrated corporate functions, globally optimized decisions and fast and easy access to accurate information, enterprise software has become an essential part of the operations of large businesses in many industries. By 1998, over 20,000 firms around the world spent system provides consistency and visibility ₹ 17 billion on enterprise software, following annual growth rates that ranged from 30 per cent to 50 per cent. In addition to direct spending on the software itself, companies often spend a multiple of licensing costs on services related to implementation and maintenance. Companies are beginning use enterprise software to automate front-office activities such as sales and marketing, call centre operations, product configuration, lead-tracking and customer relationship management.

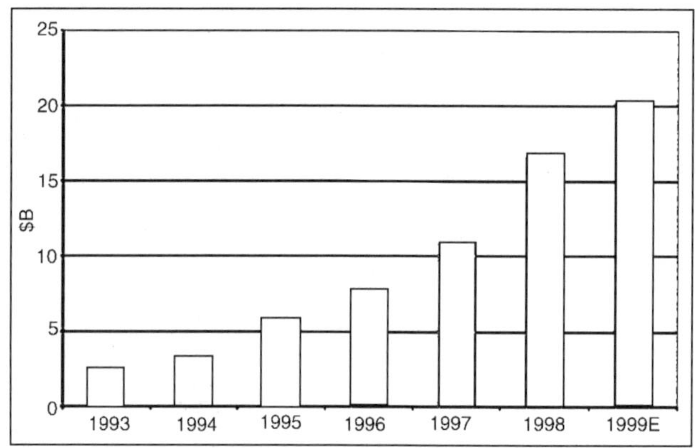

Fig. ERP Software Market Revenues

Growth of the Enterprise Software Industry

A number of trends drove the growth of the enterprise software market. First, an integrated information architecture improves business performance. Once a major company in an industry adopts enterprise software, competitors may be compelled to follow suit to stay competitive. Second, there has been a major shift towards the use of packaged applications. This is partly related to the "Y2K bug" and the European Union's conversion to a single currency, which induced companies to replace their legacy systems with packaged software effectively "outsourcing" the solution to the ERP vendor. Third, many companies were abandoning legacy software due to the demands of electronic commerce and front office applications on the front end and linking to suppliers and business partners at the back end.

Similarly, the emergence of ERP-based "vertical applications" that address the enterprise software needs of a specific industry have caused many companies to purchase ERP packages. Finally, rapid advances in computer and software technologies combined with the explosive growth of the Internet have led many companies to rethink their business practices, to put a greater emphasis on their use of IT, and to invest in a more robust enterprise architecture. Competition in the enterprise software business is fierce, with hundreds of software producers fighting for market share. The market has both companies that offer an integrated suite of applications and those that address specific business process. The first group consists of five companies known in industry parlance as JBOPS J.D. Edwards, Baan, Oracle, PeopleSoft, and SAP AG. These companies attempted to create "end-to-end" solutions for the entire enterprise, hoping that corporate customers will purchase almost all of their critical enterprise applications from a single vendor.

The reasoning behind this strategy is twofold.

First, it is increasingly important for enterprise applications to communicate and interact with each other seamlessly. For example, a company can commit to a more reliable delivery time if its sales order entry and manufacturing software packages are integrated; if the same vendor produces all of the software, applications can integrate more tightly.

Second, customers may prefer to rely on one major vendor for most of their software needs, because having a single vendor simplifies contracting and relationship management and creates a single point of accountability for all software problems.

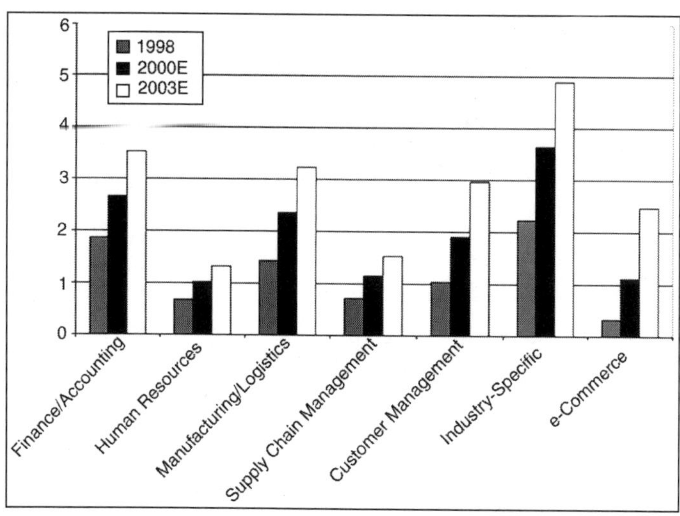

Fig. ERP and ERP-Related Packaged Application Market

On the other hand, scores of companies that make innovative products compete to provide software solutions for customer relationship management, supply chain management, electronic commerce and purchasing. These companies offer software that can be "bolted on" to the existing ERP backbone and, together, provide a flexible "bestof- breed" portfolio of solutions in different areas. Players in the area of customer relationship management include Siebel Systems, Clarify, Remedy, Epiphany, Broadvision and Trilogy. These firms produce software to help with customer support, product configuration, one-to-one marketing and sales-force automation. Leaders in ecommerce software are too numerous to list, but some examples are GE Information Systems, Sterling Communications, Ariba Technologies and Commerce One. Supply chain management software helps companies optimize their production processes and logistics across the entire supply chain; Technologies and Manugistics are leaders in this area. The size of the packaged application market by category, and market forecasts for the years 2000 and 2003, are shown in Figure.

COMPONENTS/MODULES

- Transactional Backbone
  - Financials
  - Distribution
  - Human Resources
  - Product lifecycle management
- Advanced Applications
  - Customer Relationship Management
  - Supply chain management software
    a. Purchasing
    b. Manufacturing
    c. Distribution
  - Warehouse Management System
- Management Portal/Dashboard
  - Decision Support System

These modules can exist in a system or can be utilized in an ad-hoc fashion.

MEANING AND DEFINITION OF ENTERPRISES

To be able to understand the problem at hand, it is important that we articulate the issue we are discussing. SSEs are defined differently in different countries. It is true that a SSE in the United States may be a large enterprise in India and a very large enterprise in Uganda. While the absolute figures involved in the definition of these enterprises may differ, there are some underlying similarities in the concept used in the definitions. The following are common measures of defining SSE.

SIZE DEFINITIONS

The legal definition of "small" varies by country and by industry. In the

United States the Small Business Administration establishes small business size standards on an industry-by-industry basis, but generally specifies a small business as having fewer than 500 employees for manufacturing businesses and less than $7 million in annual receipts for most non-manufacturing businesses.

The definition can vary by circumstance – for example, a small business having fewer than 25 full-time equivalent employees with average annual wages below $50,000 qualifies for a tax credit under the health care reform bill Patient Protection and Affordable Care Act. In the European Union, a small business generally has under 50 employees. However, in Australia, a small business is defined by the Fair Work Act 2009 as one with fewer than 15 employees.

By comparison, a medium sized business or mid-sized business has under 500 employees in the US, 250 in the European Union and fewer than 200 in Australia. In addition to number of employees, other methods used to classify small companies include annual sales (turnover), value of assets and net profit (balance sheet), alone or in a mixed definition. These criteria are followed by the European Union, for instance (headcount, turnover and balance sheet totals). Small businesses are usually not dominant in their field of operation.

ADVANTAGES OF SMALL BUSINESS

A small business can be started at a very low cost and on a part-time basis. Small business is also well suited to internet marketing because it can easily serve specialized niches, something that would have been more difficult prior to the internet revolution which began in the late 1990s. Adapting to change is crucial in business and particularly small business; not being tied to any bureaucratic inertia, it is typically easier to respond to the marketplace quickly. Small business proprietors tend to be intimate with their customers and clients which results in greater accountability and maturity. Independence is another advantage of owning a small business.

One survey of small business owners showed that 38 per cent of those who left their jobs at other companies said their main reason for leaving was that they wanted to be their own bosses. Freedom to operate independently is a reward for small business owners. In addition, many people desire to make their own decisions, take their own risks, and reap the rewards of their efforts. Small business owners have the satisfaction of making their own decisions within the constraints imposed by economic and other environmental factors.

However, entrepreneurs have to work very long hours and understand that ultimately their customers are their bosses. Several organizations also provide help for the small business sector, such as the Internal Revenue Service's Small Business and Self-Employed One-Stop Resource.

PROBLEMS FACED BY SMALL BUSINESSES

Small businesses often face a variety of problems related to their size. A frequent cause of bankruptcy is undercapitalization. This is often a result of poor planning rather than economic conditions—it is common rule of thumb that the entrepreneur should have access to a sum of money at least equal to the projected revenue for the first year of business in addition to his anticipated expenses. For example, if the prospective owner thinks that he will generate $100,000 in revenues in the first year with $150,000 in start-up expenses, then he should have no less than $250,000 available. Failure to provide this level of funding for the company could leave the owner liable for all of the company's debt should he end up in bankruptcy court, under the theory of undercapitalization. In addition to ensuring that the business has enough capital, the small business owner must also be mindful of contribution margin (sales minus variable costs).

To break even, the business must be able to reach a level of sales where the contribution margin equals fixed costs. When they first start out, many small business owners underprice their products to a point where even at their maximum capacity, it would be impossible to break even. Cost controls or price increases often resolve this problem. In the United States, some of the largest concerns of small business owners are insurance costs (such as liability and health), rising energy costs and taxes. In the United Kingdom and Australia, small business owners tend to be more concerned with excessive governmental red tape. Another problem for many small businesses is termed the 'Entrepreneurial Myth' or E-Myth. The mythic assumption is that an expert in a given technical field will also be expert at running that kind of business. Additional business management skills are needed to keep a business running smoothly. Still another problem for many small businesses is the capacity of much larger businesses to influence or sometimes determine their chances for success.

MARKETING THE SMALL BUSINESS

Finding new customers is the major challenge for Small business owners. Small businesses typically find themselves strapped for time but in order to create a continual stream of new business, they must work on marketing their business every day. Common marketing techniques for small business include networking, word of mouth, customer referrals, yellow pages directories, television, radio, outdoor (roadside billboards), print, e-mail marketing, and internet.

Electronic media like TV can be quite expensive and is normally intended to create awareness of a product or service. Many small business owners find internet marketing more affordable. Google AdWords and Yahoo! Search Marketing are two popular options of getting small business products or services in front of motivated Web searchers. Successful online small business marketers are also adept at utilizing the most relevant keywords in their site content.

Advertising on niche sites can also be effective, but with the long tail of the internet, it can be time intensive to advertise on enough sites to garner an effective reach.

Creating a business Web site has become increasingly affordable with many do-it-yourself programmes now available for beginners. A Web site can provide significant marketing exposure for small businesses when marketed through the Internet and other channels. Some popular services are WordPress, Joomla and Squarespace. Social media has proven to be very useful in gaining additional exposure for many small businesses.

Many small business owners use Facebook and Twitter as a way to reach out to their loyal customers to give them news about specials of the day or special coupons and generate repeat business. The relational nature of social media, along with its immediacy and 24-hour presence lend intimacy to the relationship small businesses can have with their customers, while making it more efficient for them to communicate with greater numbers. Facebook ads are also a very cost-effective way for small businesses to reach a targeted audience with a very specific message. In addition to the social networking sites, blogs have become a highly effective way for small businesses to position themselves as experts on issues that are important to their customers.

This can be done with a proprietary blog and/or by using a backlink strategy wherein the marketer comments on other blogs and leaves a link to the small business' own Web site. A solid public relations strategy that utilizes speaking engagements, press releases, feature stories, events and sponsorships can also be a very cost-effective way to build a loyal following for a small business.

FRANCHISE BUSINESSES

Franchising is a way for small business owners to benefit from the economies of scale of the big corporation (franchiser). McDonald's restaurants, TrueValue hardware stores, and NAPA Auto Parts stores are examples of a franchise. The small business owner can leverage a strong brand name and purchasing power of the larger company while keeping their own investment affordable. However, some franchisees conclude that they suffer the "worst of both worlds" feeling they are too restricted by corporate mandates and lack true independence. However, in some chains, such as the aforementioned TrueValue and NAPA, franchises may have their own name alongside the franchise's name.

SMALL BUSINESS BANKRUPTCY

When small business fails, the owner may file bankruptcy. In most cases this can be handled through a personal bankruptcy filing. Corporations can file bankruptcy, but if it is out of business and valuable corporate assets are likely to be repossessed by secured creditors there is little advantage to going to the expense of a corporate bankruptcy. Many states offer exemptions for small business assets so they can continue to operate during and after personal bankruptcy. However, corporate assets are normally not exempt, hence it may be more difficult to continue operating an incorporated business if the owner files bankruptcy.

Certification and Trust

Building trust with new customers can be a difficult task for a new and establishing business. Some organizations like the Better Business Bureau and the International Charter now offer Small Business Certification, which certifies the quality of the services and goods produced and can encourage new and larger customers. These services may require a few hours of work, but a certification may reassure potential customers.

Contribution to the Economy

Small business (less than 500 employees) accounts for around half the GDP and more than half the employment. Regarding small business, the top job provider is those with less than 10 employees, and those with 10 or more but less than 20 employees comes in as the second, and those with 20 or more but less than 100 employees comes in as the third (interpolation of data from the following references). The most recent data shows firms with less than 20 employees account for slightly more than 18 per cent of the employment. Of the 5,369,068 employer firms in 1995, 78.8 per cent had fewer than 10 employees, and 99.7 per cent had fewer than 500 employees.

SOURCES OF FUNDING

Small businesses use several sources available for start-up capital:

- Self-financing by the owner through cash, equity loan on his or her home, and or other assets.
- Loans from friends or relatives
- Grants from private foundations
- Personal Savings
- Private stock issue
- Forming partnerships
- Angel Investors
- Banks
- SME finance, including Collateral based lending and Venture capital, given sufficiently sound business venture plans

Some small businesses are further financed through credit card debt—usually a poor choice, given that the interest rate on credit cards is often several times the rate that would be paid on a line of credit or bank loan. Many owners seek a bank loan in the name of their business, however banks will usually insist on a personal guarantee by the business owner. In the United States, the Small Business Administration (SBA) runs several loan programmes that may help a small business secure loans. In these programmes, the SBA guarantees a portion of the loan to the issuing bank and thus relieves the bank of some of the risk of extending the loan to a small business. The SBA also requires business owners to pledge personal assets and sign as a personal guarantee for the loan. Canadian small businesses can take advantage of federally funded programmes and services.

PRICE POLICY IN PUBLIC ENTERPRISES

In public enterprises, the pricing function is "diffused in excess of the minister, the department, and the managers". Even when the government, through the minister concerned, decides in relation to the common price-profit policy, the actual details of the price structure will have to be worked out through the management of the undertaking. In common as distant as the public enterprises are concerned, the government decides the pricing policy while the managers of scrupulous enterprises decide the price structure within the common framework of the Government's price policy.

PERFORMANCE OF PUBLIC SECTOR

Prior to 1991 when New Economic Policy was announced, while the government has been pushing ahead with more and more public sector undertakings, there has been considerable criticism in relation to the poor performance, and in some cases utter failure of government undertakings in the country. For the reasons mentioned earlier the performance of public enterprises cannot be judged solely on the foundation of profit criteria. Some of the public enterprises were running on profit while several others were running on losses. The in excess of-all picture reveals that flanked by 1960-61 and 1977-78 percentage of profit after tax to total paid-up capital and reserves had ranged flanked by 0.2 to 4.6 per cent. Therefore through thc criterion of "profit after tax" the performance of the public sector has been poor.

Since 1991-92, gross profit as a ratio of capital employed (rate of return on capital) has shown a separate improvement. It increased from 12 per cent in 1991-92 to 16 per cent in 1995-96. In the subsequent years it has been in the range of 13 to 15 per cent. Reviewing the situation it was mentioned: "In absolute conditions net profits (after tax) of Central government public enterprises rose considerably from ₹ 2,400 crores in 1991-92 to ₹ 9600 crores in 1995-96. The rate of return as measured through net profits to capital employed rose to 10 per cent in 1995-96, which is the highest in the decade.

Though, as in previous years, the petroleum sector enterprises contributed the overwhelming bulk of these profits- ₹ 2899 crores out of the total 3789 crores in 1989-90 (76.6 per cent of total). Therefore, the 200 odd non-petroleum enterprises contributed a meagre sum of ₹ 883 crores. While this reflected an improvement in excess of the net profit of ₹ 431 crores in 1988-89, the ratio of net profits to capital employed in non-petroleum sector enterprises was barely 1.3 per cent in 1989-90." Clearly there is substantial scope for improving financial performance of non-petroleum Central government enterprises.

Throughout 1992-93 gross profit as a proportion of capital employed declined to 11 per cent. Net profit of public enterprises declined from ₹ 3789 crores in 1989-90 to ₹ 2272 crores in 1990-91. The net rate of return declined from 4.5 per cent in 1989-90 to 2.2 per cent in 1990-91, the lowest since 1984-85. Throughout 1991-92 it declined further to 2.1 per cent. The petroleum sector, as in the earlier years, accounted for bulk of the net profit ₹ 1779 crores out of the total of ₹ 2475 crores. But 1991-92 being a year of foreign swap crisis, resource crunch and a year of common slackening of industrial manufacture, the public sector also suffered the impact of overall economic deceleration.

As noted before, it is not appropriate to treat profits as the sole criterion of efficiency of the public sector. The gains to employees and welfare expenditures on employees in public enterprises are to be noted in this connection. The real emoluments per employee in the public sector went up from ₹ 11210 in 1978-79 to ₹ 17339 in 1991-92. The annual growth rate of real emoluments works out to 3.43 per cent throughout this period. Further, as against ₹ 420 in 1968-69, the average annual expenditure per employee on welfare behaviours increased to ₹ 4427 in 1988-89.

A total sum of ₹ 974 crores in the form of houses, educational facilities, medical care, etc., was spent in 1988-89 for the benefit of employees. The public sector through assuming responsibility of rehabilitation of sick units (instance, textile mills in private sector) had to bear a considerable burden in order to save 1.6 lakh employees from the spectrum of unemployment. This social responsibility explains to some extent the lower profitability of public sector.

Through the criterion of capability utilisation also, the public sector performance is establish to be better (relative to the private sector) through some studies. The foreign swap earnings of public enterprises also constitute a performance indicator. The value of exports of central public sector enterprises increased from ₹ 502 crores in 1972-73 to ₹ 6366 crores in 1989-90. Physical productivity events also are to be used as performance indicators.

Privatisation

One of the major concerns often expressed with respect to privatisation is that with a transfer of management into private hands, the interest of employees might suffer. Government has chosen to put in necessities into the shareholder agreements, executed as a part of strategic sales, to ensure that there is no retrenchment of employees at least for a period of one year after privatisation, and even thereafter, retrenchment to be possible only under the Voluntary Retirement Scheme (VRS) as applicable under Department of Public Enterprises (DPE) guidelines or the Voluntary Separation Scheme, which was prevailing in the company prior to disinvestments, whichever is more beneficial for the employee. These provisions have been incorporated to enhance employee's welfare. It is motivating to note that while much is made of the likely adverse impact of disinvestments on employment, in fact, in excess of the last 10 years, as accounted through the PSE Survey 2000-01, public sector undertakings have seen a net reduction in employment from a level of 2,179 million employees in 1991-92 to a level of 1,742 million in 2000-01, or a reduction of 20 per cent in excess of this period. Till March 31, 2001, 3.69 lakh employees had opted for VRS. In comparison, the retrenchment of employees after disinvestment has been marginal. In eight disinvested PSUs and five disinvested ITDC Hotels, against an initial employee strength of 27,967 at the time of disinvestments, only 2,119 employees were retrenched through VRS, and another 910 for other reasons. As against a total of 3,029 post disinvestment separations, 855 fresh appointments have been made resulting in a net reduction of 2,174 employees or in relation to the 7.8 per cent employees, compared to the employment level at the time of disinvestments.

ENTERPRISES IN INDIA

The main thrust to the joint sector came during the post-1970 period. Prior to India's independence a number of Joint Enterprises were established by a few erstwhile Princely States. Air India International provides another notable example. The company was established by the Tatas in 1948. The Government of India provided 49 per cent share in its equity.

The Government subsequently acquired an additional 2 per cent equity from the Tata Sons Ltd to convert it into a government company. In spite of the government holding 51 per cent of the equity the Air India continued to be under the management of the Tatas until it was fully taken over by the Government of India in 1953.

There were twelve other undertakings in 1966-67, in which the Central Government had a substantial stake in equity capital without having direct managerial control. In a few cases equity participation by foreign enterprises in the public sector enterprises was also allowed. Madras Fertilizers Ltd. for example, was established as a joint enterprise in participation with Amoco Inc. (USA) and National Iranian Oil Co.(Iran).

The same foreign companies were partners in Madras Refineries Ltd too. Cochin Refineries Ltd. was established with the participation of the Phillips Petroleum Co. (USA) and Duncan Brothers Ltd.; Lubrizol India Ltd.; with the Lubrizol Corporation (USA); and Triveni Structurals Ltd., with Voest Alpine (Austria). Maruti Udyog Ltd., is one of the latest cases where a foreign private corporation has been invited to join hands with the Government. A feature of all the above cases appears to be that public sector holdings are of majority nature and these are managed by Government nominated boards. The Industrial

Policy Resolution (IPR) of 1956 had classified industries into three main categories, depending on the role that the state was to play in each industry;

- The industries, the future development of which will be the exclusive responsibility of the state are referred to as Schedule-A industries.
- The industries which will be progressively state-owned and in which the state will generally take the initiative in establishing new undertakings and wherein private enterprise will be expected to supplement the efforts of the state in developing these industries are specified in Schedule - B.
- The non-scheduled Industries are left to the initiative and enterprise of the private sector. The IPR, 1956 envisaged that the state would help the private sector in fulfilling the role assigned to it within the planning framework and the industrial policy in force from time to time. In doing so, the state will continue to foster institutions to provide financial aid to these industries, and special assistance will be given to enterprises organised on co-operative lines for industrial and agricultural purposes. In suitable cases, the State may also grant assistance to the private sector. Such assistance, especially when the amount involved is substantial, will preferably be in the form of participation in equity capital, though it may also be in part in the form of debenture capital.

KEY LAWS

Information Technology Act, 2000 In May 2000 the Indian Parliament passed the Information Technology Bill now known as the Information Technology Act, 2000. The Act covers cyber and related information technology laws in India. Some of the issues addressed by the Information Technology Act, 2000 include:

- Chapter II states that any subscriber can authenticate an electronic record with his digital signature, and subsequently any person can verify that document by using the subscriber's public key.
- Chapter III states that all electronic records and digital signatures have legal acceptance. The chapter also confers rights to the Central Government to make rules with respect to digital signatures.
- Chapter IV deals with the attribution, acknowledge-ment and dispatch of electronic records and digital signatures.
- Chapter VI deals with the regulation of the certifying authorities. The chapter also lists the powers of the controller to investigate any contraventions to the provisions of the Act.
- Chapter VII and VIII state the conditions under which a digital signature may be suspended or revoked.
- Chapter IX states that any person who accesses, downloads, copies,

extracts data without authorized means or permission is punishable. The section also states that any person tampering with, damaging, denying unwarranted access to or manipulating any computer/ computer system shall be liable to pay damages by way of compensation not exceeding INR 10 million to the affected persons. Introducing viruses or causing disruptions in a computer are also punishable under the Act.

- Chapter X describes the role of the Cyber Regulations Appellate Tribunal.
- Chapter XI deals with offences such as wrongful loss or damage or destruction of information, deletion or alteration of any information in a computer network, 'hacking' etc and prescribes their punishment. It also includes offences such as tampering with computer source documents; publishing obscene information, misrepresentation, and breach of confidentiality and privacy.
- Chapter XII states that if a network provider/ intermediary can prove that he has taken diligent steps to prevent the offence he has been charged with, or that it was unintentional, he is not punishable under the Act.

Intellectual Property Right Laws for Computer Software Under Indian law, computer programmes have copyright protection, but no patent protection. A software programme is an algorithm and patent law does not protect algorithms per se. The term 'software' includes computer programmes, databases, computer files, preparatory design material and associated printed documentation, such as users' manuals.

Under the Indian Copyright Act, copying from an engraving is an infringement of the copyright, but an engraving produced independently from the same picture is not. Copyright laws generally do not protect the owner from independent creation or reverse engineering. Therefore, many software and hardware companies have been able to take advantage of the copyright law's lack of protection against reverse engineering.

India has one of the most modern copyright protection laws in the world. A major development in the area of copyright was the amendment to the Copyright Act of 1957 in 1999, to make it fully compatible with the provisions of the TRIPS Agreement. Known as the Copyright (Amendment) Act, 1999, this Act came into force on January 15, 2000.

The 1994 amendment of the Copyright Act of 1957 brought sectors such as satellite broadcasting, computer software and digital technology under Indian copyright protection. The present Copyright Act conforms fully to the TRIPS obligations. The other important development during 1999 was the issuance of the International Copyright Order, 1999, which extended the provisions of the Copyright Act to nationals of all World Trade Organization (WTO) member countries. As per the provision in the Indian Copyright Act, 1957 and as amended in 1994-1995, any person who knowingly makes use on a computer of an infringing copy of computer programme shall be punishable. According to Section 63 B, copyright infringement attracts a minimum jail term of seven days. The Act further provides for fines, which shall not be less than INR 50,000, but may extend up to INR 200,000, and a jail term up to three years or both.

The Ministry of Information Technology has taken also several initiatives to upgrade security standards in India. These include setting up organizations such as the Standardization, Testing and Quality Certification (STQC) Directorate, the Computer Emergency Response Team (CERT), the Information Security Technology Development Council (ISTDC), etc.

TECHNOLOGICAL POLICY

PREAMBLE

Political freedom must lead to economic independence and the alleviation of the burden of poverty. We have regarded science and technology as the basis of economic progress. As a result of three decades of planning, and the Scientific Policy Resolution of 1958, we now have a strong agricultural and industrial base and a scientific manpower impressive in quality, numbers and range of skills. Given clear-cut objectives and the necessary support, our science has shown its capacity to solve problems.

The frontiers of knowledge are being extended at incredible speed, opening up wholly new areas and introducing new concepts. Technological advances are influencing life-styles as well as societal expectations. The use and development of technology must relate to the people's aspirations. Our own immediate needs in India are the attainment of technological self-reliance, a swift and tangible improvement in the conditions of the weakest sections of the population and the speedy development of backward regions. India is known for its diversity.

Technology must suit local needs and to make an impact on the lives of ordinary citizens, must give constant thought to even small improvements which could make better and more cost-effective use of existing materials and methods of work. Our development must be based on our own culture and personality. Our future depends on our ability to resist the imposition of technology which is obsolete or unrelated to our specific requirements and of policies which tie us to systems which serve the purposes of others rather than our own, and on our success in dealing with vested interests in our organizations: governmental, economic, social and even intellectual, which bind us to outmoded systems and institutions.

Technology must be viewed in the broadest sense, covering the agricultural and the services sectors along with the obvious manufacturing sector. The latter stretches over a wide spectrum ranging from village, small-scale and cottage industries (often based on traditional skills) to medium, heavy and sophisticated industries. Our philosophy of a mixed economy involves the operation of the private, public and joint sectors, including those with foreign equity participation.

Our directives must clearly define systems for the choice of technology, taking into account economic, social and cultural factors along with technical considerations; indigenous development and support to technology, and utilization of such technology; acquisition of technology through import and its subsequent absorption, adaptation and upgradation; ensuring competitiveness at international levels in all necessary areas; and establishing links between the various elements concerned with generation of technology, its transformation into economically utilizable form, the sector responsible for production (which is the user of such technology), financial institutions concerned with the resources needed for these activities, and the promotional and regulating arms of the Government.

This Technology Policy Statement is in response to the need for guidelines to cover this wide-ranging and complex set of inter-related areas. Keeping in mind the capital-scarce character of a developing economy it aims at ensuring that our available natural endowments, especially human resources, are optimally utilized for a continuing increase in the well-being of all sections of our people. We seek technolo-gical advancement not for prestige or aggrandisement but to solve our multifarious problems and to be able to safeguard our independence and our unity.

Our modernization, far from diminishing the enormous diversity of our regional traditions should help to enrich them and to make the ancient wisdom of our nation more meaningful to our people. Our task is gigantic and calls for close co-ordination between the different departments of the Central and State Governments and also of those concerned, at all levels, with any sector of economic, scientific or technological activity, and, not least, the understanding and involvement of the entire Indian people. We look particularly to young people to bring a scientific attitude of mind to bear on all our problems.

AIMS AND OBJECTIVES

Aims

The basic objectives of the Technology Policy will be the development of indigenous technology and efficient absorption and adaptation of imported technology appropriate to national priorities and resources. Its aims are to:

- Attain technological competence and self-reliance, to reduce vulnerability, particularly in strategic and critical areas, making the maximum use of indige-nous resources;
- Provide the maximum gainful and satisfying employment to all strata

of society, with emphasis on the employment of women and weaker sections of society;

- Use traditional skills and capabilities, making them commercially competitive;
- Ensure the correct mix between mass production technologies and production by the masses;
- Ensure maximum development with minimum capital outlay;
- Identify obsolescence of technology in use and arrange for modernization of both equipment and technology;
- Develop technologies which are internationally competitive, particularly those with export potential;
- Improve production speedily through greater efficiency and fuller utilization of existing capabilities, and enhance the quality and reliability of performance and output;
- Reduce demands on energy, particularly energy from non-renewable sources;
- Ensure harmony with the environment, preserve the ecological balance and improve the quality of the habitat; and
- Recycle waste material and make full utilization of by-products.

Self-Reliance

In a country of India's size and endowments, self-reliance is inescapable and must be at the very heart of technological development. We must aim at major technological break-throughs in the shortest possible time for the development of indigenous technology appropriate to national priorities and resources. For this, the role of different agencies will be identified, responsibilities assigned and the necessary linkages established.

Strengthening the Technology Base

Research and Development, together with science and technology education and training of a high order, will be accorded pride of place. The base of science and technology consists of trained and skilled manpower at various levels, covering a wide range of disciplines, and an appropriate institutional, legal and fiscal infrastructure.

Consolidation of the existing scientific base and selective strengthening of thrust areas in it are essential. Special attention will be given to the promotion and strengthening of the technology base in newly emerging and frontier areas such as information and materials sciences, electronics and bio-technology. Education and training to upgrade skills are also of utmost importance. Basic research and the building of centres of excellence will be encouraged.

Skills and skilled workers will be accorded special recognition. The quality and efficiency of the technology generation and delivery systems will be continuously monitored and upgraded. All of this calls for substantial financial investments and also strengthening of the linkages between various sectors (educational institutions, R&D establishments, industry and governmental machinery).

PRIORITIES

The time scales involved in the generation of technology are long, even with imported elements. Therefore, relevant technologies in all areas of priority, particularly where large investments are to be made, should be clearly identified well in advance. The cost and time element involved in the import of technology and indigenous development will be given consideration. Components which could be assigned to the various institutions which are capable of developing them or which could be built up for such activities will be identified. Ministries concerned with large investments and production activities in areas such as food, health and energy will be provided with appropriate technical support through suitably structured S&T groups.

Employment

Human resources constitute our richest endowment. Conditions will be created for the fullest expression and utilization of scientific talent. Measures will be taken for the identification and diffusion of technologies that can progressively reduce the incidence of poverty and unemployment, and of regional inequalities.

The application of science and technology for the improvement of standards of living of those engaged in traditional activities will be promoted, particularly household technologies. Technologies relevant to the cottage, village and small industries sector will be upgraded. In the decentralized sector labour must be diversified and all steps taken to reduce drudgery. In all sectors, the potential impact on employment will be an important criterion in the choice of technology.

Energy

Energy constitutes an expensive and sometimes scarce input. Therefore, the energy requirements both of a direct and indirect nature for each product and each production activity and the associated technology employed will be analysed. Measures will be devised to avoid wastage or non-optimal use of energy. Fiscal measures as necessary will be introduced to ensure these. Research and Development in the energy sector will aim at improving the efficiency of its production, distribution and utilization, as well as improvement of efficiency in processes and equipment.

Efficiency and Productivity

Technologies already employed will be evaluated on a continuing basis to realise maximum benefits in terms of increased production and lower costs, specially in the public sector enterprises. Every effort should be made to utilize by-products and wherever possible to recycle waste materials, especially those from urban areas. Programmes to make use of easily available and less costly materials will be supported.

ENVIRONMENT

Development should not upset the ecological balance for short as well as long-term considerations. Poorly planned efforts to achieve apparently rapid development, ignoring the long-term effect of many technologies on the environment, have resulted in serious ecological damage.

It is, therefore, essential to analyse the environmental impact of the application of each technology. Due regard will be given to the preservation and enhancement of the environment in the choice of technologies. Measures to improve environmental hygiene will be evolved.

SOME SPECIFIC AREAS

In technology development special emphasis will be focused on food, health, housing, energy and industry. In particular, stress will be laid on:

- Agriculture including dry-land farming;
- Optimum use of water resources, increased production of pulses and oilseeds;
- Provision of drinking water in rural areas, improvement of nutrition, rapid reduction in the incidence of blindness, eradication of the major communicable diseases (such as leprosy and tuber-culosis), and population stabilization;
- Low-cost housing;
- Development and use of renewable non-conventional sources of energy;
- Industrial development

INDIGENOUS TECHNOLOGY

Fullest support will be given to the development of indigenous technology to achieve technological self-reliance and reduce the dependence on foreign inputs, particularly in critical and vulnerable areas and in high value-added items in which the domestic base is strong. Strengthening and diversifying the domestic technology base are necessary to reduce imports and to expand exports for which international competitiveness must be ensured.

Inventions

The spirit of innovation and invention is the driving force behind all technological change. We must awaken our science and technology to the exciting challenges of our times, provide incentives to encourage inventors, and direct their efforts to areas of special importance. The system of rewards and incentives will be strengthened for inventions, innovations and technological breakthroughs and their utilization. The fullest opportunity will be provided to make use of inventions.

Enhancing Traditional Skills and Capabilities

Traditional skills and capabilities will need to be upgraded and enhanced, using knowledge and techniques generated by advances in science and technology. Technologies which will result in low-cost production and in products marketable close to the point of manufacture, particularly in the rural sector, will be promoted. Support will be given to technologies which reduce pressure on items in short supply and utilize improved local materials and methods. Government will give preference to products of such technologies in its own purchases. The adoption of technologies that can promote decentralized production will be helped through the support to design, marketing, quality control and other services.

Ensuring Timely Availability

The time cycle from scientific research to utilization is a long one. Hence the need to initiate action well in advance to identify and ensure timely availability and delivery of new technologies. Encouragement and support (fiscal, commercial and administrative) will be given to the production and user organizations to be associated with and participate in technology development efforts at appropriate stages.

UPGRADATION TO PREVENT OBSOLESCENCE

Technology is constantly on the move. The base of indigenous technology should be capable of utilizing world-wide advances and adapting them to local needs. The creation and strengthening of institutional structures for keeping track of international developments will receive urgent attention.

A strong central group will be constituted to undertake technology forecast and technology assessment studies and will inter alia draw up programmes of purposeful research. Arrangements will be made to provide high-level scientific advice in major sectors of the economy. Where big investments are involved or a large volume of production is envisaged, it will be incumbent on the Ministry or agency concerned to provide a technology forecast covering its requirements over a ten-year or longer period and evolve a strategy for development based on priorities.

DEMAND FOR INDIGENOUS TECHNOLOGY

Our country has already invested significant amounts in setting up research and development facilities as well as design consultancy and engineering capabilities. The technological potential inherent in this system of interlinked capabilities must be fully utilized, and in turn provide a fillip for further development from within the system. Incentives will, therefore, be provided to users of indigenously developed technology, and for products and processes resulting for such use.

PREFERENTIAL TREATMENT

In view of the cost of technology development and the time necessary for successful marketing of a new or improved product, indigenously developed items are invariably at a disadvantage compared with imported products or those based on imported technologies and brand names. Support must therefore be provided through fiscal and other measures, for a limited period, in favour of products made through indigenously developed technologies, care being taken to ensure quality.

FISCAL INCENTIVES

Suitable financial mechanisms will be established to facilitate investment on pilot plants, process demonstration units and prototype development in order to enable rapid commercial exploitation of technologies developed in laboratories. Linkages between scientific and technological institutions and development banks will be strengthened. Gaps in technology will be identified and suitable corrective measures taken with adequate allocation of resources.

Fiscal incentives will be provided in particular to: promote inventions; increase the use of indigenously developed technology; enhance in-house Research and Development in industry; and efforts directed to absorb and adapt imported technology.

DESIGN ENGINEERING

Capabilities in design engineering are essential for the translation of know-how to commercial production. This is particularly important in areas relating to: agricultural production; agro-industries; metallurgical, chemical and petrochemical processes; machine tools; industrial machinery and capital goods; as well as for the construction and erection of entire plants.

Building up and enhancing these capabilities will have a catalytic beneficial impact on the utilization of indigenous efforts that have resulted in product and process know-how. Existing design engineering capabilities will be strengthened and upgraded, and interaction encouraged between design engineering organizations, academic and research institutions and industry. Wherever gaps exist, design engineering capabilities will be developed and nurtured.

Engineering Consultancy

Engineering consultancy is a vital area for ensuring speedy technological and industrial development. It ensures the appropriate utilization of indigenous materials, plant and machinery. Engineering consultancy provides an essential link between R&D institutions and industry, and thus promotes effective transfer of technology. Capability for total systems engineering, process development and project management should be developed with collaboration if required. Wherever capability exists, utilization of Indian consultancy engineering organizations will be promoted.

Even where foreign technical collaboration or consultancy is considered unavoidable, association of designated Indian consulting engineering organizations would be preferred. Indigenous engineering consultancy, in both private and public sectors, will be promoted on a sound professional basis in the context of the overall national perspective of technological self-reliance.

In-house R&D

In-house R&D units in industry provide a desirable and essential interface between efforts within the national laboratories and the educational sector as well as production in industry. Appropriate incentives will be given to the setting up of R&D units in industry and for industry including those on a cooperative basis. Enterprises will be encouraged to set up R&D units of a size to permit the accomplishment of major technological tasks.

TECHNOLOGY ACQUISITION

A policy directed towards technological self-reliance does not imply technological self-sufficiency. The criterion must be national interest. Government policy will be directed towards reducing technological dependence in key areas. Advantage should be taken of technological developments elsewhere. This can also be achieved through well-defined collaborative arrangements in research and development. At any given point of time, there will be a mix of indigenous and imported technology. However, technology acquisition from outside shall not be at the expense of national interest. Indigenous initiative must receive due recognition and support.

In the acquisition of technology, consideration will be given to the choice and sources of technology, alternative means of acquiring it, its role in meeting a major felt need, selection and relevance of the products, costs, and related conditions. A National Register on Foreign Collaboration will be developed to provide analytical inputs at various stages of technological acquisition.

Principles of Acquisition and Technology Assessment

Where the need to import technology is established, every effort should be made to ensure that it is of the highest level, consistent with requirements and resources. The technology import will be so planned as to have effective transfer of basic knowledge (know-why) and to facilitate further advancement. Where the import of technology is contemplated, the level to which technology has been developed, or is in current use, within the country, shall be first evaluated. Lists of technologies that have been adequately developed to the extent that import is unnecessary will be prepared and periodically updated; in such areas no import of technology would normally be permitted; and the onus will be on the seeker of foreign technology, be it industry or a user Ministry, to demonstrate to the satisfaction of the approval authority that import is necessary. Technology assessment systems will be reviewed. A technology assessment mechanism consisting of competent groups will render advice in all cases of technology import relating to highly sophisticated technology, large investments and national security. Aspects of employment, energy, efficiency and environment will be kept in view.

The basic principles governing the acquisition of technology will be:

- Import of technology, and foreign investment in this regard, will continue to be permitted only on a selective basis where: need has been established; technology does not exist within the country; the time taken to generate the technology indigenously would delay the achievement of development targets.
- Government may, from time to time, identify and notify such areas of high national priority, in respect of which procedures would be simplified further to ensure timely acquisition of the required technology.
- There shall be a firm commitment for absorption, adaptation and subsequent development of imported know-how through adequate investment in Research and Development to which importers of technology will be expected to contribute.

UNPACKAGING

Technology to fulfil a particular need consists of many components. It is necessary to develop capability to break down the total package of technology required for a purpose into components, some of which may be readily available or could be indigenously developed, and other that will need to be imported. Norms and guidelines for such unpackaging will be evolved.

Absorption of Technology

There shall be a commitment to ensure an adequate scale of investment in R&D for the absorption, adaptation and, wherever possible, improvement on and generation of new technology, making fullest use of overall national capabilities. Only thus can self-reliance be ensured and a technology generation process established firmly. Appropriate mechani-sms will be evolved at the stage of technology assessment to ensure the absorption of imported technology.

Technological Information

The availability of an efficient system of collection and analysis of relevant technological information, including cost and other economic aspects, is a prerequisite for the appropriate choice of technologies. This will considerably enhance the possibility of obtaining favourable terms and conditions in acquisition of technology. Such a technology information base will be established.

TECHNOLOGY TRANSFER- DIFFUSION

Special efforts need to be made for the diffusion of technology in use to all beneficiaries who can employ them optimally. Appropriate measures shall be evolved to facilitate technology diffusion, including: horizontal transfer; technological support for ancillaries from large units; technology inputs to small units; and upgradation of traditional skills and capabilities. International Competitiveness and Technology Exports. It is necessary to maintain international competitiveness in products, services and technologies that have export potential. Conditions for the marketing of indigenous technology and of products based on it will be improved. It is important in all such cases to conform to the highest international standards.

Technical Cooperation among Developing Countries

A concerted effort will be made to participate fully in technical cooperation among developing countries. Encouragement will be provided for participation in technology development programmes with other developing countries which can contribute to mutual national development.

Protection: Legislative Framework

Development of technology calls for large investments and often involves considerable risk. Encouragement will be given to obtaining necessary protection in all cases of indigenous technology development. A mechanism will be set up to ensure that national interests arising from the generating of technology are fully protected internationally in terms of industrial property rights.

IMPLEMENTATION

The success of the Technology Policy and the speed with which the various facets of the policy are implemented will depend to a considerable extent on a system for efficient monitoring, review and guidance and a scheme of incentives and disincentives. Government will evolve instruments for the implementation of this Technology Policy and spell out in detail guidelines for Ministries and agencies of Government as well as for industries and entrepreneurs.

Success in implementation demands a conscious integrated approach covering technology assessment, development, acquisition, absorption, utilization and diffusion, and connected aspects of financing, based on overall national interests, priorities and the attainment of the most challenging technological goals. Above all, the entire population must be imbued with self-confidence and pride in national capacity. Indian Science and Technology must unlock the creative potential of our people and help in building the India of our dreams.

Bibliography

Alan Rushton, Phil Croucher and Peter Baker: *The Handbook of Logistics and Distribution Management*, Viva Books, Delhi, 2010.

Anil Kumar Chojar: *Supply Chain Management : Theories and Applications*, Deep and Deep Publication, Delhi, 2012.

Ashish Bhatnagar: *Textbook of Supply Chain Management*, Word Press, Delhi, 2011.

Bholanath Dutta: *Sales and Distribution Management*, I.K. International, Delhi, 2011.

Chae An.: *Supply Chain Management on Demand: Strategies and Technologies, Applications With contributions by numerous experts*, Springer, New York, 2000.

Dyckhoff: *Supply Chain Management and Reverse Logistics*, Springer, New York, 2001.

FRAZELLE: *Supply Chain Strategy: The Logistics of Supply Chain Management*, Tata McGraw-Hill, Delhi, 2003.

Graeme Shanks: *Second Wave Enterprise Resource Planning Systems: Implementing for Effectiveness*, Cambridge University Press, New York, 2001.

IYER: *Toyota's Supply Chain Management*, Tata McGraw-Hill, Delhi, 2009.

J. Paul Sundar Kirubakaran: *Supply Chain Management*, Serials Publication, Delhi, 2008.

Jayashree Dubey and M L Sai Kumar: *Supply Chain Management*, New Century Publication, Delhi, 2007.

John T Mentzer: *Supply Chain Management*, Response Books, Delhi, 2001.

Knolmayer: *Supply Chain Management Based on SAP Systems*, Springer, New York 2005.

Kulkarni: *Supply Chain Management: Concepts and Cases (Book + CD)*, Tata McGraw-Hill, Delhi, 2004.

Mukesh Bhatia and N.J. Kumar: *Supply Chain Management : Concept Theory and Practices*, Regal Publication, Delhi, 2012.

N.H. Mullick and Mohd. Altaf Khan: *Sales and Distribution Management*, Enkay Publication, Delhi, 2011.

N.H. Mullick and Mohd. Altaf Khan: *Supply Chain Management*, Enkay Publication, Delhi, 2011.

Nada R. Sanders: *Supply Chain Management: A Global Perspective*, Wiley, Delhi, 2012.

Neha Kapil: *Enterprise Resource Planning*, Saloni Publication, Delhi, 2004.

Pankaj Madan and Neeraj Anand: *Supply Chain Management : Concept Planning and Execution*, Global Vision Publication, Delhi, 2012.

Pingali Venugopal: *Sales and Distribution Management : An Indian Perspective*, Response Books, Delhi, 2008.

S L Gupta: *Sales and Distribution Management*, Excel Books, Delhi, 2003.

S. S Mishra: *Social Accountability In Global Supply Chain Management*, Taxmann Publications, Delhi, 2009.

Samjay Thakur: *Retail Store and Supply Chain Management*, Oxford Book Company, Delhi, 2012.

Simchi-Levi: *The Logic of Logistics: Theory, Algorithms, and Applications for Logistics and Supply Chain Management, 2e*, Springer, New York 2007.

Stadtler: *Supply Chain Management and Advanced Planning, 2e*, Springer, New York, 1993.

Sunil Sharma: *Supply Chain Management : Concepts, Practices and Implementation*, Oxford University, Delhi, 2010.

Tapan K. Panda and Sunil Sahadev: *Sales and Distribution Management*, Oxford University Press, Delhi, 2005.

Index